# ADULT EDUCATION AND PHENOMENOLOGICAL RESEARCH

## New Directions for Theory, Practice, and Research

### Sherman M. Stanage

Professor of Philosophy
and
Professor of Leadership and Educational Policy Studies
Northern Illinois University

## ROBERT E. KRIEGER PUBLISHING COMPANY
Malabar, Florida
1987

Original Edition 1987

Printed and Published by
**ROBERT E. KRIEGER PUBLISHING COMPANY, INC.**
**KRIEGER DRIVE**
**MALABAR, FLORIDA 32950**

**Library of Congress Cataloging-in-Publication Data**

Stanage, Sherman M. (Sherman Miller)
  Adult education and phenomenological research.

  Bibliography;  P.
  Includes index.
  1. Adult education. 2. Phenomenology. I. Title
LC5219.S675    1987    374    86-32204
ISBN 0-89874-907-7

10  9  8  7  6  5  4  3  2

# ADULT EDUCATION
# AND
# PHENOMENOLOGICAL RESEARCH

## *New Directions for*
## *Theory, Practice, and Research*

# TABLE OF CONTENTS

*For*

**Anna Maude Garison Stanage**
*and*
**Sherman P. Stanage**

# ACKNOWLEDGEMENTS

This book probably would not have been written had Michael Collins and Paul Ilsley not been students in a number of my graduate courses in philosophy at Northern Illinois University. I will always be grateful to them for posing fundamental questions and problems which led me to apply my long-standing specializations and interests in phenomenology, value theory, and philosophy of the social sciences and of the human sciences to many areas of theory, practice, and research in adult education. These are the kinds of intellectual debts which cannot be repaid in any manner short of one's own recommitment as a scholar and teacher upon each and every occasion that a brilliant student raises the most relevant kinds of questions.

There are other students with whom I have been privileged to work in the general contexts of philosophy and adult education, and especially in my seminars and workshops in phenomenology and adult education. Hopefully, they will not be too embarassed if I both name them and thank them for their contributions to the nourishing and the actualizing of my feelings, my experiences, and my 'consciousings' as a philosopher and as an adult educator who expresses his own love of wisdom partially along the pathways laid out in this essay.

I have always encouraged my students to be my critics. The finest of these have always been the most critical and among those persons whose views have been of the greatest benefit in my work as a teacher and scholar. Those students in more recent years who must be named include: Joseph Agnello, Rebecca Bachar, Ming Bao, Sharon Bruce, Deborah Brue, Dieter Bussigel, Irene Carr, Scipio A. J. Collin, III, Alvin Davis, Susanna Davison, Willard Draper, Trenton Ferro, Anna Gobledale, Paula Hardin, Robert Hartmann, Mickey Hellyer, John Hill, Brenda Hodges, Clifford I-Aharanwa, Keith Krasemann, Jane Leicht, Sylvia Mann, Dana Maxfield, Joan McCollom, Helena Mauceri, Raymond Molitor, Steven Murphy, Dianne Poppl, Allan Quigley, Margaret Rodeghero,

Isabelle Sabau, Kelly Salsbery, Richard Spaine, Gabriele Strohschen, Daniel Swanson, Sripen Supapidhayakul, Alice Thorson, Theodora Thurwachter, and Julie Wendorff.

I am deeply indebted to each and all of the members of the faculty in adult education at Northern Illinois University who have both encouraged my work in philosophical investigations in adult education and who have critiqued its results: Phyllis Cunningham, Thomas Heaney, Robert Mason, John Niemi, Richard Orem, Edwin Simpson, Robert Smith, and Dean William Young; and to Ronald Cervero and Sharan Merriam of the University of Georgia.

My special gratitude for all her services rendered in the preparation of the manuscript is reserved for Cheryl Fuller, word processing operator in the office of the College of Liberal Arts and Sciences. Dean James Norris of the College of Liberal Arts and Sciences and Dean Jerrold Zar, Associate Provost for Research and Dean of the Graduate School, deserve my special thanks for having made important services available to me in the course of the preparation of the manuscript. I am grateful to artist Mike Phelps for his fine illustrations.

Throughout it all, my wife Diane, and my daughters, Ruthe, Deborah, Kelley, Lisa, Suzanne, and Christine, have nourished me with deep love and encouragement. Without knowing it, they have helped me move through many of the feelings which have emerged as concepts in what follows.

Many of the views, claims, and arguments which are laid out in the book have been presented in different form at meetings of adult educators, especially to meetings of the Adult Education Research Conference in Montreal, Raleigh, and Syracuse, and to meetings of the Midwest Research-to-Practice Conference in DeKalb and Ann Arbor. Papers presenting earlier and different versions of some of the ideas have appeared in *Adult Education Quarterly* (36, No. 3, Spring 1986, 123-129), *Philosophy and Rhetoric* (2, No. 2, 1969, 81-90), *Human Studies* (2, July 1979, 131-158), *Educational Theory* (26, No. 1, Winter 1976, 53-71), *The Southwestern Journal of Philosophy* (now *Philosophical Topics*) (1, Nos. 1-2,

Summer 1971, 72-80), *Pacific Philosophy Forum* (later
*Philosophy Forum)* (7, 1968, 4-46).

The author and the publisher gratefully acknowledge
permission from the publishers of the above journals for
permission to use the materials cited, and to the
publishers listed below for permission to quote from the
works noted.

**American Association for Adult and Continuing Education,**
for the article, "'Unrestraining' Freedom: Adult
Education and the Empowerment of Persons," by Sherman M.
Stanage, in *Adult Education Quarterly,* Volume 36, No. 3,
Spring 1986, New York: American Association for Adult
and Continuing Education, 1986.

**Basil Blackwell,** for selections from *Philosophical
Investigations* by Ludwig Wittgenstein, and translated
from the German by G. E. M. Anscombe, Oxford: Basil
Blackwell, 1958.

**Dover Publications, Inc.,** for selections from *On the
Improvement of the Understanding, The Ethics, and
Correspondence,* by Benedict de Spinoza, New York: Dover
Publications, 1951.

**Hackett Publishing Company, Inc.,** for selections from
*Discourse on Method and Meditations on First
Philosophy,* by Rene Descartes, and translated from the
Latin by Donald A. Cress, Indianapolis, Indiana: Hackett
Publishing Company, Inc., 1980.

**Harvard University Press,** for selections from *Collected
Papers of Charles Sanders Peirce,* Volume I, edited by
Charles Hartshorne and Paul Weiss, Cambridge,
Massachusetts: Harvard University Press, 1960.

**Harvard University Press,** for selections from *The
Republic,* by Plato. Reprinted by permission of the
publishers and the Loeb Classical Library from *The
Republic* by Plato, translated by Paul Shorey, Cambridge,
Massachusetts: Harvard University Press, 1935.

**Holt, Rinehart and Winston, Inc.,** for a selection from *Logic: The Theory of Inquiry,* by John Dewey, New York: Henry Holt and Company, Inc., 1938.

**Martinus Nijhoff Publishers,** for a selection from Edmund Husserl, *Cartesian Meditations,* translated from the German by Dorion Cairns, from pages 1-3, Dordrecht, Holland: Martinus Nijhoff Publishers, 1977. Copyright (c) 1977 by Martinus Nijhoff Publishers, Dordrecht, Holland; and for a selection from Alfred Schutz, "On Multiple Realities," in Alfred Schutz, *Collected Papers,* Volume I: The Problem of Social Reality, edited and introduced by Maurice Natanson, from pages 208-209, Dordrecht, Holland: Martinus Nijhoff Publishers, 1962. Copyright (c) 1962 by Martinus Nijhoff Publishers, Dordrecht, Holland.

**Northwestern University Press,** for a selection from *Edward Husserl: Philosopher of Infinite Tasks,* by Maurice Natanson, Evanston, Illinois: Northwestern University Press, 1973; and for a selection from Alexander Pfänder, *Phenomenology of Willing and Motivation,* translated from the German by Herbert Spiegelberg, Evanston, Illinois: Northwestern University Press, 1967.

**W. W. Norton and Company, Inc.,** for selections from *Meditations on Quixote,* by José Ortega y Gasset, translated from the Spanish by Evelyn Rugg and Diego Marin, New York: W. W. Norton and Company, Inc., 1961. Copyright (c) 1961 by W. W. Norton and Company, Inc.

**Oxford University Press,** for selections from *An Essay on Metaphysics, The Idea of History,* and *Speculum Mentis,* all by Robin G. Collingwoood, Oxford: Oxford University Press, 1940, 1956, and 1924 (respectively).

**Routledge and Kegan Paul Ltd.,** for a selection from Plato, *Theaetetus* (197a-199c), in Francis MacDonald Cornford, *Plato's Theory of Knowledge: The Theaetetus* *and the* **Sophist** *of Plato Translated With a Running Commentary,* London: Routledge and Kegan Paul Ltd., 1935.

**Charles Scribner's Sons,** for selections from *I and Thou,* by Martin Buber, translated from the German by Walter Kaufmann, New York: Charles Scribner's Sons, 1970.

**Syracuse University Publications in Adult Education,** for selections from *Relentless Verity; Education for Being-Becoming-Belonging,* by James Robbins Kidd, Syracuse, New York: Syracuse University Publications in Adult Education, 1973.

*Acquaintance with [philosophy] must come rather after a long period of attendance on instruction in the subject itself and of close companionship, when, suddenly like a blaze kindled by a leaping spark, it is generated in the soul and at once becomes self-sustaining.*

Plato, *Letter VII\**

# PREFACE

When James Robbins Kidd was awarded Syracuse University's William Pearson Tolley Medal for Distinguished Leadership in Adult Education (in October 1973), he concluded his acceptance address by affirming:

> *Education for being-becoming-belonging. Education for living and for dying. It's not the kind of concept that is much admired by people these days, people who want to see all learning objectives specified in lucid statements of behavioral changes to be carried out in short, manageable steps. I have offered little that is orderly or symmetrical, little that can be easily computerized, little that lies snugly inside traditional disciplines, little for which governments or foundations have announced grant programs. I have suggested much that is perplexing, withstands easy curriculum design, casts some doubt on many present goals and programs, and may seem to demand a range of method and content that will defy attainment of any quality.*
>
> *I have reminded us of some qualities and forces that mark or should mark the education and self-education we foster. If I am right in my assertion that being-belonging-becoming should be found at the central core of adult education, at least four tasks are needed:*

*1) **Conceptualization** - to take these tangled and tattered strands of ideas and make of them a woven garment;*

*2) **Persuasion** - persuading men and women to give care and attention to what in themselves is most human;*

*3) **Curriculum** - to develop the content and learning experiences that will enrich and enlarge us to goals for the advancement of the entire human family;*

*4) **Method** - to choose and organize and refine the means to learning that help men and women to be free.*

*What is needed is wisdom that none of us possess except through sharing: and I mean wisdom, not sophisticated slickness . . .[1]*

Of the four tasks Robie Kidd cited, this book is concerned primarily (but surely not exclusively) with **conceptualization,** with the largely philosophical task of taking some "tangled and tattered strands of ideas" from within adult education practices and theories and making of them "a woven garment." This book presents a new way of conceptualizing some old phenomena toward the formulation of new perspectives, a way whose investigations may be seen as fundamental to any philosophy of adult education.[2] Old ground is being cleared in preparation for locating the footings and foundations of new ideas for practices and research.

The way is **phenomenology.**[3] The old phenomena are adults, education, and philosophy. None of these is a single phenomenon, but the rich in-gathering of the countless flowing phenomena we catch and capture in passing in the human sciences.[4] An understanding of this way leads to new programs of learning for the adult learner, adult educators, and the subject-matter of adult education, and to a new paradigm of research, new research programs, and the subsequent emergence of new problems.

Most philosophers would agree that four questions centrally characterize the study of philosophy:

**Who Am I?**
>    **What Can I Know?**
>        **What Ought I To Do?**
>            **What May I Hope?**

These four questions, however, are not exclusively philosophical problems. We all face these questions in some degree, and the meaning that a person's life has is founded in one's personal responses to these questions. These questions and our meaningful responses to them are every bit as crucial during the adult years as in those youthful ones we worry so much about. Moreover, the varieties of resolutions which have been proposed for these questions and problems have been basic to the development of philosophical approaches to education and to the institutions of intelligence through the centuries. Much of what it ought to mean to be an educated adult involves working at the creation and construction of personally meaningful responses and answers to these questions.

Whereas all of us face these problems, not all adults find themselves ready, willing, or able to deal with them effectively. Fears, confusions, boredom, and failures in our lives exact heavy tolls. These obstacles, and countless others not detailable outside the lives of individual persons, have been the subjects and themes of a long and rich--and immensely popular--so-called 'self-help' literature.[5]

This book explicitly addresses the four fundamental questions, Who Am I?, What Can I Know?, What Ought I To Do?, What May I Hope?, as vital questions in the lives of adults. It also speaks to the ways in which individual adult lives can achieve realization of their fullest growth potential.

The book consists of an Introduction and six Parts. It is very important to understand the somewhat unusual overall sequence and arrangement of the Parts, chapters, and other sections of the book. The Parts are arranged so that the reader may move through considerations of definitions of adult education; clarifications of what phenomenology is, what scientific methods are and how all of this is related to selected problems in adult education; reflections on what it means to be an adult; on what education and philosophy are in relationship to one another; and finally a clarification of what phenomenology is as a new kind of research and program of research in adult education.

Each Part has three chapters which discuss matters of great importance to the topics clustered together in that Part. But there are special clusterings of the numbered chapters: 1, 4, 7; 2, 5, 8; and 3, 6, 9. I explain these special relationships immediately below. One very important reason for relating them in these special ways is that they provide philosophical foundations in various ways for theory and practice, and especially for research, in adult education.

The Introduction positions us all--author and readers--and offers a way toward self-knowledge, self-help, and discipline. The Introduction also tries to clarify the roots of this work and the originations and beginnings of careful investigations into those unique phenomena presented for reflection by adults, by education, and by philosophy.

Part I briefly introduces **phenomenology,** discusses 'linguistic phenomenology' and the personal language of learning to learn within the adult lifeworld, and relates phenomenology to certain familiar activities in scientific methods. It also discusses phenomenology's great importance not as one of countless other philosophical schools, types, and 'isms', but as the necessary basis for all philosophy and for all sciences (Edmund Husserl's claim).[6]

Part II presents a phenomenological investigation of the personal world of an adult, as an illustration and example of the uses of phenomenology, and closes with a discussion of some of the most basic issues and problems necessarily involved in the development of any philosophy of adult education. These matters include investigations of assumptions, goals, means, ends, and philosophical methods in adult education. As philosophically significant problems, these underlie many of the problems normally dealt with in the literature of adult education, for example, the content and context of adult education, adult learning procedures, and the great variety of 'how-to' approaches.

Parts III through V each offer brief phenomenological accounts of **feeling, experiencing,** and **consciousing,** respectively. Part III, **Adults,** presents a phenomenology of **feeling**, a discussion of habit and habituating the will-to-learn, and an account of the 'everydayness'[7] of the adult lifeworld.[8] The 'everydayness' of the lifeworld of the adult is the medium in and through which the continuing learning throughout the adult years must arise and become vital. A nuclear understanding of this 'everydayness' of living-in-the-world can only come through adults' own perceptions of their feelings, habits, and the special forms of 'everydayness' in which each one individually is immersed.

Part IV, **Eduction** (genuine 'education'), consists of a brief phenomenology of **experiencing**, a discussion of the importance of the phenomenon of relevance in education, and accounts of literal, technical, and metaphorical languages as these demonstrate degrees of both competency and performance, for example, in the special disciplinings[9] conducting us through adult learning. Each of us carries language, and our languages carry our cultures. New constitutions within our lives such as new facts, values, and careers become relevant to us, and these new relevancies occasion new and often unfamiliar words, languages, motivations, and perspective transformations.[10] These are especially critical issues within the 'everydayness' of the adult lifeworld.

Part V, **Philosophy,** offers a brief phenomenology of **consciousing,** a view of the 'metaphorizing' of a person's life, and concludes with an account of that vital life of the adult which courses through inquiry, care, and service within our lifeworld. These qualities of individual lives have profound impact upon the nurture of an enhanced quality of life, not only for adults but for all persons.

Part VI focuses on special problems concerning research in adult learning and education. It discusses ways in which phenomenological investigations constitute a new paradigm of research, a new program of research in and through adult education,[11] and lays out a variety of clusters of new problems for adult education research.

I have just rehearsed important contents and claims of each Part of the book. I hope that readers will find this book compelling in its messages for adult learners, renewing for teachers, a voyage in new and adventurous directions for both theory and practice in adult education, and appropriate to many new and emerging learning needs of adult lives. Moreover, I hope that it becomes a motivating journey along the rich pathways and vitality of individual willing toward 'self-help'.

If the book proves itself in these and many other ways, this will be partly because readers have found that their contact with the book has been instrumental in assisting them to discover and to create a variety of new and rich layers of meaning in their professional lives. It will also be because these new layers of personal meaning will have emerged at levels and in ways most unexpected. Old, paralyzing, and destructive habits, for example, may well give way to new, energizing, and constructive habits toward the birth and rebirth of goals and lives of service through more fundamental vocational commitments and more satisfying professional careers.

Although I discuss new paradigms of research in Part VI, some important points may be introduced here. Chapters 1, 4, and 7 present phenomenological accounts of **feeling, experiencing,** and **consciousing,** respectively. I use the acronym, **FEC,** to bring these human dynamisms intimately together; hence, I speak of the **FEC Structure** in adult learning. The **FEC Structure** is the structure of **person**[12] which all persons have. The **FEC Structure,** properly fleshed out, is my answer to the

first philosophical question, **'Who Am I?'**, in the special context of adult education. It also becomes a
fundamental sector of this new paradigm of research in
adult education as a human science. A clear understanding of this structure is crucial to the adult learner
and to the adult educator. It is the general paradigm
of **person** into which fit all of the other structures of
**person** that persons manifest or express, or which
persons may be said to be.

Chapters 2, 5, and 8 discuss habit, relevance, and
metaphors. I bring these together as the **HRM Structure**
in adult learning and education. The **HRM Structure**,
carefully developed, offers my response at present to
the second philosophical question, **'What Can I Know?'**,
in the context of adult education. It also presents
itself as another region of this new paradigm of research. For example, What does it mean to be an educated adult? Who should decide this, and on the basis
of what criteria?

Chapters 3, 6, and 9 discuss 'everydayness', languages of relevancy, and the vital life, respectively.
My term, **EvLV Structure,** gathers together the close
relations these have for adult learning and continuing
education. This **EvLV Structure,** properly developed and
understood, emerges as my response to the third philosophical question, **'What Ought I To Do?'** Still another
clustering of research programs within this new paradigm
of research emerges. This concerns less the question of
what a person ought to do through specific modes of
action and conduct in daily life, and much more the
question of the significance of both rational and moral
choices involved throughout possible learning, professional, and career directions in one's life.

After reading this essay the reader should begin to
understand how the entire essay addresses the fourth
special question, **'What Can I Hope?'** Dare I suggest
that from among the hopes and expectations within our
'everydayness' we may select some which become special
'oughts-to-be' within our professional and personal
lives? Any hopes fulfilled will significantly affect
learning and teaching, teaching and the taught, and the

grounding and legitimization (if and whenever needed) of the subject-matter of adult learning.

There may be readers who feel that the four philosophical questions--as they have uniquely and idiosyncratically arisen in your lives--are not answered for you. Fair enough. I urge you to consider once again that one of the most important marks of adulthood must be the realization that whatever the ways in which originations are felt, and beginnings come to be present in our lives, each of us individually must shoulder the full burden of nourishing our growth. 'Self-help' is a virtue which adults must rediscover. Understanding additional marks of adult selfhood should lead one to understand the life-enhancing virtues of 'self-help' and thereby reduce the chronic over-dependency of adult learners upon the wrong kinds of practices, paradigms, and programs of adult education, and consequently the over-reliance upon 'experts', 'specialists', 'facilitators', and the like. Remember that I speak only of over-dependency here!

There may well be variations of this criticism which will point to the unanswerability of these four philosophical questions in some degree, either in principle or for individual persons and special circumstances. But consider the possibilities for adult growth and change. Consider the possible fruits of your careful reflection upon these questions. Consider how your personal answers to these questions might emerge once you have moved consecutively through more layers (and these layers more varied) of meaning than you ever thought you could. These realizations can become the first practical results of your reflections upon adult education and phenomenology.

Finally, each of us can draw support from Bertrand Russell's characteristically eloquent testimony to the value of philosophical reflection on any subject matter:

*Philosophy is to be studied, not for the sake of any definite answers to its questions, since no definite answers can, as a rule, be known to be true, but rather for the sake of the questions themselves; because these questions enlarge our conception of what is possible, enrich our intellectual imagination, and diminish the dogmatic assurance which closes the mind against speculation; but above all because, through the greatness of the universe which philosophy contemplates, the mind also is rendered great, and becomes capable of that union with the universe which constitutes its highest good.*[13]

# INTRODUCTION

## Defining Adult Education: A New Way of Thinking about Some Old Phenomena

A phenomenological parable about the complexities, perplexities, and ironies of defining adult education as a discipline or field . . . consider

> How many trees make up a forest? How many houses a city? . . . Forest and city are two things essentially deep, and depth is fatally condemned to become a surface if it wants to be visible.
>
> I have now around me as many as two dozen grave oaks and graceful ashes. Is this a forest? Certainly not. What I see here is some trees of the forest. The real forest is composed of the trees which I do not see. . . . The forest will be breaking up into a series of successively visible portions, but I shall never find it where I am. The forest flees from one's eyes.
>
> The forest is always a little beyond where we are. It has just gone away from where we are and all that remains is its still fresh trace. The ancients, who projected their emotions into corporeal and living forms, peopled the forests with fugitive nymphs. Nothing could be more exact and expressive. As you walk along, glance quickly at a clearing in the bush and you will notice a quivering of the air as if it were

*hastening to fill the void left by the sudden departure of a slender, naked form.*

*From any spot within its borders the forest is just a possibility: a path along which we could proceed, a spring from which a gentle murmur is brought to us in the arms of silence and which we might discover a few steps away, snatches of songs sung in the distance by birds perched on branches under which we could pass. The forest is the aggregate of possible acts of ours which, when carried out, would lose their real value. The part of the forest immediately before us is a screen, as it were, behind which the rest of it lies hidden and aloof.*

"The Forest," in Jose Ortega y Gasset, *Meditations on Quixote*[1]

*The meaning of adult education . . . is the continued effort to learn by those past school age whether busily employed or not in earning their livelihood; its purpose is to produce and sustain the healthy mind in the healthy body. It can go on daily by thought, by observation, by reading, by making, and it has a special value if pursued in common with others. Life will be in-finitely richer for it; sympathy will be quickened, selfishness will shrink, false pride will be subdued. The thing is worth doing; let us do it!*

D. H. S. Cranage, in
R. St. John Parry, ed., *Cambridge Essays on Adult Education,* 1922, in the aftermath of the publication of the *1919 Report.*[2]

## A. Originations

An introduction serves important functions: (1) It places a subject-matter, a topic, a theme, before us. It locates and positions this subject-matter in our presence. (2) It **pre**-positions me the writer and you the reader relevantly in the presence of the subject-matter, topic, or theme. (3) Quite literally (and in keeping with the fundamental etymology of the word), the introduction leads us inward.

This inwardness takes two forms. A person moves inside a subject-matter and thereby comes to know it better and better. One also moves into oneself more reflectively, and this is the most important form of inwardness effected by any introduction. To know a subject and oneself either better than before or reflectively for the first time is necessarily both to know oneself and the world far better. These are among such diverse happenings as when the host introduces guests and when the teacher introduces a course to the students. In this way, also, I lead you through to phenomenology of adult learning and education with this action of writing.

Introductions involve two kinds of sources or "starts" in our lives. I distinguish these as *originations* and *beginnings*. In this section I have been dealing with originations and origins. The passages below from Albert Cobham and the philosopher René Descartes may be described as originations.

Originations are risings and arisings through which we infer that there must be and must have been sources, something logically prior to the rising and the arising. This is what we can call a source or origin. This source or origin does not have to be a specific human action, act, or event. But the special focus of originations properly is upon the act or fact of something-- even a thought about someone's action or your own prior action--as arising or as springing up from something else; or upon the derivation of something as existing in reference to, and by virtue of, its source. Originations are instances of giving origin to, of giving rise to, of leading something to arise or begin, to initiate, to bring into existence. They are cases in which something about our lives, for example, is derived or deduced from specified sources, is perceived as commencing from something else.

But I should like to go further as I try to conduct each reader into places, positions, states of being, and conditions in relation to my themes of adults, education, and phenomenological research. This introduction carries within it the following account of one student's experiences through education. Alfred Cobham offers an account of his feelings, his experiences, and his thoughts about adult education and the realization of its meaning for his life in England. Date it 1922, in the aftermath of that historic event, the publication of the *1919 Report,* the *Report of the Committee on Adult Education* (Cd. 321, 1919).[3] Cobham said that "the essay is written from the point of view of a working-man, a craftsman with a lifelong experience of working-men of the wage-earning class."

> I know the difficulties and soul-destroying conditions that surround the lives of very many of the workers; I know the oppression and languor of unvarying toil at uninteresting and unpleasant tasks, the jading weariness of repeating the same mechanical movements every minute for fourteen hours a day, month by month, year after year. I know what it is to see my boyhood and youth pass away without any opportunity for education such as the Forster Act gave to those of later birth. I know what it is not to know, and to be conscious of not knowing, what it is to feel a real mind-hunger. I have many times stood wistfully, cravingly looking into a book-shop window much as a penniless urchin looks into that of a confectioner. I have known these things and I sometimes ponder them regretfully. There is this consolation, however. The opportunity came to me when I understood the need for it, and I sometimes even feel thankful that I was not born in better circumstances. I might have had a "sound business education" thrust upon me and lost my soul; I was, in fact, lured into the verdant fields of literature where I found its appropriate sphere.

For twenty five years I have lived in a University Extension atmosphere doing University Extension work and it has brought into my life a great joy, which is ample justification for my plea for widespread Adult Education. . . .

I was well on in manhood before I took seriously to systematic study. Finding myself woefully behind what I felt I ought to be, I resolved to make an effort to mend my condition. But how?[4]

*But how?* Indeed! Answers to this question are seductively presented, but surely not fully available in those legendary "nuts-and-bolts" or "how-to-do-it" brochures, manuals, and books which are so ubiquitously in use as immediate and relatively unreflective aids in: (1) individual-oriented apprenticeships, correspondence courses, internships, and tutorials; in (2) group-oriented situations involving clinics, community development organizations, conferences, demonstrations, institutes, laboratories, study groups, "short" courses, trips, tours, travel, and workshops, and in (3) conjunction with such techniques as 'brainstorming', 'buzz groups', group discussions, interviews, panels, and 'role playing'.[5] These aids and the contexts of their uses may be quite valuable, but what are the theoretical and philosophical foundations for these practical approaches?

In fact, Cobham did not answer his own question in any of these ways, as we shall see shortly. One of the principal claims throughout this book is that approaches to "how-to" questions and problems in the context of adult learning, teaching, and evaluation must be based on careful and consistent theory and philosophy of adult education. One reason for this is that when a person has an immediate need to know (as distinct from a mediated need to know)[6] anything at all, this, too, requires reflection, and the briefest reflection is already entrance into theory and philosophy.

I believe that this claim runs directly counter to much prevailing opinion, belief, and practice within the institution of adult education at the present time. I return to this claim again and again. It is extremely important.

For the moment I want to lead you further into the possibilities of phenomenological research in adult education through the words of the philosopher René Descartes, one of the supreme cartographers of consciousness in the history of Western philosophy. The setting is France. The date is 1637.

> As soon as age permitted me to escape the tutelage of my teachers, I left the study of letters completely. And resolving to search for no other knowledge than what I could find within myself, or in the great book of the world, I spent the rest of my youth traveling, seeing various courts and armies, frequenting peoples of varied humors and conditions, gathering varied experiences, testing myself in the encounters which fortune sent my way, and everywhere so *reflecting* upon what came my way that I could draw some profit from it. For it seemed to me that I could discover much more truth in the reasonings that each person makes concerning matters that are important to him, whose outcome ought to cost him dearly later on if he has judged incorrectly, than in those reasonings that a man of letters makes in his private room, which touch on speculations producing no effect, and which for him have no other consequence except perhaps that the more they are removed from common sense, he will derive all the more vanity from them, for he will have to employ that much more wit and artifice in attempting to make them probable. And I have always had an especially great craving for learning to distinguish the true from the false, to see my way clearly in my actions, and to go forward with confidence in this life.

It is true that, while I spent time merely observing the customs of other men, I found hardly anything about which to be confident and that I noticed there was about as much diversity as I had earlier found among the opinions of philosophers. Thus the greatest profit I derived from this was that on realizing that many things, although they seemed very extravagant and ridiculous to us, did not cease being commonly accepted and approved by other great peoples, I learned to believe nothing very firmly concerning what I had been persuaded to believe only by example and custom; and thus I gradually freed myself from many errors that can darken our natural light and render us less able to listen to reason. But after spending many years thus studying in the book of the world and in trying to gain experience, *I made up my mind one day also to study myself and to spend all the powers of my mind in choosing the ways which I ought to follow.* For me this procedure was much more successful, it seems, than if I had never left either my country or my books.[7] (My emphasis)

We note that Mr. Cobham's question, *But how?*, is Descartes's question, as well. They were both adults, but separated in their respective early years by the widest possible divergence in their individual life-worlds. Reflect on the similarities clearly manifested in these two extreme cases of adult education, each concluded with superb success. For example, are these extreme cases really mutually exclusive ones, even if Cobham's life was that of a workingman of the wage-earning class and René Descartes's life an elitist one in terms of educational and cultural advantages? Extreme cases they may be, in economic and cultural terms, but is there not some spectrum or continuum which brings into close proximity even the ranges of diversity attested in these extreme cases?

Actions introduce ideas, or the necessity of ideas, and ideas introduce actions. There are special actions

we call feelings, experiences, and consciousings. Both immediate and mediate needs to alter the enervating bad habits of my life, for example, and the desire to do so, may be feelings. These are the first steps--actions of a supremely important kind, if you will--toward the necessary replacement of these habits by positive and life-generating habits. A destructive habit cannot simply be destroyed. But it can be replaced by a more satisfying and healthier habit. Education--especially *adult* education successfully pursued--consists largely in the replacement of life-destructive habits by life-regenerative habits. 'Experience', by formal definition if not in common understanding, is actional, and con-sciousings are activities of knowing.

Hence we can say that feelings, experiencings, and consciousings are actions every bit as much as physical activities like those required in writing these words. And insofar as some actions introduce ideas, these actions are new personal actions; they lead persons or things into a particular position, state, condition, or relation with respect to some other person or thing.

But ideas also introduce actions. Ideas, concepts, conceptions, thoughts, notions, images, and impressions all introduce actions. They lead to, they conduct persons to their feelings, experiencings, and conscious-ings themselves, direct us into awareness, acquaintance, and knowledge. Introductions hence are actions which both direct ideas to persons and persons to ideas.

In the light of this descriptive account of origina-tions, the discussions of certain phases of their lives by Alfred Cobham and René Descartes above are excellent case studies of *originations,* although extreme cases of differing kinds of lifeworlds. In these ways, more-over, an introduction is an origination. I return to these matters a bit later.

## B. Beginnings

An introduction is also a *beginning.* Beginnings are typically the actions of persons in opening up operations respecting their lives. That is, through beginning something a person sets himself up effectively to do something. A beginning is a first point of contact with one's own project, the entering upon and into something, the act of taking that absolutely necessary first step of working through a problem. The alcoholic begins his long way back into productive and creative life from disease, malaise, and spiritual discontent through the acceptance of a personal problem and through the refusal of that next drink of alcohol. The journey does begin with the first step. The first step and the *beginning* are identical. Beginning something is starting it on its own career, giving origin (as distinct from being an origin) to it, bringing it into existence, creating it.[8]

Once again I turn to personal records of individual decisions constituting beginnings which have been offered by Alfred Cobham and Rene Descartes.

Let us consider Cobham's statement first.

No municipal science and art schools then existed in the town in which I still live; no University Extension nor W.E.A. Tutorial Classes; only Popular Lectures at the Y.M.C.A. *I decided to attend these, and they deepened my determination.*

Twenty-five years ago, that enthusiast, Miss Rigby, secretary of the local branch of University Extension, insistently urged me to take a ticket for a course of Extension lectures. *I hesitated and invented excuses for refusing.* I felt that I should find myself surrounded by consciously superior people, from which class I had already caught many a chill. She persisted, and ultimately succeeded in persuading me. I went to the first lecture and discovered to my great surprise how much I had misjudged, as it has been so frequently misjudged, the spirit and conduct of University Extension. The *humanness* and *sympathy* of the lecturer, the *goodwill* and *kindness* of the committee, the *comradeship* and *helpfulness* of the members, at once *won my regard and have sustained it* ever since.[9] (My emphasis)

A passage from Descartes's *Meditations on First Philosophy*, presents his words describing the beginning of his passage through to philosophy. It will be obvious, I believe, why I describe Descartes's 'beginning' as an extreme case: He asserts that he will ". . . at once attack those principles which supported everything that I once believed." It is rare indeed that any of us do this--begin reconstructions of our lives in this manner--but once done, this extreme reflecting action is sufficient in itself to warrant characterizing a person who does it as a *philosopher,* as one who truly does *love wisdom.*

Several years have now passed since I *first realized* how many were the false opinions that in my youth I took to be true, and thus how doubtful were all the things that I *subsequently built* upon these *opinions. From the time I became aware of this, I realized that for once I had to raze everything in my life, down to the very bottom, so as to begin again from the first foundations, if I wanted to establish anything firm and lasting in the sciences.* But the task seemed so enormous that I waited for a point in my life that was so ripe that no more suitable a time for laying hold of these disciplines would come to pass. *For this reason, I have delayed so long that I would be at fault were I to waste on deliberation the time that is left for action.* Therefore, now that I have liberated my mind from all cares, and I have secured for myself some leisurely and carefree time, *I withdraw in solitude. I will, in short, apply myself earnestly and openly to the general destruction of my former opinions.*[10] (My emphasis)

Thus far we have before us personal testimony as evidence of highly successful adult education from two disparate sources, an English workingman and a French philosopher. It seems clear that both of them speak as one voice with the German philosopher Edmund Husserl, the founder of twentieth-century phenomenology, in attempting to guide us, not to instruct but to show us and describe for us what they 'saw' in their personal lifeworlds. They have, as he has, I believe, claimed the right to speak according to their best lights-- primarily to oneself, and correspondingly to other persons. Surely Descartes and Husserl have lived through the most serious and reflective of philosophical existences. This is the burden of the testimony of their philosophical influences through the years.

I believe that there is a special sense in which Cobham did this as well during the adult years of his education. There is indeed a philosophical continuum which unites these three men. I come to this point later (in discussions of Plato and John Dewey), but first it is helpful to cite R. G. Collingwood's words as entirely reflective of the aims of adult education:

> All thought exists for the sake of action. We try to understand ourselves and our world only in order that we may learn how to live. The end of our self-knowledge is not the contemplation by enlightened intellects of their own mysterious nature, but the freer and more effectual self-revelation of that nature in a vigorous practical life. If thought were the mere discovery of interesting facts, its indulgence, in a world full of desperate evils and among men crushed beneath the burden of daily tasks too hard for their solitary strength, would be the act of a traitor: the philosopher would be better to follow the plough or clout shoes, to become a slum doctor or a police-court missionary, or hand himself over to a bacteriologist to be inoculated with tropical diseases.[11]

To these claims we might add that "to be old," wrote
Martin Buber, ". . . is a glorious thing when one has
not unlearned what it means to **begin**." I do not know
many of you, my readers, but there is a sense in which
contact may also be established through this essay on
meaningfulness and through friendships which may be
established as we venture forth--**begin**, as it were--
together.

## C. Learning Through Practice: Common Sense Through Philosophical Inquiry

The classic account in Western philosophy of a con-
tinuum in which distinctions are made between degrees
and kinds of knowledge and ways of knowing is offered by
Plato in the *Republic.* The passages are known as the
"Simile of the Line."[12] Socrates is talking to Glaucon,
Plato's brother:

> Conceive then, said I, as we were saying, that
> there are these two entities, and that one of
> them is sovereign over the intelligible order and
> region and the other over the world of the eye-
> ball, not to say the sky-ball, but let that pass.
> You surely apprehend the two types, the visible
> and the intelligible.
> I do.
> Represent them then, as it were, by a line
> divided into two unequal sections and cut each
> section again in the same ratio--the section,
> that is, of the visible and that of the intelli-
> gible order--and then as an expression of the
> ratio of their comparative clearness and obscur-
> ity you will have, as one of the sections of the
> visible world, images. By images I mean, first,
> shadows, and then reflections in water and on
> surfaces of dense, smooth, and bright texture,
> and everything of that kind, if you apprehend.
> I do.
> As the second section assume that of which
> this is a likeness or an image, that is, the

animals about us and all plants and the whole
class of objects made by man. . . .

By the distinction that there is one section
of it which the soul is compelled to investigate
by treating as images the things imitated in the
former division, and by means of assumptions from
which it proceeds not up to a first principle but
down to a conclusion, while there is another
section in which it advances from its assumption
to a beginning or principle that transcends
assumption, and in which it makes no use of the
images employed by the other section, relying on
ideas only and progressing systematically through
ideas. . . .

This then is the class that I described as
intelligible, it is true, but with the reserva-
tion first that the soul is compelled to employ
assumptions in the investigation of it, not
proceeding to a first principle because of its
inability to extricate itself from and rise above
its assumptions, and second, that it uses as
images or likenesses the very objects that are
themselves copied and adumbrated by the class
below them, and that in comparison with these
latter are esteemed as clear and held in honor.

I understand, said he, that you are speaking
of what falls under geometry and the kindred
arts.

Understand then, said I, that by the other
section of the intelligible I mean that which the
reason itself lays hold of by the power of dialectic, treating its assumptions not as absolute
beginnings but literally as hypotheses, under-
pinnings, footings, and springboards so to speak,
to enable it to rise to that which requires no
assumption and is the starting point of all, and
after attaining to that again taking hold of the
first dependencies from it, so to proceed down-
ward to the conclusion, making no use whatever of
any object of sense but only of pure ideas moving

on through ideas to ideas and ending with ideas. . . .

And now, answering to these four sections, assume these four affections occurring in the soul--intellection or reason for the highest, understanding for the second, belief for the third, and for the last, picture thinking or conjecture--and arrange them in a proportion, considering that they participate in clearness and precision in the same degree as their objects partake of truth and reality.

I employ an upward metaphor in the following diagram of the 'simile of the line'. My reason for doing so is that Plato's account of the kinds and ways of knowing at the very end of Book VI of the *Republic* is followed in the opening pages of Book VII by his well-known "myth of the cave." In those pages Plato tells the story of the pilgrimage of the soul of one person (Socrates, probably) as the story of his ascent from below, from the bowels of a cave.

My judgment is that these two accounts must be read as two inseparable forms of a single message articulating the process of inquiry and knowing. The *first,* the "simile of the line," is the formalized statement of this way. The *second,* the "myth of the cave," is the story of the relationship of ignorance and the growth away from ignorance through several kinds of education. Both together may be read clearly as a parable of adult learning and the continuing saga of an adult's education. Plato's "simile of the line" is schematized in the figure on the next page.

## Plato's SIMILE OF THE LINE

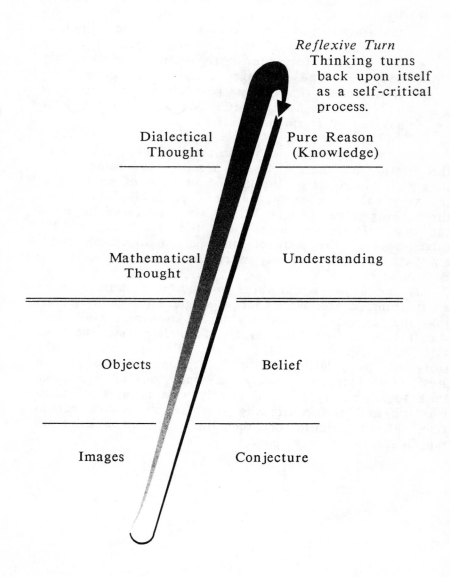

*Reflexive Turn*
Thinking turns
back upon itself
as a self-critical
process.

Dialectical
Thought

Pure Reason
(Knowledge)

Mathematical
Thought

Understanding

Objects

Belief

Images

Conjecture

One might read John Dewey's *Logic: The Theory of Inquiry*[13] as a central text in the philosophy of adult learning and education. It clearly addresses problems of adult education. I shall discuss a number of points I believe to be relevant to adult education and which are found in Chapter Four of Dewey's work, "Common Sense and Scientific Inquiry."

There Dewey is primarily concerned with a number of similarities between commonsense inquiry and scientific inquiry. The former is the kind of questioning and problem solving which takes place within, as the *Oxford English Dictionary* puts it, "the good sound practical sense," or through the use of "combined tact and readiness in dealing with the ordinary affairs of life." Commonsense inquiry deals with questions and problems regarding "situations of use and enjoyment." Dewey also cites another definition of common sense: "The general sense, feeling, judgment of mankind of a community." He claims that both significance and meaning are conveyed in these two definitions when they are taken together as definitions of common sense.

Many additional characteristics of significance and meaning within everyday life and the life of common sense are explored in that chapter. The criteria for judging significance, meaning, and worth are practical, largely arbitrary, and changing; commonsense inquiry is 'qualitative' as distinct from mathematical inquiry; it is teleological (end-seeking, or purposive), nonspecialized, and presented in nontechnical language; there may be some order and system in commonsense inquiry, although it deals normally with the most generalized kinds of problems.

It is within and throughout the domains of common needs of 'everydayness' and commonsense inquiry that scientific inquiry arises.

(1) Scientific subject-matter and procedures grow out of the direct problems and methods of common sense, of practical uses and enjoyments. They (2) react into the latter in a way that enormously refines, expands and liberates the contents and the agencies at the disposal of scientific subject-matter to that of common sense.

## Dewey's PROCESS OF INQUIRY

### Scientific Inquiry

1. Greater refinement in ways of knowing our world.
2. Criteria are less arbitrary and less changing.
3. More quantitative.
4. Knowledge is more intrinsic.
5. More specialization.
6. Technical language.
7. Higher degrees of order and system.
8. More specific problems.

*Reflexive Turn*
Thinking turns back upon itself as a self-critical process.

### Commonsense Inquiry

1. More concerned with the use and enjoyment of things.
2. Criteria for judgments are more arbitrary and changing.
3. More qualitative.
4. Teleological knowledge (purposive and end-seeking).
5. Less specialization.
6. Nontechnical language.
7. Lesser degrees of order and system.
8. Generalized problems.

When it is taken to be final, it generates those controversial problems of epistemology and common sense, separation and opposition of metaphysics that still dog the course of philosophy. When scientific subject-matter is seen to bear genetic and functional relation to the subject-matter of common sense, these problems disappear. Scientific subject-matter is intermediate, not final and complete in itself.[14]

Dewey characterizes scientific inquiry in the most general sense as a process of refining various ways of knowing the world; its criteria for evaluating and assessing significance, meaning, and knowledge are less arbitrary and less changing (although still often arbitrary and surely changing) than common sense; its judgments tend to be more quantitative, even mathematical; much scientific inquiry is directed toward intrinsic ends (ends which Dewey characterizes as knowing for the sake of knowing); much of scientific inquiry is instrumental, practical and specialized; much of it is carried on through technology and complex technical languages; it is characterized by a high degree of order and system.

These descriptions are descriptions of distinct (but, of course, for Dewey, inseparable) ways of inquiring within the process of *inquiring* into the constitutions and structures of the lifeworlds of persons. Individual persons may conduct these inquiries, and communities of interested persons may conduct cooperative inquiries, into these questions and problems within the generalized problematic situations within the 'everydayness' of these lifeworlds.[15] Dewey's process of inquiry was schematized on the previous page.

I have tried to dramatize Dewey's two distinct ways of inquiry--both of them through a process of questions/possible answers . . . questions/possible answers (and so forth)--on the previous page. The "upward" metaphor I use in the diagram must not be interpreted in any moral or ethical evaluative sense, although the latter are present in Plato's earlier account. Neither kind of inquiry is necessarily 'better' than the other in Dewey's context, although his ethical theory laying out the construction of the good was developed within the parameters of his account of the relation of common sense and scientific inquiry. What we have here instead is a set of very careful and helpful phenomenological distinctions which can be recorded as one attempts to meet the problematics within the 'everydayness' of our lives. The *reflexive turn* at the 'top' of both schemata represents ultimately the use to which even the most refined ways of inquiry might be put in the midst of the problematics of our 'everydayness'.

The discussions of knowing, knowledge, and the known in the views of Plato and Dewey share common characteristics, among them the following ones which I cite because of their importance for our purposes: (1) Both as philosophers and adult educators they begin by describing knowledge as persons' perceptions within the everyday world. (2) Neither thinker allows perception to constitute the whole of knowledge, or knowledge properly so-called, since both require that a clearer definition of what knowledge is must include the perceptual, but move beyond it into judgments about the world which can be verified or falsified as a part of the quest for true knowledge or truth. (3) Both of them characterize knowledge more fully as judgment marked by both definition and more precise discourse. (4) Both Dewey and Plato present knowledge as a continuum of inquiry.

An important clue to the principal difference between their accounts, however, is contained in the very words 'knowing' and 'knowledge'. Dewey may be said to offer a phenomenological description of 'knowing' as personal inquiry (both as personal and as public knowledge) that moves through wide ranges of description of all these elements: enjoyment and use of things within the world; judging and judgments; quantitativeness; qualitativeness; purposiveness; specialization; language expression, from the metaphorical uses of language through the literal uses to the technical uses of language; order and system; and generalization/specialization. Dewey's account is richly descriptive of what happens in the

movement of commonsense inquiry (that is, inquiry founded in the common sensing of phenomena, which also have
their properties in the public domain characterized as
public knowledge).

Plato presents not so much a descriptive account, but
a much more reflective and speculative rendering of
'knowing' and the 'known', with normative judgments
attending these. That is, the 'higher' a person's
'knowing' and 'knowledge' move along the continuum of
inquiry which the 'simile of the line' is, the greater
degree of clarity there is in the knowledge portrayed,
and the better grasp and kind of knowledge a higher
state of mind has. Plato's way of saying it is that
this is the manner in which knowledge ought to be understood, and especially and fully so from the vantage
level of the 'pure reason' of 'dialectical thought'.
Hence, Plato may be read as laying out an epistemology,
or a theory of knowledge, whereas Dewey's description
both enfleshes Plato's epistemological position, and in
turn is itself illuminated by Plato's careful reflective
terms.

In the light of what I discussed in Sections A and B
above, originations and beginnings, Dewey's description
may be seen as an example of 'originations', and Plato's
more speculative and epistemological statement becomes
an excellent example of what I mean by 'beginnings'.
'Originations' mark the way in which things may have
emerged, whereas 'beginnings' are always logged in and
pegged through personal reflection. The relationships
between them are rather like the ebbs and tides of
history as lived by persons actually living through the
pragmatic actions of their lives, as distinct from the
written story of those personal actions in history as
they are brought together in a plausible tale. Telling
the story necessitates that the lives of those persons
as lived become the determinate subject-matter of certain kinds of systematic investigations which formally
have come to be known as the discipline of history. The
lives as lived are 'originations'. The tale as told
recounts 'beginnings'. Read together, both kinds of

accounts are fused together and create a rich intellectual clearing in which to introduce the subject-matter
of adult education as a rigorous human science.

## D. The Subject-matter of Adult Education: Adult Education as Rigorous Human Science

Conceptualization, persuasion, curriculum, and method
were the tasks Robie Kidd claimed must be the first
priorities for adult educators. He also mentioned
*sharing*. Whereas *philosophers* have often been
viewed as the most solitary kinds of persons, ironical-
ly, *philosophy* may be that discipline among all of the
formal disciplines of knowledge most desperately in need
of shared and cooperative work. In this respect, therefore, it can be seen as closely aligned with the pursuit
of adult education, since sharing and cooperation are
the foundation of the latter. And the relationship is
much closer, since philosophizing is typically (but not
always) something that only adults may do successfully.
Both Plato and Aristotle claimed that persons ought to
be mature adults before beginning the study of
philosophy.

I have already alerted you to the fact that this is
an essay on meaning, as any phenomenological investigation must be. Meaningfulness is always cast in personal
and intersubjective terms. Hence my hope is that all of
us--including the author--may move through greater self-
knowledge as we move through the essay. If this happens, then we ourselves will be persuaded and persuasive
of others in what we try to do here. When we feel and
when we think we try to position these feelings and
these thoughts in our lives through language. And we
want to try out their meaning and worth by sharing them
intersubjectively with other persons.

We may even help in the development of curricula
which assist the structuring of our learning experi-
ences--and also assist us, we hope, in learning to
learn--within 'everydayness'. Of course this relates to
the ends and goals we plan as most worthy of achieving.

Clearly, method(s) and means thus become primary concerns. Therefore, although I try to perform the task of conceptualization throughout, the attempt to do this without trying to be persuasive, without pointing toward the development of relevant curricula and the use of effective practical methods might be criticized by some readers as "pie-in-the-sky," disembodied, and impotent. But wait! Those other three tasks cited by Kidd, without conceptualization may be only so many voices in the wind, rudderless programs of study with much wheel-spinning generating few results of lasting consequence.

Consider the relationships of theory and practice--conceptualization and method, if you will--within adult education. Whatever protestations there may be to the contrary, practice and method in adult education do not simply take place *in vacuo* or in disembodied form. They are created out of logically prior webs and networks of ideas, presuppositions, and theories. These might not be stated or thought through. These conceptualizations may never see the light of day, but a bit of logic would bring them into explicit formulation for investigation. This is a primary task of any philosophy of adult education.

Conceptualization and practice in adult education should never be separated. They can and should be distinguished. And when distinguished, it should be recognized (1) that every conceptualization must be tested, applied, and improved if possible; (2) that every practice and method should be conceptualized and thereby improved if possible; (3) that conceptualization and method must go hand in hand in all inquiries within the human sciences; and (4) adult education--insofar as it is a science--is a human science. But what does it mean to claim that adult education is a human science?

Almost anything goes into and passes for the theory and practice of adult education today. Almost three decades ago, two prominent adult educators defined adult education in these terms:

> Adult education includes all the activities with an educational purpose that are carried on by people outside the ordinary business of life.[16]

> [Adult education is] an educational program that is planned and organized to assist adults in meeting their responsibilities as individuals and as members of society.[17]

In 1976, the General Conference of UNESCO adopted what has become accepted as the 'world definition' of adult education:

> The term *adult education* denotes the entire body of organized educational processes, whatever the content, level, and method, whether formal or otherwise, whether they prolong or replace initial education in schools, colleges, and universities as well as in apprenticeship, whereby persons regarded as adult by the society to which they belong develop their abilities, enrich their knowledge, improve their technical or professional qualification, or turn them in a new direction and bring about changes in their attitudes or behavior in the two-fold perspective of full personal development and participation in balanced and independent social economic, and cultural development. . . .[18]

Gordon G. Darkenwald and Sharan B. Merriam have defined adult education in the following terms, fully aware that this definition "does not address other important concerns such as the content, sponsorship, methodology or purposes of adult education: Adult education is a process whereby persons whose major social roles are characteristic of adult status undertake systematic and sustained learning activities for the purpose of bringing about changes in knowledge, attitudes, values or skills."[19]

These definitions are sufficient to suggest the great diversity of definitions of adult education. Jerold W. Apps wrote that "this field, concerned with the education of adults, might seem elusive, ambiguous, contradictory, and perplexing."[20] Operationally defined, adult education theory and practice are frequently whatever persons who call themselves adult educators (or who are labeled this by others) say or do as experts, professionals, or specialists. Truly, there may be many mansions in adult education as constructed and practiced, but most--as theory--are built upon foundations of sand shifting with the waves of fashionable but fleeting practices. Practices have preceded and unreflectively dictated theories almost exclusively. This particular asymmetrical relationship of practice and theory is not always bad, but practices should be under constant examination. This examination, however, always invokes reflection, and reflection necessarily occurs within a theoretical framework. Therefore, it is always better to understand what theoretical structure undergirds practices. And it is always best that theories and practices relevant to each other be consistent with one another.

Relevant and productive research in adult education requires that the theory and practice of adult education be consistent with each other. If the research is fitting, pertinent, and applicable to the study of and the leadership of adults, it is all the more likely to bring forth desired results and to lead to additional-- and initially unforeseen--problems for research projects and research programs. Theory and practice stand or fall together within the specific circumstances of well-formed projects.

It is frequently difficult to tell what relevant research or productive research is in adult education because a large number of special methodological problems remain unresolved at the core of what adult education is perceived to be. In this section I discuss several of these from a phenomenological perspective. These include the questions of whether adult education is a discipline, whether it has a subject-matter, and how it is defined in theories appropriate to it and in the light of its practices. I will (1) argue that although adult education is not a discipline, it does have a definable subject-matter; (2) present a strategy for moving from current operationalizing definitions of what adult education is to a normative definition of what it is in theory and practice; (3) state and clarify this normative definition of the subject; and (4) show how adult education thereby may be seen as the paradigm of rigorous human science.

## Adult Education and the Conception of a Discipline

It has been customary (although grossly misleading) to distinguish between 'physical' sciences such as physics, and 'social' sciences such as economics and to claim that all sciences are included in one or another of these classifications. In addition, it is fashionable to distinguish as 'humanities' other kinds of studies such as philosophy. The problem is that theories and practices of adult education do not fit into any of these classifications. They are disciplines, but is adult education a 'discipline?'

Answering this question in the affirmative requires that the education of adults (and even adult learning per se) be addressed as the training of physical, mental, and/or moral powers of adult persons through instruction, control, exercise, and the inculcation of good habits. It also requires accounts of the state or condition of orderly conduct resulting from this systematic training, or accounts of the states of order and control which result from this instruction. As a discipline, adult education would be considered a carefully circumscribed branch of knowledge or instruction.

Clearly, adult education is not a discipline. This conclusion significantly disposes of a large number of methodological problems. For example, adult educators no longer should feel guilty about, or be censured for, "not being scientific enough." They should not be duty bound to have their research conform to one or another of the "hard" or "soft" sciences, or attempt to imitate one of these, or have their most relevant and crucial research methods or programs be dictated either by one of these or by one of the "humanities" disciplines.

## The Subject-matter of Adult Education

Does adult education have a subject-matter? A subject-matter is the 'matter' operated upon in an act or process, or the 'matter' or phenomena out of which something is created. It is material for public discourse or public expression in language. A subject-matter is anything with which thought, deliberation, or discussion is concerned. It is anything treated or dealt with in reflective ways, or that with which a science deals, even a body of facts or ideas with which a study is concerned.

Adult education does indeed have a clear and distinct subject-matter, one which literally stares us in the face. But trees have obscured the presence of the forest. Because practices have almost always seemed more pressing and have preceded theories and theory-building in unreflective ways, adult educators have never clearly formulated their essential subject-matter and its structures. Consequently, they have either not founded their disparate practices in consistent philosophical theories at all, or they have done so only in piecemeal and logically inconsistent ways. The principal reason why they have done so is that they have selected different kinds and degrees of phenomena unreflectively as more relevant than others. And what scales of relevance have they used?[21]

Elias and Merriam have offered a rich and useful account of the major theoretical directions adult educators have taken.[22] They call these 'philosophies' of adult education: 'liberal', 'progressive', 'behaviorist', 'humanist', 'radical', and 'analytical' philosophies. Each of these positions is an attempt at conceptual clarity, coherence, and consistency in the application of its concepts, but this is the special focus of the "analytic" approach. Each position shows how its relevant data emerge from circumscribed concerns, but 'behaviorism' is a deliberate reductionism carefully explored. Each position seeks some kind of change among people, whether the change is personal, community-based, or more global; but 'liberal', 'progressive', and 'radical' adult education clearly emphasize (even if in quite different ways) an over-arching concern for effecting transformations. 'Humanistic' adult education is person-centered and focuses on the active and voluntaristic cooperation of participants.

Considered as coordinate to one another in explanatory power but mutually exclusive, each approach sometimes has been proclaimed normatively to be *the* philosophy of adult education with resolutions to all relevant problems (at least in principle). Clearly they each have drawn their most perspicuous insights from different sets of phenomena and have performed their most crucial experiments and studies in the light of these differences. Clearly, however, all of their devotees claim to be dealing with persons in one way or another, although it is not always evident what essential structure of **person** or **personhood**[23] is under investigation such that one approach can claim to be logically different from the others. What is **person** or **personhood**, as distinct from persons? It is important to make this distinction as clear as possible. Suppose that 'adult education' is a generic concept combining theory and practice rather than a class concept. In philosophy concepts generally are treated as 'genuine concepts' which overlap one another, whereas in mathematics and the physical sciences concepts are treated generally as 'class concepts' which are mutually exclusive. Plato's concepts of Goodness, Truth, and Beauty are classic examples of generic and overlapping concepts, whereas in mathematics the concepts of 'circle', 'triangle', and 'square' are mutually exclusive concepts. 'Class concepts' are alleged to provide the greater ground for 'objectivity'.[24]

A classification of the different kinds of philosophical foundations for adult education practices (as grouped into mutually exclusive classes) would give way to a phenomenological investigation of the phenomena presented by the thoughts and actions (with thought and action overlapping as generic concepts) of persons. This latter analysis would not be limited rigidly, or through the mutual exclusions necessary to 'objectivistic' classificational methods, to just one or another set of phenomena selected through one of these specific 'philosophical approaches' for the sake of 'objectivity'. All phenomena manifested by persons initially would be equal candidates for investigation. Suppose, further, that **person** is the essential subject-matter of adult education. Not persons or people, but **person**. The distinctions between **person** and person are crucial to this essay. **Person** is the full eduction of what persons are and have in common; it makes possible communication on the basis of intersubjectivity within the coexistence of persons.

Suppose that both the sense of an enduring self, the capacity for self-recognition, and the reflexive capacity for new, unfamiliar, and nonhabitual acts and actions are among but do not exhaust the essential structures of what we mean by **person**. They are among the countless eductions of **person**. Moreover, we note that in any rigorous scientific investigation the methods of investigation emerge from within the phenomena under investigation. In the most originative sense, a science (from the Latin **scientia**) is the systematic investigation of a determinate subject-matter. This is the full bedrock of rigorous science.

If these suppositions are granted, a phenomenology of the essential structures of adult education uncovers a *provisional* definition of adult education: **adult education is the enactment of, and the systematic investigation of the phenomena constituting the adult eductions of person, specifically of persons' free and deliberate motives for acting.**[25]

Person's free and deliberate motives for acting are not 'caused' except in the special sense distinguished by R. G. Collingwood below. Collingwood claimed[26] that the word 'cause' in English (from the Greek $\alpha\iota\tau\iota\alpha$ and the Latin **causa**) has a variety of meanings which lead to great ambiguities in its usages. He identified at least three of these senses, respectively, as used in the writing of history, in the practical sciences of nature such as medicine and engineering, and in the theoretical sciences of nature such as physics and chemistry. Collingwood further claimed that the relation between these three senses of 'cause' is an historical relation: Number I being the earliest of the three, Number II a development from it, and Number III a development from that. Collingwood wrote:

> Sense I. Here that which is 'caused' is the free and deliberate act of a conscious and responsible agent, and 'causing' him to do it means affording him a motive for doing it.
> Sense II. Here that which is 'caused' is an event in nature, and its 'cause' is an event or state of things by producing or preventing which we can produce or prevent that whose cause it is said to be.
> Sense III. Here that which is 'caused' is an event or state of things, and its 'cause' is another event or state of things standing to it in a one-one relation of causal priority: i.e., a relation to such a kind that (a) if the cause happens or exists the effect also must happen or exist, even if no further conditions are fulfilled, (b) the effect cannot happen or exist unless the cause happens or exists, (c) in some sense which remains to be defined, the cause is prior to the effect; for without such priority there would be no telling which is which. If C and E were connected merely by a one-one relation such as is described in the sentences (a) and (b) above, there would be no reason why C should be called the cause of E, and E the effect of C, rather than vice versa. But whether causal priority is temporal priority, or a special case of temporal priority, or priority of some other kind, is another question.
> Sense I may be called the *historical* sense of the word 'cause', because it refers to a type

of case in which both C and E are human activities such as form the subject-matter of history. When historians talk about causes, this is the sense in which they are using the word, unless they are aping the methods and vocabulary of natural science.

Sense II refers to a type of case in which natural events are considered from a human point of view, as events grouped in pairs where one member in each pair, C, is immediately under human control, whereas the other, E, is not immediately under human control but can be indirectly controlled by man because of the relation in which it stands to C. This is the sense which the word 'cause' has in the *practical sciences of nature,* i.e., the sciences of nature whose primary aim is not to achieve theoretical knowledge about nature but to enable man to enlarge his control of nature. This is the sense in which the word 'cause' is used, for example, in engineering or medicine.

Sense III refers to a type of case in which an attempt is made to consider natural events not practically, as things to be produced or prevented by human agency, but theoretically, as things that happen independently of human will but not independently of each other: causation being the name by which this dependence is designated. This is the sense which the word has traditionally borne in physics and chemistry and, in general, the *theoretical sciences of nature.*[27]

Whereas much adult education research is carried out in accordance with an overt or covert commitment to a presupposition of causal relationships relating to persons' behavior, and involve unreflectively Sense III of 'cause' above (and cannot possibly make sense in dealing with persons as having free and deliberate motives for acting), phenomenological investigations require that alleged 'causal' relationships and theories about 'causal' relationships be put aside. I issue this disclaimer often in this essay, but if 'cause' is to be admitted into the discussion at all it must be used in Sense I above, as "the free and deliberate act of a conscious and responsible agent, and 'causing' him to do it means affording him a reason for doing it". There-fore, I propose that both researchers and practitioners work with the adult eductions of **person** without causal theories, or in ways involving 'cause' in Collingwood's Sense I above. Sense II of 'cause' may be used with some justification, also, if causes are to be admitted in any degree. The points we have just explored are fundamental to what a human science is. I suggest, finally, that a number of research projects of a theoretical and historical nature are ready for the plucking here.

Each of the principal philosophies of adult education identified by Elias and Merriam can be demonstrated to have distinctive, overlapping, and cooperative locations within the systematic investigation of **person**. Each position, when reflectively reworked, and with consis-tent interfacings of its theories and practices, will be seen to be a phase, region, or sector of the investiga-tion of the generic essence of adult education as gener-ic concepts of research and will be better able to lay out its research programs in the light of distinguish-able relevancy systems.[28] Although not a discipline, adult education does have a subject-matter. The adult eductions of **person** constitute this subject-matter. Indeed, adult education has always had this subject-matter, but adult educators almost never have formulated it clearly enough. Surely, they have not done so in formal definitions in their writings.

## Adult Education as Rigorous Human Science[29]

Affording motives, which is the reason-giving pro-cess, is crucial. (1) From the adult educator's per-spective a person can be given reasons for acting. This means either that a person's actions can be understood in the light of certain reasons, or that a person may be given, and accept as one's own, reasons for acting. Or it may be both at once. Affording motives in this perspective means that *reasons why* are being given. (2) From the adult learner's perspective, one may be given, and may accept as one's own, certain reasons for acting. Or it may mean that one's own reasons for acting have been educed from oneself. Affording motives in this perspective means that *reasons for* are being given.

Phenomenologists have long argued that there are kinds of studies which can be called 'human sciences.' A phenomenological investigation is always a human science. Moreover, a central claim of this essay is that adult education is the paradigm of rigorous human science. A human science is an orderly and systematic investigation and description of a person's (and persons') felt experiences of direct phenomena through the various forms in which selected and relevant phenomena may appear or be manifested. Realizing, evidencing, and certifying are three of the many possible ways in which we speak of our processes of awareness both of facts within our lifeworlds and of our commitments as persons. Within our adult lifeworlds we learn most fundamentally and lastingly through the assurances of facts situated within our commitments and beliefs. Facts within values; values situating facts--both of these flow inextricably through indeterminately long streams of time and space.

A *human science* deals necessarily with both facts and values and does not formally exclude the latter in the midst of its scientific investigations. A *fact* is any phenomenon intersubjectively structured, explored, investigated, and analyzed as an objecting agreement of intersubjectively felt experience. A *value* is any phenomenon intersubjectively structured, explored, investigated, and analyzed as a subjecting agreement of intersubjectively felt experience.

## Conclusion

I have tried to show in this section that although adult education is not a discipline, it does have a subject-matter; that this subject-matter can be clearly defined; that this subject-matter can be systematically investigated such that adult education can be viewed as the paradigm of rigorous human science. If I have succeeded in showing this, the implications for research are immense. Not the least of these implications is that adult educators, in investigating **person**, assist in providing reasons for the actions of others and for their own actions, and thereby lead us all toward enriched understanding of **person** and consequently of the actions which have been taken or could be taken by persons.

I know of no 'discipline' in which the subject-matter comes to be more enriched for personal uses whereby persons become transformatively empowered to assume greater charge of their own destinies than within the practices of adult education located within this normatively conceived scientific foundation--and whereby persons come to have motives for acting and go on to act on these.

Now, what follows from the claims in the Preface and in this Introduction? How do we perform the promise of an essay in meaningfulness which seeks to investigate some of the most central phenomena presented by adults within the 'everydayness' of their lifeworld as they (ought to) help themselves through continuing learning? My answer is that this *essay* follows. Literally, an essay is the action and process of trying, testing, experimenting, and perhaps 'proving'. I shall try to perform these promises and address Robie Kidd's *task*s through philosophical investigations characterized most fundamentally as phenomenological.

*What is phenomenology?*

# PART I

## Phenomenology, Linguistic Phenomenology, and Scientific Methods

*Phenomenology is, in the 20th century, mainly the name for a philosophical movement whose primary objective is the direct investigation and description of phenomena as consciously experienced, without theories about their causal explanation and as free as possible from unexamined preconceptions and presuppositions.*

Herbert Spiegelberg,
"Phenomenology," in the
*Encyclopedia Britannica*, 1965[1]

To say briefly and yet intelligibly what phenomenology is and intends is something desired by many but at this time hardly possible . . . Let us begin by picturing the situation which we surveyed when we analyzed the total content of thinking. The thinking subject from whom the whole variety of thought-forming acts of thinking proceeds, aiming his sights at a completely unlimited variety of objects in all possible fields of objects, develops, as these objects confront him now in this, now in that, kind of consciousness, successively with respect to the objects comprised in the surrounding world, the whole abundance of thought products of various

kinds, as we have partly enumerated them above.
Phenomenology shifts the point of sight of its
investigation first into thinking subject and
focuses from this place on the objects within the
object world of this thinking subject; it then
takes hold of the thoughts and the opinions which
the thinking subject harbors about the object
and, in so doing, refrains from taking any stand
with regard to these opinions, while taking the
objects and the object worlds merely as the
counterparts (seen thus or so by the subject) of
his thinking consciousness, without allowing
itself any [claims to] transcendent knowledge of
these objects. For only from the point of sight
of that thinking subject and only as intentional
counterparts of that consciousness are these
objects visible to it from its standpoint.
Phenomenology, therefore, also leaves aside all
knowledge obtained elsewhere and all the sciences
of these objects, because it places itself in
thought before the beginning of all such science.
From the point of sight moved into the thinking
subject it looks *first* at the intentional objects
and the opinions of that subject, particularly at
the acts of consciousness which pertain to these
objects and opinions, and *next* to the modes of
givenness of the objects and the modes of thought
of the opinions. Indeed, even the subject into
which it transfers its point of sight is left
behind unheeded. Viewing in this manner it takes
inventory first of what there is to be seen
within the scope so staked out. It does not
raise at all the question of the reality of what
can thus be intuited, not even with regard to the
acts of consciousness, but only pays attention to
the what and the properties, as well as the
mutual relations, of what is to be found there.
The most cautious and most circumspect
description of what is intuited is then followed
especially by the tracing of the essential and
necessary affinities in the various

distinguishable strata of the whole, both between
the elements of the same stratum and between the
elements of different strata. *In particular, the
way in which certain elements or complexes stand
in relation to certain others as their ultimate
fulfillment and foundation is pursued in detail
and by cautious probing. Thus phenomenology
passes constantly through the different spheres:
namely, those of the acts of thinking, the
consciousness of objects, the opinions, and the
intentional objects.* (My emphasis)

> Alexander Pfänder,
> in *Phenomenology of
> Willing and Motivation*[2]

**Introductory Remarks**

A phenomenological approach to adult education opens
up new directions for research and uncovers new layers
of clarity in perceptions, conceptions, action, and
practices. This means that new ventures in programming,
curricula, teaching, and research become manifest con-
textually within all learning/teaching appropriately
characteristic of adults. It means, moreover, that the
personal ventures of adult self-help, of adult self-
willing and self-motivating decisions, plans, and
actions, also may come to be seen in clearer focus
through phenomenological investigations.

Part I begins with introductory definitions of phenomenology by Herbert Spiegelberg and Alexander Pfänder,
not simply as another case among countless philosophical
traditions, "isms," or "schools," but as the inevitable
and necessary basis for all philosophies and for all
sciences. To call it a 'basis' is not to say that it is
a *complete* basis or even a completable basis for all
philosophy or for all science. I do not make these
claims. Every conceptual system or edifice requires its
foundation just as every physical edifice does. Foundations may change, but they are foundations and foundational all the same. So it is with phenomenology. It
is founding, foundational, and a foundation for all
philosophies and for all sciences. All of these, both

as originations and beginnings, are disclosed through phenomenological investigations, as Edmund Husserl claimed.

In what follows, I offer introductory sketches of phenomenology, 'linguistic phenomenology', and briefly relate central aspects of phenomenological methods to a number of the activities characterized as scientific methods. The juxtaposition of these two clusters of methods of inquiry, search, and criticism ought to attest very clearly, at least, Edmund Husserl's claims that phenomenology is the most rigorous of sciences: Even the most rigorous scientists in the very early stages of a research project do the kind of investigation which could be termed phenomenological investigation, and in the final or interpretational stages of research projects, interpretations of the phenomena and the results of the investigations and experiments might well move along phenomenological lines.

## A. Phenomenology

'Phenomenology' is a formidable word. The word points to a selection from a range of intellectual instruments and tools; it empowers them with special force toward exploration of the vast reaches of the conscious vital lives of persons. Through the consciousing[3] processes laid out by phenomenological exploration, descriptions, and analyses, our experiencings and feelings as persons are also shown forth toward further understanding.

Yes, 'phenomenology' is a formidable word. What does it really mean? How does phenomenology relate to philosophy? How does it relate to adults and to their learning and education?

A person is a human being who thinks, a 'self,' an 'I,' a 'subject.' The discovery, through philosophy, of this thinking 'I' is at the same time the discovery that this subject, self, this 'I', in thinking, is always *thinking-of*. Thinking-of is always an action performed by a person who is reflective, and who is therefore performing reflexive actions of thought[4] toward the object(s)[5] of that person's conscious life.

A person is never merely conscious, but always *conscious-of*. Hence I have used the term 'consciousing,' literally *knowing-with*, in this same way because knowing-with is built into the etymology of the concept of consciousness. Phenomenological analysis discloses that the vital relation of knowing-with is logically prior to any concrete instance of a person's being conscious-of another 'object', whether person, color, hope, fear, or indeed any other 'object' in the person's consciousing of a personal lifeworld.

These objects of one's conscious life may be feelings, experiencings, ideas, hopes, problems, physical objects, and any other phenomena within the 'everydayness' of one's lifeworld. This is what Pfänder points to in speaking of a person's

> . . . aiming his sights at a completely unlimited variety of objects in all possible fields . . . as these objects confront now in this, now in that, kind of consciousness, successively with respect to the objects comprised in the surrounding world, the whole abundance of thought products of various kinds, as we have partly enumerated them above.[6]

Phenomenological research is committed to *neither* idealism and its ultimate grounding in the subject, self or I, *nor* to realism's ultimate grounding in the object, thing, physical unit "out there" in an external world. Phenomenological investigations start with *both* the thinking subject, the 'I,' *and* the object world of this thinking subject. Hence, phenomenological research consists of investigations of both the thinking subject and what is thought by this thinking subject. Most significantly, phenomenological investigations move cartographically along the contours of both these maps at the same time. These two forms of investigations may be distinguished in time or they may be performed at different times, but although they are distinguishable investigations with distinctive research strategies and tactics they are inseparable research enterprises.

All presuppositions used in these enterprises are under constant examination. Thus Pfänder writes:

> Phenomenology shifts the point of sight of its investigations first into the thinking subject and focuses from this place on the objects within the object world of this thinking subject; it then takes hold of the thoughts and the opinions which the thinking subject harbors about the object and in so doing refrains from taking any stand with regard to these opinions, while taking the objects and the object worlds merely as the counterparts (seen thus or so by the subject) of his thinking consciousness without allowing itself [any claims] to transcendent knowledge of these objects.[7]

Since its presuppositions of method are always under scrutiny, phenomenological investigations place to one side 'all knowledge obtained elsewhere,' put it in 'brackets' or within parentheses, so to speak, and put all of this on the shelf for further investigation and analysis. Hence, it leaves aside, that is, it does not affirm, deny, debate, rebut, or attempt to refute, any of the special sciences of objects of the world, whether of an 'external world' or of a world of purely subjective consciousness.

Recall from the Introduction that Alfred Cobham, finding himself 'woefully behind what I felt I ought to be, resolved to make an effort to mend my condition. But how?' And René Descartes sought to begin a personal reconstruction of knowledge at the very bottom '. . . so as to begin again from the first foundation, if I wanted to establish anything firm and lasting in the sciences.'

How does one begin? I claim that the journeys from originations through to beginnings of the investigations undertaken by both Cobham and Descartes were of the same kind, although perhaps without the same degree of motivating force of radical doubt or single-minded intensity toward the reconstruction of their former opinions and intellectual conditions. They both undertook their philosophical journey while deeply immersed within the 'everydayness' of their lifeworlds. They said this explicitly.

Edmund Husserl describes this journey in the determination of problems and the formulation of methods as a movement through to phenomenology. His example is the life and work of Descartes.

Every beginner in philosophy knows the remarkable train of thoughts contained in the *Meditations*. Let us recall its guiding idea. The aim of the *Meditations* is a complete reforming of philosophy into a science grounded on an absolute foundation. That implies for Descartes a corresponding reformation of all the sciences, because in his opinion they are only nonself-sufficient members of the one all-inclusive science, and this is philosophy. Only within the systematic unity of philosophy can they develop into genuine sciences. As they have developed historically, on the other hand, they lack that scientific genuineness which would consist in their complete and ultimate grounding on the basis of absolute insights, insights behind which one cannot go back any further. Hence the need for a radical rebuilding that satisfies the idea of philosophy as the all-inclusive unity of the sciences, within the unity of such an absolutely rational grounding. With Descartes this demand gives rise to a philosophy turned toward the subject himself. The turn to the subject is made at *two* significant levels.

*First*, anyone who seriously intends to become a philosopher must 'once in his life' withdraw into himself and attempt, within himself, to overthrow and build anew all the sciences that, up to then, he has been accepting. Philosophy-- wisdom (**sagesse**)--is the philosophizer's quite personal affair. It must arise as *his* wisdom, as his self-acquired knowledge tending toward universality, a knowledge for which he can answer from the beginning, and at each step, by virtue of his own absolute insights. If I have decided to live with this as my aim--the decision that alone can start me on the course of a philosophical development--I have thereby chosen to begin in absolute poverty, with an absolute lack of knowledge. Beginning thus, obviously one of the first things I ought to do is reflect on how I might find a method for going on, a method that promises to lead to genuine knowing. *Accordingly the Cartesian Meditations are not intended to be a merely private concern of the philosopher Descartes, to say nothing of their being merely an impressive literary form in which to present the foundations of his philosophy. Rather they draw the prototype for any beginning philosopher's necessary meditations, the meditations out of which alone a philosophy can grow originally.*

When we turn to the content of the *Meditations,* so strange to us men of today, we find a regress to the philosophizing ego in a *second* and deeper sense: the ego as subject of his pure *cogitationes.* The mediator executes this regress by the famous and very remarkable method of doubt. Aiming with radical consistency at absolute knowledge, he refuses to let himself accept anything as existent unless it is secured against every conceivable possibility of becoming doubtful. Everything that is certain, in his natural experiencing and thinking life, he therefore subjects to methodical criticism with respect to the conceivability of a doubt about it; and, by excluding everything that leaves open any possibility of doubt, he seeks to obtain a stock of things that are absolutely evident. When this method is followed, the certainty of sensuous experience, the certainty with which the world is given in natural living, does not withstand criticism; accordingly the being of the world must remain unaccepted at this initial stage. The meditator keeps only himself, qua pure ego of his *cogitationes*, as having an absolutely indubitable existence, as something that cannot be done away with, something that would exist even though this world were non-existent. Thus reduced, the ego carries on a kind of solipsistic philosophizing . . .[8] (My emphasis)

From this point, the 'I'--and let us now simply say I, or you--looks at and examines both the objects we are thinking-of within our consciousness and our opinions about these objects, particularly with respect to the individual and unique actions of our consciousness[9] which present these objects and opinions for our scrutiny. Next we look at the modes of givenness of these objects and the modes of thought of the opinions we have. This means that we explore both the manner, appearance, and form in which something is manifested and the ways in which we are thinking-of it.

In Part II, Section A, I discuss many of the steps, stages, phases, episodes, or moments of phenomenological methods, and I try to clarify Pfänder's statements through what I term a phenomenology of the personal world, the lifeworld, of an adult. I offer it there as a case study and as an example of phenomenological research in adult education.

## B. Linguistic Phenomenology and the Personal Language of Learning to Learn Within the Adult Lifeworld

In addition to the general aims of phenomenology laid out briefly above, there is a special way of doing phenomenology which is of great significance, in my judgment, to theories and practices in adult education. This special form may be termed *linguistic phenomenology*. Basically, this kind of phenomenology is a continuing attempt to draw together into a cohesive whole selected principles and practices from linguistic philo-

sophy as found in J. L. Austin's brilliant work and
certain principles and practices like those discussed in
the previous section.

I shall now try to lay out, albeit in rudimentary and
incomplete form, a version of this way of doing phenomenology in an effort to show how it is significant in
study, teaching, and research in adult education, and
especially so in the investigation of the phenomenon of
'learning to learn.' In doing so, I offer an investigation of a special case of adult eduction of
**person**,[10] the case of '**person**-talk.' Learning to learn
is an adult eduction of **person** of a special reflexive
kind, and its clearest presentation is through
linguistic phenomenology. The immediate question is:
what is linguistic phenomenology?

In his Presidential Address to the Aristotelian
Society in 1956, J. L. Austin claimed that

> In view of the prevalence of the slogan 'ordi-
> nary language', and of such names as 'linguistic'
> or 'analytic' philosophy or 'the analysis of
> language', one thing needs specially emphasizing
> to counter misunderstandings. When we examine
> what we should say when, what words we should use
> in what situations, we are looking . . . not
> *merely* at words (or 'meanings', whatever they
> may be) but also at the realities we use the
> words to talk about; we are using a sharpened
> awareness of words to sharpen our perception of,
> though not as the final arbiter of, the phenome-
> na. For this reason I think it might be better
> to use, for this way of doing philosophy, some
> less misleading name than those given above--for
> instance, 'linguistic phenomenology'. . .[11]

A few years later, during the colloquium on analytic
philosophy held at Royaumont, France, Austin offered
more substance to his description of "linguistic phenomenology":

> We use the multiplicity of expressions which the richness of our language furnishes us in order to direct our attention to the multiplicity and the richness of our experiences. Language serves as interpreter for observing the living facts which constitute our experience, which, without it, we would tend to overlook. . . . The diversity of expressions which we can apply attracts our attention to the extraordinary complexity of the situation on which we are called upon to speak. This means that language illumines for us the complexities of life.[12]

The *second* important use of the phrase to which I call our attention is Herbert Spiegelberg's use of it in a paper, "Linguistic Phenomenology: John L. Austin and Alexander Pfänder." Addressing a section of the XIIIth International Congress of Philosophy in Mexico City, in 1963, Professor Spiegelberg wanted to show how:

> Austin's type of analysis . . . was moving beyond mere linguistic analysis toward a supplementary study of the phenomenon which led to an explicit phenomenology. From the other side Pfänder . . . [claimed that] phenomenology proper, presupposes a conceptual analysis under the name of 'clarification of meaning,' to be guided largely by what we mean by the terms of our ordinary language.[13]

The phrase 'linguistic phenomenology' may well be no more than a name in search of a method or process. Still, the invocation of the name is heuristic, itself a discovering of a certain kind. I believe that linguistic phenomenology has a special significance for philosophy of adult education.

It is a way of articulating as precisely as possible the distinctions within what adults say in direct investigation and description of phenomena which we feel, experience, and conscious (know-with). In this context, a phenomenon is (literally) any showing-of-itself-in-itself, or anything taken as an instance-of-itself, to be focused upon. Linguistic phenomenology is a way as free as possible from unexamined, preconceptions and presuppositions; thus, it is 'presuppositionless' in Husserl's special sense: its presuppositions are under constant reexamination.

There is one complex cluster of phenomena in particular to which the investigations of linguistic phenomenology uniquely apply within the theory and practice of adult education. These are the phenomena to which we may refer as the adult eductions of **person**. A **person** is a special kind of phenomenon, a special showing-of-itself-in-itself, a special instance-of-itself, to be focused upon. When we investigate this phenomenon we necessarily do so initially as linguistic phenomenologists, I believe.

A person is a speaker and a spoken-to, 'Man is the speaking animal.'[14] 'Speech is not merely a tonal system, a neurological montage. Rather, it represents a constitutive element in human reality, so that the function of language only assumes its full meaning within the context of the total human experience . . . the essence of speech must be sought for in the act of speaking.'[15]

Speaking is the constituting and reconstituting process of encountering that is the personal reality of each one of us. Particularly does speaking in its full sense--the sense including all the gestural dimensions as well as the phonetic ones--bring about for the speaker and the spoken-to 'a certain structural co-ordination of experience, a certain modulation of existence, exactly as a pattern of my bodily behavior endows the objects around me with a certain significance both for me and for others.'[16] Speaking is the philosophical foundation for understanding the phenomena fundamental to the process of learning to learn.

The authentic discovery of myself as a person *is* the discovery that I can speak. In speaking, and as I speak, I am both speaker and spoken-to; 'and since the discovery of myself as a person is also the discovery of other persons around me, it is the discovery of speakers and hearers other than myself.'[17] Thus, from the first, the feeling, the experiencing, and the consciousing which speaking is as expression contain in themselves the structure, the feeling, experiencing, and consciousing of speaking to others and of knowing that others speak to me.

If one has a new feeling, a new experiencing, a new consciousing, he must express it to others. A person must say it in order to see whether it is a good one; it must be expressed to other persons, 'in order that finding them able to share it, he may be sure that his own [consciousing] of it is not corrupt.'[18]

We may distinguish between: (1) **person**-speaking[19] and (2) **person**-spoken-to. As **person**-speaking, I directly present, I directly articulate my feelings, my experiencings, and my consciousings. As **person**-spoken-to, I seek to understand the person who speaks to me, who presents himself through the course of my own direct exploration, description, and analysis of what I feel, experience, and conscious the other **person**-speaking.

Although we may distinguish these two modes of **person**, we cannot separate them. The initiation of a dialogue is not immediately its completion. To present anything is to bring it before, to bring it into the presence of. In the law, for example, to present something is to lay it before the court as an object of inquiry. And in grammar, the present tense is the presenting, or the presenting tense; it is speaking in the here and now.

Thus, the distinguishable but inseparable modes of **person** constitute the dialogue which is the encountering, question-answering, and speaking. In questioning, we doubt, we dispute, we ask, we inquire. In answering, we swear against, we reply, we have a successful meeting, we comply, we fulfill, we are in some conformity, we correspond, we bring some suitability to the question. All of this has ample illustration in the marketplace, in legislative bodies, in the courts, in scientific inquiries, and in doing philosophy after the model of one kind or another of radical doubt, as we have seen it done in the extreme case in Descartes' *Medita-*

*tions,* for example. Speaking through question-answer-question--and so forth--is itself the base of the continuity of learning to learn.

Moreover, the model of questioning-answering itself is inquiry. To inquire is to seek in, to seek within, to seek into, to seek toward, to ask, to investigate, to examine. It has the full sense of seeking 'out' what is 'in.' A full inquiry, then, is an ordered questioning-answering process, a discourse. Inquiry is a dialogic process of bringing 'out' what is 'in,' explicitizing what is implicit; almost literally, it is unraveling what is entwined.

Questioning-answering is the invocation of **person** in the **person**al world. Questioning-answering constitutes the **person**al world, and the personal world is **person**. I have already distinguished two modes of **person**, (1) **person**-speaking, and (2) **person**-spoken-to. Now we may make a distinction between two kinds of **person**-speaking: (1) **person**-talk, and (2) *talk-about* **person**.

**Person**-talk is what I propose to term my talking to Joseph who is present to my talking, whether I am talking-about John or about anything else. **Person**-talk is not *talk-about* **person**. I do not, indeed cannot, *talk-about* myself. **Person**-talk is my own articulation, myself offered to another person. My talk presents me; it is myself presented. I present myself in any present talk, and I could present myself in present talk in some other way, but in my **person**-talk I choose this way out of an indeterminately large repertory of ways. **Person**-talk is **person**-presenting, **person**-articulating. **Person**-talk does not convey information; rather, it directly presents. I present myself in and through my speaking. Information and facts about persons are based upon this speaking as expression.

The following passage from Claire Smith's paper[20] contains an excellent example of **person**-talk as I intend it.

I lived life blindly, from minute to minute....
I still have chewed finger-nails, the scars, the
   freckles that mark me myself and no one else.
From the time I was a one-celled being born to Mr.
   and Mrs. Smith....
I was a jealous child, jealous of those around me...
I grew up alone.
I blamed my parents for all the sorrow they were
   causing me.
I did not understand, nor did I try to understand
   their plight.
From my beginning came a certain part of my
   personality, an insecurity which is still a
   part of me.

Each of these characterizations is literally a speaking-out, a selecting and a firming-up of central or decisive characteristics of this individual person and no other. These are choices made from within a repertory of possible facets and dimensions. **Person** flows through these characterizations. If any other method of description were attempted in an interpretation of this **person**-talk, the way of linguistic phenomenology would be basic to it, as a way of attempting to articulate as precisely as possible the distinctions in what is said to us in the course of the direct investigations and descriptions of phenomena as we feel, experience, and conscious these . . . as **person**-talk to us. For example, a behavioral account or a content analysis might be offered of a person's speaking and speech acts, but they would not be able to penetrate to the level of symbolic interaction and meaning(s) which **person**-talk is, and so linguistic phenomenological investigations underlying these approaches would still be necessary. But their results would tend to negate the value or the necessity of the former approaches, although these might still be helpful for reasons other than assistance toward understanding the adult eductions of **person**.

Talk-about persons is all talk about persons to which a person talked-about makes no contributions, whether that person be present to the situation in which the talk takes place, or whether he be absent. All talk regarding persons absent to the situation in which the talk takes place is talk-about persons.

Talk-about **person** focuses on speaking as a kind of yearning for dialogue, but for dialogue which is not placing and timing itself in a given situation. Perhaps talk-about **person** is only potential dialogue in search of the two or more persons who could actualize it, for a dialogue requires at least two persons speaking-across to one another. And in talk-about **person**, the spoken-about is not responding in the situation. It does not articulate **person** to us; it does not bring us face to face, or person to person, with one another. All talk-about **person** involves our view-of-another. It turns us in that person's direction, but it is not his speaking to us in response to our turning to him. It is our placement of him within a situation and circumstances, a process in which he himself has no articulative, constitutive place.

Thus, **person**-speaking is both **person**-talk and talk-about **person**. But in the former, the focus is on the direct presenting and **pre**senting of oneself. In the latter, the focus is on the indirect presenting and **pre**senting of oneself, for what a person says about another person must always be placed in the context, structure, or perspective of the speaker. An example from therapy comes to mind. Therapy proceeds ultimately through **person**-speaking, and whereas **person**-talk is the raw data and evidence of the therapeutic process, what the patient also says about other persons--for example, parent, friend, 'other'--surely relates significantly to the progress from the appearance of symptoms through possible cure.

Linguistic phenomenology, as I have said, is a way of doing philosophy, a way of articulating as precisely as possible (never-ending in its precising) the distinctions in what we say in the course of the direct investigations and descriptions of phenomena as persons feel, experience, and conscious these. I believe that linguistic phenomenology is a singularly appropriate way of investigating **person**-talk, and **person**-talk is at the core the subject-matter of adult education and adult learning. It is also fundamental to the process of the adult eductions of learning to learn and of learning how to learn.

Let me suggest how this is the case through a brief phenomenological account of learning to learn in this context of learning who and what **person** is. (I discuss in detail the process of learning how to learn in Part IV, C., below.) Suppose that someone claims that the most important feature of learning and education is learning how to learn, or learning to learn, and that the really good student is one who has learned to learn. One response might be that the phrase 'learning to learn' is redundant since genuine learning already contains within it whatever meaning the phrase could have, or add, to learning per se. For example, if learning is coming into possession of knowledge, facts, skills, and procedures and having these ready at hand[21] for use whenever relevant to some situation, then one has not really learned anything unless and until one has learned (that) he has learned them, i.e., has come to know (that) he knows them. Having learned something then would mean that one knows (that) he knows this. And it suggests that this 'knowing I know' and 'learning to learn' have become habituations in the experiencings and consciousings of all good students.

This analysis seems accurate for all learning from experience when experience is modelled primarily as a relatively passive receptivity to instruction and discipline. Therefore, the more crucial this passive receptivity model of experiencing is in a person's views the more significant questions about the processes of learning to learn become. The reason is that the phrase in this case refers to a felt acknowledgement that one ought to break away from this model, or that it does not articulate the process of learning richly enough and must be altered to accommodate some view beyond a model of mere passivity. But the more the adult learner or adult educator is committed to a model of experience as active and actional in all learning, the less important this process of learning to learn becomes. Why is this the case? Because learning to learn is a phenomenon which is already built into the conception of the full, rich model of experience as an active reaching out into the world and grasping sectors of it.[22]

In either case, however, it is still worthwhile to focus on the phenomenon 'learning-to-learn' and see what a brief phenomenological investigation further uncovers. First, learning *how* to learn is logically founded in 'learning-to-learn', since the adverb 'how' simply presents the way(s) in which 'learning-to-learn' takes place. Second, 'learning-to-learn' refers to persons' distinguishable reflections on both learning and on what is learned. Learning and the learned thereby have both become the focused objects of 'learning-to' as actualized through the many ways of 'learning how'. This is analogous to the phenomenon of 'thinking-of' as always requiring an 'object' of thinking. Next, because it is always reflective, 'learning-to-learn' is also reflexive. It is consciousing moving in a double direction simultaneously, with two intended 'objects' of consciousness: (1) one direction is toward the learning process itself, and (2) the other direction is toward the 'object(s)' learned.[23] Finally, 'learning-to-learn' is possible at the levels of **person** distinguished as experiencing and consciousing, or reflection. But it is concretely successful only insofar as habituations of consciousings, or reflection, are instantiated in the lives of persons. I deal further with this matter and with its relation to the 'will-to-learn' in Chapter 2.

I have not been arguing in this section that linguistic phenomenology is appropriate for describing talk-about anything or everything in the world, or even a way of evaluating what we say about all of the distinctions within the world. Obviously all of my talk about microscopic and macroscopic worlds is *talk-about*. None of it is **person**-talk except in the sense that what I say is **person**-talk constituted of my eduction of **person**.

It is possible to distinguish a *weak sense,* and a *strong sense* of 'linguistic phenomenology.' Consider the *weak sense* first. Each of us as a person speaks and articulates a network of relationships. Each of us speaks and articulates a kind of constancy of encounter, a focusing of feelings, tryings, and knowings-with. In these ways, each of us is in a lifeworld which we already know in part. We come to know better and better. We will never be content with our temporary gains, even if resigned never to achieve knowingly an ultimate goal.[24] Our feelings, our experiencings, and our consciousings we attempt to express, and these attempts we come to know as the speaking we do. In speaking and in being spoken-to we come to know our lifeworld and our circumstances. In coming to know our lifeworld better we are also reconstituting it and repositioning ourselves within it. These are among the important adult eductions. We are learning, and in doing so we are learning to learn and learning how to do it. We are continuing our education.

To recognize all of this is not yet to do the philosophy necessary to the full articulation of what we feel we feel, experience as experience, and know that we know. In this *weak sense,* linguistic phenomenology is improperly so-called. To be sure, even it is an attempt to constitute more clearly the network of relations which a person in some sense already is, the more thorough and more precise standings of our feelings, our experiencings, and our 'knowings-with.' But in this *weak sense,* the investigations may fail, and fall back as receding waves *either* into mere language analysis (because they might not really heed the rich adult eductions of the **person**-talk of **person**-speaking), *or* into simple phenomenological description (because they might fail to investigate and analyze the concepts and other rich language forms in the eductions of **person**-talk of **person**-speaking).

In the *strong sense,* linguistic phenomenology, properly so-called, focuses upon **person**, a special showing-of-itself-in-itself, a special instance-of-itself. Linguistic phenomenology first attempts to articulate as precisely as possible the distinctions (among inseparables) within **person**-talk. Linguistic phenomenology *then* will gather the clusterings of all instances of **person**-talk for orderly and systematic description and investigation. It will focus upon key examples of uses of these either as instances-of a structure, or as a structure-of instances. *Thirdly,* it will position these structures at levels of feelings, experiencings, and consciousings of **person**-talk. These are among the sorts of things I try to do in Part II, Section A.

Further, the **person**-talk of persons is the direct phenomenon as felt, experienced, and conscioused, for linguistic phenomenology. Again, the sensible articulation and elucidation of the language of personal feeling, personal experiencing, and personal consciousing at specifiable levels and in specifiable degrees and kinds at which **person**-talk takes place will be investigated by a linguistic phenomenology. These last two steps are the unique phenomenological side of what I am calling a linguistic phenomenology.

I have maintained that the investigation, exploration, and analysis of **person** is the direct investigation, exploration, and analysis of **person**-talk as we feel, experience, and conscious this. It is inquiry into **person**-talk, and inquiry into **person**-talk is the entry into the questioning-answering speaking, or the encountering dialogue of adult eductions of **person**: the doubtings, disputings, askings . . . the swearings-against, the replies, the relatively successful meetings, compliances, fulfillings, conformities, correspondings, and suitabilities which arise as questionings posed and answerings tentatively supplied . . . only to become the suppositions, the **pre**-suppositions of more questionings. . . .[25] Evaluating these matters is the process of learning, of possessing and having relevantly available to our needed rise, the continuity of meanings which we come both to possess and to have in hand for our needed use. This is knowledge as well, for what we have learned we know, and what we know we have previously learned somehow, in some situation, in the midst of some circumstances, for the main reason that something has become relevant to us. How we do this is how we learn. Learning how to learn is knowing how to learn, understanding the constitutive phenomena we now understand as the adult eductions of **person** which are expressed by adults. Therefore, learning how to learn is coming to know better and better *both* the processes of investigating phenomena (the noetic intentionality of learning itself as an ongoing process in persons) *and* what is thereby known (the noematic intentionality of the learned, the attended-to, the grasped, the conscioused 'objects' of persons).

Husserl's terms 'noesis', 'noetic', 'noema', and 'noematic' can be used very fruitfully.[26] What becomes clearly evident is that the investigations of a linguistic phenomenology can be very useful in research into the phenomena of adult eductions of learning-to-learn.

## C. Phenomenology and Familiar Steps in Scientific Methods

It is clear that phenomenology and 'the scientific method(s)' (or just plain 'science') are *not* opposed or mutually exclusive kinds of investigations. A major claim of this book is that phenomenological investigations work the soils of science; that sciences could not long endure--and surely could not attest spectacular success--without the kinds of investigation here claimed as 'phenomenological' being undertaken in some degree. Moreover, problems encountered along the way as adults continue their learning present stellar opportunities for showing how the grounds for 'scientific approaches' and phenomenological approaches, and as a consequence so-called 'quantitative' and 'qualitative' approaches, necessarily are fused in all work in adult education. As a field of study and scientific investigation, adult education is a *human science.*

I wish to be both clear and practical on these points. One important further step in this direction is to show how phenomenological methods and steps in scientific methods exhibit this necessary fusion of grounds and concepts. I take this clarifying step immediately below. Part VI will discuss phenomenology as a new paradigm and program of research in adult education.

In the remainder of this section I shall discuss briefly certain actions, procedures, and conceptualizations which persons as scientists (within the relevancy systems 'science' necessitates) perform and employ. I do this in the left-hand column. In the right-hand column I relate certain essentials of phenomenological methods to the generalized scientific methods.

My discussion of the phenomenological methods has been inspired by the brilliant and sustained research in phenomenology, and especially in the history of the phenomenological movement, performed over many decades by Herbert Spiegelberg.[27]

For example, each edition of his distinguished work *The Phenomenological Movement* (published in three editions through 1986), has concluded with a section entitled "The Essentials of the Phenomenological Movement." This section is of inestimable value for anyone who wishes to apply phenomenological methods to any subject-matter. This is especially true, in my judgment, in the case of practitioners and researchers in adult education. I recommend strongly that students and professionals in adult education study with the greatest care these 'essentials' of the phenomenological method that Spiegelberg discusses in detail, and which are the prototype for my development of the essentials of phenomenological methods as I present them in this section.

The 'positive steps of the phenomenological method', as Spiegelberg lays them out, are:

(1) Investigating particular phenomena.
(2) Investigating general essences.
(3) Apprehending essential relationships among essences.
(4) Watching modes of appearing.
(5) Watching the constitution of phenomena in consciousness.
(6) Suspending belief in the existence of phenomena.
(7) Interpreting the meaning of the phenomena (hermeneutics).

My discussion below lays out and clarifies certain phases, steps, and stages of methods in phenomenological investigation, which I put to detailed use in Part II, Section A., where a phenomenology of the personal world of an adult is offered.

### 1. Observation and Our Processes of Intuiting Phenomena

| Observation | Our processes of intuiting phenomena |
|---|---|
| In all orderly and systematic thinking about any determinate subject-matter, every observing is already a perceiving, a watching, a 'keeping-toward' as performed by a person. These are processes through which we take careful notice of any subject-matter. Further, in the tradition of orderly and systematic thinking, intersubjectivity is already present in any person's observations, and all observations are already theory-laden (Norwood Hanson.)[28] In scientific observations, intersubjective observations become the accurate observations of trained observers. Intersubjective perceivings and observings are the basic structurings making possible the cross-checkings, verifications, etc., of | In its root sense, to intuit something is to 'see' something. The term conveys the sense of (1) a person's capturing the first approximations (in their togetherness) of seeing, hearing, smelling, tasting, and touching when a person focuses or concentrates on a phenomenon, or cluster of phenomenon, that is, on a subject-matter; and the sense (2) of a person's moving through to the deeper, further sense of 'really hearing,' 'really seeing,' etc. In intuiting phenomena, therefore, we focus upon the uniqueness of the phenomena themselves as reducible to nothing other or less than what they themselves are. Husserl's motto always was 'Zu den Sachen Selbst' (to the things themselves.) |

scientific observation. In these ways information arrived at intersubjectively is already public information, and it becomes the ground of the 'objective' knowledge considered characteristic of the sciences.

A brief note on the nature of the reductive process may be instructive. To reduce a given subject-matter is to draw it together as constituting a whole, a unity, but to do so in such a way that the sheer bulk or plenum of data which constitutes the subject-matter in its totality (a totality deemed ultimately unknowable in all of its possible exfoliations) is pared away to the essentials which situate the subject-matter as focused. That is, a reduced plenum becomes a determinate subject-matter.

But the principle of reduction requires the presuppositions that the subject-matter be a complex reality which is equal to the sum of the parts into which it is conceptually divided and reduced, and that these parts somehow determine the subject-matter. Thus, a model is involved, a model which draws a subject-matter together by leading it back to its simplest parts and which claims that the more complex and temporally later is necessarily a function of the less complex and earlier,[29] for example, as one might presume to 'explain' a subject-matter by reducing it to its 'causes.'[30]

Reductionist views are legion, and are employed by much of the presentday conception of the social sciences which still follows largely in the wake of Descartes's mathematical method and model of the sciences. Reductions, even if and when claimed as necessary to a given model used for treating some subject-matter, are always constructed along the lines of what is perceived (whether by one person or many persons) as being *relevant*. Therefore, reliance upon a reductionistic model of dealing with persons raises the subject of relevance and relevancy systems to the highest level of philosoph-

ical significance. These issues are discussed principally in Part IV, Chapter 6.

## 2. Classification and Our Processes of Describing Particularizings of Phenomena

### Classification

### Our processes of describing particularizings of phenomena

When we classify anything we arrange or put into a class or classes some phenomena on the basis of resemblances and differences between these phenomena. We make judgments about certain phenomena and things as belonging to, or as not belonging to, certain types, categories, kinds, etc., in terms of common properties and non-common properties. Basic to the process of classification are the activities of describing particularizings of phenomena, i.e., intersubjective analyses and intersubjective descriptions.

(1) Intersubjective analyzing

(2) Intersubjective describing

The methods of phenomenology, through fundamental intersubjectivity, pursue two principal ways of particularizing determinate subject-matter. They deal, *first*, with a part of a subject as distinct, but not separate, from the whole, as one might speak of the actor's 'part' in a play. Thus, to particularize a phenomenon is to focus on some one, or more, part(s) of the individual constituents, to take a part and concentrate on it for special investigation and exploration. These investigations can only take place through the general explorations of the structurings of given phenomena along the lines of their particular and distinct ingredients and configurations. *No* subject-matter should necessarily be reduced to parts of the whole which it is as if this were simply a necessary step in scientific procedure. The *second* way of particularizing phenomena is to describe phenomena, to portray, represent, and communicate distinctly (by means of properties and qualities) the uniqueness of these phenomena.

Both ways are ways of selecting out, and firming-up central, essential, and decisive characteristics of given phenomena. These are ways of getting at other possible--and differing--facets and varying dimensions of any given subject-matter.

### 3. Hypothesization, Generalization, and Our Processes of Describing the Relatings of Phenomena

| Hypothesization and Generalization | Our Processes of Describing the Relatings of Phenomena |
|---|---|
| A *hypothesis* is 'a placing under'. It is a tentative theory or supposition provisionally adopted in order to understand | (1) As a whole<br><br>(2) Through the appearings of phenomena |

'facts' (or what I would call the intersubjective agreement of felt experience) and to guide in the investigation of other 'facts' relating to given phenomena. *Theories* suggest a much greater range of possible evidence, and a greater likelihood of higher and higher degrees of probability of accuracy of meaning and 'truth'. *Laws* suggest statements of order and relationships regarding phenomena which are regarded as more and more invariable under given conditions. Therefore, in all orderly and systematic thinking about determinate subject-matters, all hypothesizings are provisional conclusions drawn from data and 'known facts' (feelings, experiencings, and consciousings which become the bases of intersubjective agreements of felt experiences) and are used as structuring foundations for further explorations and investigations of phenomena.

(3) Through the phenomena taken as Whole

(4) Through its (their) shading perspectives

(5) Through varying modes of clarity

The methods of phenomenology make it possible to describe both *what* a phenomenon is as it appears and the ways of its appearing. The grounding of particulars and the seeing of essentials which are meanings and intendings of particulars are the relatings of phenomena. A phenomena may be explored 'as a whole' through its temporal lives (through the invocation of time and timing concepts). Again, a phenomenon may be explored in its appearings-to-us. Both of these ways are ways of describing *what* appears.

We can also describe the relatings of phenomena through explorations of the *ways* in which something appears to us. In the *first* place, we can come to feel, experience, and to conscious (know-with) better and better what we have already felt, experienced, and conscioused previously in part. *Secondly,* we can recognize modifications of the phenomenon as 'perspectives-shading-off' of the phenomenon as it is seen toward the outer edges or fringes of manifestation as a phenomenon. A *third* way of seeing the ways of appearing of some phenomena is to describe the modes of clarity or the degrees of clarity and distinctness through which the phenomenon appears.

## 4. Explanation, Understanding, and Watching the Constitution of Phenomena in Our Consciousness

### Explanation and Understanding

To explain something is to 'make it level', to flatten it out, and to place it within more and more familiar contexts. This means that one may place 'facts' before 'values' in certain kinds of investigations typically called 'scientific' investigations. To explain a phenomenon is to give it meaning, to give reasons concerning it, and to account for it. It is to

### Watching the Constitution of Phenomena in Consciousness

This requires that we place-together in sequence some of the essential steps through which a phenomenon is constituted (intersubjectively) in our consciousness. The result of such a process would be the determination of the typical structures of a constituted object in consciousness (consciousing in an object directly) by means of the analysis describe its form and structure by tracing its origins and development through the sequencing of its steps of rising, developing, and structuring of it as a subject-matter which is the clear focus of our selective attention.

of the sequential steps of the acts of constitution.

## 5. Experimentation and Our Open-ending Explorations of Phenomena

### Experimentation

'Experiment' and 'experience' arise from the same etymological root. They both focus on *what* persons do and on *how* they do what they do. Literally, when we *try* to do anything at all, this is both our experimenting and our experiencing. We usually reserve the term 'experience' for those episodes through which we speak of our own tryings, our own attempts within, or the attempts of an egoistic 'I', or 'my' attempts.

Normally we use the term 'experiment' when we focus on what someone else is experiencing (as we view that person from the out-

### Our Open-ending Explorations of Phenomena

The methods of intersubjectivity require an open-ending investigation of phenomena. Perhaps this open-endedness signals an unfinished--or even unfinishable task in principle--for the precise parameters of the overlap of all 'subjects' and 'objects' cannot be precisely indicated in any field of inquiry, or in any disciplined investigation. This openness requires that we 'bracket', 'suspend judgment on', 'parenthesize', 'hold in abeyance' *all* questions or concerns relating to the 'existence', 'nonexistence', 'possibility' or 'impossibility', or

side) or (in another sense) when we seek to do something specific with and about our own experience. But in this latter sense we can say that experimentation is reflexive experience. The most crucial problem here, I think, is the model of experience we use whenever we experience, or wish to study experiences of others, or our experiences of others. For example, how reductionistic or how eductive will our model(s) be?

'causal origins' of given phenomena. This suspension and openness should be evident in each of the steps, stages, or dimensions of the methods of phenomenological intersubjectivity. This suspension of certain kinds of questions and judgments and this openendedness require that we think and act as if the phenomena may be felt, experienced, and conscioused apart from any prior considerations of possible 'causal' sequences which might have given rise to it. Whatever else may be involved, this commitment to open-endedness is a plea that we not necessarily reduce all phenomena to their 'parts', as various forms of behaviorism', logical positivism, logical empiricism, and linguistic analysis (each of these individually and severally followed by fields of science and scientific programs of research in adult education research) have done. Thus it is that we can speak, for example, of intuiting persons, describing persons' particularizings, and describing persons' relatings by focusing upon them in their stream, in their processional continuation.

Also, why not, as a requirement in adult education research, require the use of at least two models (one constitutive and one eductive) in every experiment involving persons? This suggestion, if taken seriously by a sufficient number of researchers among adult educators, could have profound influence on all investigations involving **person** in adult education. Let me describe this suggested requirement very briefly.

This twofold way might lead, with the development of the necessary empirical methods, to what I call *reflexive experimentation* in both qualitatively and quantitatively based research in adult education. This would mean that *every* experiment involving persons' ideas and actions would have to state two forms of any given hypothesis, and test out hypotheses in a double sense, a *constitutive* and an *eductive* form. These may be investigated through the constitutive function of phenomenology and the eductive function of phenomenology, respectively. The constitutive form is a model of experiment founded upon the *because motives* of persons, whereas the eductive form is a model of experiment based upon the *in-order-to-motives*[31] of persons. Some of this experimentation could be done as public *praxis,* but much more remains to be the experience of a thought experiment, or a variant of Husserl's method of 'free imaginative variation'.[32] Of course, these are all *actions* and, under appropriate matrices of relevance, *acts* as well.

## 6. Prediction and Our Processes of Interpreting

| Prediction | Our processes of interpreting |
|---|---|
| To predict is to 'say-before', to say and to know what will happen before it happens. In | All interpretations involving any subject-matter involve focusing on this subject as a problem (or |

orderly and systematic thinking we predict when we are able to state the conditions under which (within which, etc.) some phenomena will manifest themselves, for example, in terms of certain specifiable spatial and temporal modes of the manifestation of these phenomena. All of this can occur only within certain agreed-upon and specifiable tolerances of error. These tolerances of error and accuracy are founded in previous intersubjective dimensions of the order and systems of method pursued. In other words, a discriminating community of trained and disciplined observers (feelers, experiencers, 'knowers', or *experimenters*) will be expected to make these judgments of prediction and later evaluations of their accuracy.

set of problems), analyzing it, describing its particularizings, and describing its relatings. Anyone of these activities is incomplete without the others, and all of them together articulate the openness, open-ending, and suspending quality of judgment. Thus, the explorations and investigations of phenomena (which together have become a topic, subject-matter or problematic theme) are personal processes of coming to feel, to experience, and to conscious better and better what we have previously felt, experienced, and consciousced in part. Predicting, controlling, and verifying (expressing meanings of and telling the 'truth' about) are specifiable ways of manifesting our processes of interpreting.

## 7. Control and Verification

### Control

To control phenomena is to exercise a directing, regulating, governing influence over these phenomena. It is to regulate or verify, as an

### Verification

To verify a phenomenon is to *make* it true somehow. To verify phenomena is to prove these phenomena (within certain structurings to be 'true', or to experienced act, activity, action, or event (or all of these), through an experiment by comparison with intersubjectively agreed-upon standards, conventions, and protocols in specified fields of inquiry and investigation.

confirm and substantiate these. It is to test the accuracy or the exactness of these. To verify is to confirm, or to 'firm up' these phenomena, and all of this is made possible by the other dimensions or steps of the methods of the sciences. These all ought to be founded, in Husserl's words, upon phenomenology as the most rigorous of all the sciences. José Ortega y Gasset defined 'truth' intersubjectively as the 'quieting of our anxieties.'33

The ideal might be to make true what we say intersubjectively about phenomena. But if we cannot claim truth in these matters, for some reasons perhaps having to do with the incompleteness of truth, then the mandate of verification is at least to make our judgments claims that become more and more meaningful and that can be conditions in terms of which we can act meaningfully.

# PART II

## Phenomenology, the Personal World, and Philosophical Problems in Adult Education

*The I of the basic word I-You is different from that of the basic word I-It.*

*The I of the basic word I-It appears as an ego and becomes conscious of itself as a subject (of experience and use).*

*The I of the basic word I-You appears as a person and becomes conscious of itself as subjectivity (without any dependent genetive).*

*Egos appear by setting themselves apart from other egos.*

*Persons appear by entering into relation to other persons.*

*One is the spiritual form of natural differentiation, the other that of natural association.*

*The purpose of setting oneself apart is to experience and use, and the purpose of that is 'living'--which means dying one human life long.*

*The purpose of relation is the relation itself--touching the You. For as soon as we touch a You, we are touched by a breath of eternal life.*

*Whoever stands in relation, participates in an actuality; that is, in a being that is neither merely a part of him nor merely outside him. All actuality is an activity in which I participate without being able to appropriate it. Where there is no participation, there is no actuality. Where there is self-appropriation, there is no actuality. The more direct the* **You** *is touched, the more perfect is the participation.*

*The* **I** *is actual through its participation in actuality. The more perfect the participation is, the more actual the* **I** *becomes. . . .*

*The person becomes conscious of himself as participating in being, as being-with, and thus as a being. The ego becomes conscious of himself as being this way and not that. The person says, 'I am'; the ego says, 'That is how I am.' 'Know thyself' means to the person: know yourself as being. To the ego it means: know your being-that-way. By setting himself apart from others, the ego moves away from being. . . .*

*The person beholds his self; the ego occupies himself with his My: my manner, my race, my works, my genius.*

*The ego does not participate in any actuality nor does he gain any. He sets himself apart from everything else and tries to possess as much as possible by means of experience and use. That is* **his** *dynamics: setting himself apart and taking possession--and the object is always* **It**, *that which is not actual. He knows himself as a subject, but this subject can appropriate as much as it wants to, it will never gain any substance: it remains like a point, functional, that which experiences, that which uses, nothing more. All of its extensive and multifarious being-that-way, all of its eager 'individuality' cannot help it to gain any substance.*

*There are not two kinds of human beings, but there are two poles of humanity.*

*No human being is pure **person**, and none is pure ego; none is entirely actual, none entirely lacking in actuality. Each lives in a twofold I. But some men are so **person**-oriented that one may call them persons, while others are so ego-oriented that one may call them egos. Between these and those true history takes place.*

*The more a human being, the more humanity is dominated by the ego, the more does the I fall prey to inactuality. In such ages the **person** in the human being and in humanity comes to lead a subterranean, hidden, as it were invalid existence--until it is summoned. (My emphasis on **person**.)*

--Martin Buber, *I and Thou*[1]

## Introductory Remarks

It is appropriate early in this discussion of adult education and phenomenological research to offer an example of a phenomenological investigation in sufficiently detailed terms for it to be instructive to both educators and students in adult education. This example must be an investigation devoted to the subject-matter of adult education consistent with the claims I made in Part I about the proper subject-matter of adult education. Accordingly, this first section in Part II is a phenomenological investigation of the personal world of an adult.

I urge the reader to consider the exploration of the personal world of an adult, the world of adult eductions of **person** as the focused and determinate subject-matter, along the lines of the systematic structuring methods of the human sciences. I have already stated that adult education may be claimed properly to be the most rigorous of the human sciences. In exemplifying this claim in the context of a study of the personal world of an adult, I carry the investigation through a variety of the relevant and essential phenomenological 'steps' or 'stages' of methods which were laid out briefly in Part I. Section C. And I ask the reader to remember that in that section I tried to clarify a number of the ways in which phenomenological methods are in clear accord with many of the systematic questioning and searching activities labeled 'scientific methods'.

It will become clear, following the account of the phenomenological world of an adult, that certain philosophical problems in adult education may be discerned. It is not the case that these problems simply arise as a consequence of the phenomenological account. These are already there in any case, but the ways of phenomenology may be useful in discerning the foundational nature of these problems and many more similar to these. I am urging all theoreticians and practitioners alike-- whether students or professionals or vocationalists--to go to work on these and problems of similar magnitude, to do it with the greatest persistence and stubbornness, but, above all, to do it through theories and practices consistent with one another.

Remember that Robie Kidd urged us all to 'conceptualize', to 'persuade', to develop curricula relevant to adults for 'being-becoming-belonging' in the lifeworld and 'to choose and organize and refine the means to learning that help men and women to be free'.

## A. Phenomenology and the Personal World of an Adult

Philosophy's task has always been primarily the first-hand intuiting, exploring, and describing of a phenomenon as a person feels it, experiences it, and is conscious of it. All preconceptions and presuppositions employed in this process are constantly under examination and are used as stepping-stones, as necessary bases for seeing 'first-hand'. It is, as it has always been, the special goal of the philosopher to attempt some meaningful elucidation of personal feelings, experiences, and thoughts at specifiable levels, and in specifiable degrees and kinds, that are manifested in persons' lives. The exposition of the concept of **person** via a case study that follows represents an effort to fulfill this mandate. I offer it, also, as an instance of research in phenomenology in adult education. How it is research, what kind of research it is, and how this kind of research will be of the greatest significance for the lives of adult learners and for any phenomenological investigation into the subject matter of adult education will become increasingly clearer as the essay moves forward.

The unquestioned acceptance by many scholars of the mutual exclusion of persons and their environments under the seductive guise of 'objectivity' as a freestanding truth-model has had serious consequences in our modern world. One prime result has been the explosive growth of technology effected through this commitment, with the further exacerbation of this gap between persons, their **person,** and their nature that is irrevocably brought into the human world by the unregenerate commitment to unrestrained uses of any and all technologies as virtual ends in themselves.

For example, these consequences are felt in the educative process through which both young and old are led to 'objective' facts (as if these are opposed to and completely exclusive of 'subjective' value systems which are thought to be merely personal); in the objectivizing and externalizing assembly-line approaches to more of the sustenances of life in the very midst of the depersonalization of persons; in the massive social and political forces 'out there, beyond persons', which render individual persons ever more subservient and powerless in the face of terrorism and in the light of the increasing impersonality of the power potential of modern concepts of warfare. Moreover, the philosophical investigation of persons' feelings, at least since the seventeenth century in the West, generally has been considered unacceptable to any who would undertake an orderly and systematic study of human beings. Hence it is not surprising to find in the social sciences that human beings have become, allegedly for reasons of order and system in research investigations, *objects.* I discuss this point further in Chapter 8.

## Phenomenological Research as Intersubjective Analysis

Unlike role theory, which makes the **person** external to community, in the dialogic view each person finds oneself to be a coexistence with other subjects; to be is already to be in community and to be related inter-subjectively. My account of persons thus presupposes intersubjectivity as its point of departure.

Phenomenology presupposes intersubjectivity. Inter-subjectivity is more than a presupposition, or a way of fusing subject and object in the category of **person**. It is also the presupposition of philosophical methods by which we can grasp (1) our processes of intuiting; (2) our processes of describing particularizings; (3) our processes of describing relatings; and (4) our processes of interpreting. I shall illustrate this method by using it as a way of understanding the personal world of Claire Smith as she discloses it to us in *Who Was I*, a paper written to fulfill a requirement of an introductory philosophy course (see Appendix I).

## Intuiting the Phenomenon

Intuition has meant a wide variety of things in the history of both Eastern and Western philosophy. In its root sense it evidently means 'to see' something or someone. Whereas it is surely not my aim to allow intuition the full mystical meaning it frequently conveys, neither can it be allowed to stand merely for the reductive physiological apprehensions of the world through the sense organs. My usage of the term here is an attempt (1) to capture in their *togetherness* the first approximations of 'seeing', 'hearing', 'smelling', 'tasting', and 'touching' when we focus or concentrate upon a subject-matter and (2) to move through to the further, deeper sense of *'really* seeing', *'really* hearing', and so on, through the rest of our senses.

With respect to persons, consider, for example, the following remarks: 'I have feelings, every person does, you know'. 'That person has had many of the same feelings I have had, and even similar experiences'. 'I am more conscious of that person now than I was before'. 'I'm a person, too, you know'.

The focus in any one of many possible expressions is intuitive and thus upon **person**. Anyone making such remarks is not asking someone to enter into a detailed study of persons or a study of the class of all living and breathing beings according to certain scientific procedures appropriate to the higher order we call man, the study of human physiology. Our first approximations, or sensings of a person, are intuitive, 'seeings' in the broad sense of relating, focusing, and concentrating 'seeings' into **person**.

The process of intuiting the phenomenon is the first stage in the method of intersubjectivity. Unlike the methods of objective analysis which *reduce* a phenomenon to parts already known and make it depend upon something other than and less than itself, in intuiting the phenomenon we focus upon its uniqueness, upon itself as reducible to nothing but itself. The method of intersubjectivity thus is particularly appropriate to the exploration of the phenomenon of **person** and of the adult eductions of **person**.

As we will realize when we read selections from Miss Smith's account, we know her partly as a first moment, a first 'seeing', a telling for our 'seeing' for the very first time. There is uniqueness, novelty, in her 'seeing' of herself for our intuiting of her. We understand her partly because of the agelessness of some of what she speaks. But however we do it, we must do so in some sense through our feeling, our experiencing, our consciousing of her. These are made possible by the fact that she is coming to 'see' herself more fully. To the degree that we understand what she is saying, intersubjectivity is present. Its presence, then, is structured within our **person** as well as within her **person**.

The richest ways of intuiting **person** rest upon such notions as feeling a **person**, experiencing a **person**, or consciousing (knowing and understanding) a **person**. Each of these is the person's being, being who she is, what she is, where she is, when she is, etc. These carry a sharing somehow with the other **person**, for feeling, experiencing, and consciousing are also forms and ways of relating persons to other **persons** and to things.

For example, *feeling* is necessarily a relating of a person, and something in addition, to the focusing of her immediate self ('I feel the stone', or 'I feel pain'). *Experiencing* is a doing, an encountering which is both a giving and receiving of oneself in relation to someone or something in addition. *Consciousing* is a knowing-with. Thus feeling, experiencing, and consciousing persons are made possible only by the assumption or presupposition of relatedness. But this is already built into the notion of **person**. Thus two or more human beings are necessarily presupposed whenever one speaks of persons or speaks of either human being as a person. Or as R. G. Collingwood expresses the matter,

> The discovery of myself as a person is the discovery that I can speak, and am thus a **persona** or speaker; in speaking, I am both speaker and hearer; and since the discovery of myself as a person is also the discovery of other persons around me, it is the discovery of speakers and hearers other than myself. Thus, from the first, the experience of speech contains in itself in principle the experiences of speaking to others and hearing others speak to me. How this principle works out in practice depends on how, in detail, I identify persons among my surroundings.[2]

That one speaks to a person or is spoken to by a person is the primitive phenomenon which we intuit. No concept and presupposition of either 'subjectivity' or 'objectivity' of knowledge alone can express this intuition of, or even the grounds of the possibilities of, **person**. We may say that our intuiting presents us not only with **person** but also with the richest of all possible subject-matters, *ourselves* (our self, myself, the 'I' which I feel myself to be), for as ourselves we are present in sharing with another who speaks of himself.[3]

## Describing Particularizings

The method of intersubjectivity includes two ways of particularizing its subject-matter. First, it deals with a part of a subject-matter as distinct, but not separate, from the whole, as one speaks of a person's desire to change his life and his plans to do so. Thus to particularize a phenomenon is to focus upon some one (or more) of its individual constituents, to *take* a part (say a plan which occurs to me while I am feeling bored at work), and to concentrate upon it for special investigation and exploration. One might pursue analysis by reinterpreting in clearer terms the sentences, words, and propositions that express what, when, how, etc., the phenomenon of **person** is. This kind of analysis is perhaps the most viable form of a logistic, atomistic, and reductive model characteristic of an 'objective' analysis or what we might term a version of a behavioristic analysis within adult education. But such analysis would not suffice, for what happens to the phenomenon **person** when all possible words, sentences, and propositions are analyzed? Analyzers and analyses in this vein might well be exhausted, but the **person** of Persons and their abstractly analyzed sectors of behavior would remain unfathomed. **Person**-analysis would still remain to be done. To do **person**-analysis the phenomenology of intersubjectivity is required. Intersubjective analysis is not reductive, and it can only be pursued through the exploration of the structurings of person along the lines of a person's own expression of ingredients and configurations.

An example of some of the ingredients and configurations as adult eductions of her **person** is found in Miss Smith's expression of herself as a person:

The experience through time is a synthesis of
  unique happenings
Which are mine alone and which shape me into me.
Thus man is not only a synthesis, but a synthesis of
  himself.
I who have never been a self before can now fully
Appreciate my self as something which can be
  defined, equated.
And examined.

In her exploration of herself Miss Smith calls attention to her 'uniqueness' as synthesized and as giving
rise to her and to no one else by referring to

                    . . . unique happenings
    Which are mine alone and which shape me into me.

Even if one believes that the whole is no more than the
sum of its parts, insistence upon a presupposition of
method that a whole and its parts are separate cannot
negate the fact of the phenomena of their inveterate
relatedness. The whole is a whole-**of** parts, and the
parts are parts-**of** a whole. Thus Miss Smith:

    . . . man is not only a synthesis, but a synthesis
    of himself.[4]

Here and elsewhere in my citations of Miss Smith's
paper it should be understood that the method of intersubjectivity is not merely being used as another hermeneutic device for understanding someone's written expression of oneself, for this method does not merely
give us more understanding of some personal exploration
than another method allegedly might--for example, a
Freudian 'causal' analysis of *why* Miss Smith wrote what
she did.
    I claim that in matters of the **person** world (1) the
assumption of intersubjectivity is the only possible
ground for accounting for our real 'seeing', 'hearing',
'touching' (generally 'sensing') of the **person** of persons, and (2) the method of intersubjectivity is the

only method which can be used fruitfully in the exploration and investigation of these matters. Thus Miss Smith's poetic expression, because it is personal, both assumes intersubjective relatedness and concretely expresses it, and thereby embodies and realizes it.

Analysis of **person** must be intersubjective analysis, and it can only be pursued through the general explorations of the structurings of **person** along the lines of a person's particular and distinct ingredients and configurations. One person presents himself to another, but he does so in uniquely *particular ways;* the method of intersubjectivity is a method of describing these particularizings. **Person**-perception studies, person self-help, self-willing, and self-motivation should be investigated through phenomenological research.

The *second* way of particularizing the phenomenon of persons is to describe the phenomenon or to portray, represent, and communicate distinctly, by means of properties and qualities, the uniqueness of the phenomenon **person**. The method of intersubjectivity makes particularizing possible. The call for description can come in questions like "Who is that person? Can you describe him?" The answer requires some kind of classificatory procedure, for example, in terms of size, weight, eye and hair color, etc. But these more ordinary answers are far wide of the target when compared with a person's own guideposts that are present as we are spoken-to: at the same time that we are spoken-to descriptively as listener, we are enabled, intersubjectively, to describe as speaker.

These two dimensions cannot be separated, for they are the Siamese twins of the process of describing our particularizings. Consider Claire Smith's presentation of distinct properties and qualities, the 'uniques' which particularize her **person**:

I am a living human being. . . .
I lived life blindly, from minute to minute. . . .
I still have chewed finger-nails, the scars, the
   freckles that mark my myself and no one else.
From the time I was a one-celled being born to Mr.
   and Mrs. Smith. . . .
I was a jealous child, jealous of those around
   me. . . .
I grew up alone. . . .
I blamed my parents for all the sorrow they were
   causing me.
I did not understand, nor did I try to understand
   their plight.
From my beginning came a certain part of my
   personality, and insecurity which is still a part
   of me.

Each of these characterizations is literally a selecting, a writing down, and a firming-up of central or
decisive characteristics of this unique, individual, and
particular person and no other. They are choices made
by the person herself from within a repertory of possible unique and particular tissues, facets, and dimensions. If any other method of description and analysis
were attempted in an interpretation of these passages,
the method of intersubjective descriptions must be basic
to it from a phenomenological perspective.

## Describing the Relatings

Although the process of describing the repertory of
particularizings of the phenomena of **person** could become
endlessly detailed in the case of any person--for example, as a constancy in process, or as a sameness in
variation--the method of intersubjectivity makes it
possible to describe both *what* a phenomenon is as it
appears and the countless *ways* of its appearing. Both
are dimensions of the ways of describing the relatings
of a phenomenon.
In the illustration in the passage above, several
variations of the specific ways of being of an 'I', a

unique feeling, experiencing, and consciousing self were presented:

> "I lived blindly, from minute to minute . . ./I was a jealous child . . ./I blamed my parents . . ./I did not understand. . . ."

The illustration to follow will present the relatings of **person** as a whole through routine temporal distinction of 'past', 'present', and 'future'. I do not wish to discuss at this point the very difficult philosophical questions, distinctions, and divisions of temporal consciousness in the full sense.[5] Yet, customary but falsifying classification and divisions of felt time into three modes never seems meant as a classification of **person** into three different persons. Even in invoking three fictive modes of time, we still seem to take **person** as a generic, essential thrust, for **person** may be explored 'as a whole' through its temporal strength. In this sense, all particularizings of **person** may be explored as relating to each other, with the focus of the investigation here upon the relatings of **person**.

The grounding of particulars and the seeing of essentials which are the meanings of the particulars are what I mean by the relatings of the phenomenon of **person**. Even the particularizings must be particularizings of connecting dimensions of a person. The examples below exemplify, by virtue of intersubjectively describing, the relatings of the phenomenon **person** with reference to a particular past, a particular present, and a particular future; these are relatings of a oneness, a generic essence of her **person**:

> I was a living human being,
> Living my life as a name--Claire Smith.
> I was uniquely myself on the surface,
> I am still Claire Smith, myself on the surface.
> More important, I am now what I never was before,
>   a determined inner self.
> Something I can look at and evaluate exactly as is,
>   because

It will change no more, except in my own
re-evaluation.
I will never know calculus, or zoology, or ancient
Greek history.
I will have a collection of knowledge which is
unique within itself.

The previous examples illustrate one way of describing *what* a person is, namely through temporal modes. Another way through which the method of intersubjectivity focuses upon *what* a person is, is to describe the process of discovering the phenomenon of person. In this process we discover her **person** in her appearings-to-us. The following example richly witnesses to these modes of appearing:

Has the world ceased to be?
No-
I am here, my body, my mind,
This three-pronged stool.
These defy an end to my existence,
And yet I must be dead. . .
For I can see nothing beyond me. . . .
I can remember being alive.
Yet where am I now. . . .

Describing the relatings of person also focuses upon the *ways* of the appearings of person: (1) as a whole, (2) as in some shading perspectives, and (3) in terms of the use of modes of clarity of person. It may well be that the use of intersubjective descriptions of **person** along these lines has more potential value in understanding **person** than any other dimension of the method.
In the *first* sense of focusing upon the appearing of the adult eductions of **person** as a whole, we come to feel, experience, and to conscious (know-with) as a whole, or at least better and better, what we have already felt, experienced, and consciousded previously in part. Sometimes a whole appears to us 'as a whole', we say. Consider for example:

Not until a day when I realized that I was alive did
a God mean anything. . . .
The realization of myself as a human being was
one of the greatest changes in my life . . .
I learned to appreciate exactly what it meant to be
alive.

Each of these statements concretizes a way of a person's
appearing as a whole.

The *second* sense requires that we recognize modifications of the **person** as 'perspective shading-off' or
recognize the phenomenon of **person** as an individual
person (an I, a self) feelingly reaches toward her own
exploring, explored, and always further explorable,
fringes. As an example of the dialectical exfoliation
of **person**, as a unique and nonreplicable person,
consider:

I do not like to think of myself as a prejudiced
Person and yet I am very prejudiced
I believe what I have been taught about my country
and its
Principles to be right.
I believe those opposing it to be wrong.
Upon investigation through knowledge I can see
both
Sides have merit in their existence. . . .
This is my own private collection of prejudices,
unlike
Any other, because my existence is a synthesis of
a particular
Collection of happenings unlike any other. . . .

A *third* sense in which we may describe the relatings
of the appearings of **person** may be stated as 'the modes
of clarity' or the 'degrees of clarity and distinctness'
in which the phenomenon appears.

Minute by minute, day by day, I increased in other
 ways. . . .
I learned to think and reason, to memorize and
 solve problems. . . .
Not until a day when I realized that I was alive did
 God mean anything.
The realization of myself as a human being was
 one of the greatest changes in my life.
Existence was a great shock to a dreamer.
I learned to appreciate exactly what it meant to be
 alive.
I came to the realization through fear.
As a more mature person, I attempted to realize
 myself more and dream myself less.

Each of the three examples of focusing upon the
appearings of a **person** as a whole manifests the sort of
experience we ordinarily have in mind when we affirm
that we have come to know ourselves--to know ourselves,
that is, in striking, originative, generative, and
motivating ways. For the purposes of this essay in the
use of phenomenological research in adult education,
there is a *fourth* and final sense in which we can describe the relatings of the phenomenon. This way consists in "the determination of the typical structure of
a constitution in consciousness by means of an analysis
of the essential sequence of its steps".[6] This kind of
description requires that we place together in sequence
some of the essential steps through which a phenomenon
is constituted in our own consciousness. Consider, for
example:

This is my own private collection of prejudices
 unlike
Any other, because my existence is a synthesis of
 a particular
Collection of happenings unlike any other,
These happenings forming not only my knowledge,
 my prejudices,
My future desires, but also my being.

> My friends, my enemies, my nation, my status
>    within my society,
> All these formed a part of this synthesis.
> And thus I was a person changing, indefinite,
> Ever increasing as a be-ing,
> Increasing as I lived, every minute of my life,
> Until I became what I am today, a self.

Each of the above examples is an episode, a moment, a step in Claire Smith's constituting of herself. When they are placed together in felt sequence they are both relatings of a person being expressed and described and the synthesizing unfolding of her **person**. Even her words themselves are new adult eductions as constitutings of her **person**: "Ever increasing as a being,/ Increasing as I lived, every minute of my life. . . ."
The intuiting, describing, and relating which belong to the method of intersubjectivity articulate an unfinished and unfinishable investigation, for the exact dimensions of the overlap of subject and object presupposed by the method cannot be precisely pinpointed. This openness requires that we suspend all questions pertaining to existence or nonexistence, possibility or impossibility, and even questions of the possible origins of the phenomenon.[7] Whatever else may be involved, this commitment to openness is a plea that we do not reduce a phenomenon to its abstractive units or fictive parts, as various forms of behaviorism, positivism, and analysis in use in adult education would have us do.[8] Thus it is that we can speak of intuiting **person**, describing **person's** particularizings, and describing **person's** relatings by focusing upon them in their stream, in their processional continuation. This necessary openness is richly portrayed in Miss Smith's work:

> This paper is me, and yet a realization has occurred within the time of writing and rewriting it. A realization that I have changed in my-self while writing it and it is immediately obsolete. If I were to rewrite it tomorrow or even a minute from now, it would be different than it is now,

for I cannot contain myself and describe myself
in definite terms and be a living, human being.

## Processes of Interpreting

The exploration and investigation of a phenomenon is
an ongoing, open-ended process of coming to feel, experience, and conscious better what we have preciously
felt, experienced, and conscioused in part. This process both underlies interpretation and constitutes it in
part. This process underlies interpretation and constitutes its vehicles, its carriers. The end result is
that we do come to know better and better in these ways.
In the special case of person this interpretation seeks
the meaning, or the 'sense' of adult eductions of **person**
in its encountering and transcending dimensions, rather
than in a reduced and reductive 'sense'. We come to
know persons in their **coming-to-be**--their *becoming* and
what comes to *belong* to them--rather than in terms of
their static being, or what they were, or our reductions
of them to what we think they were and are. Hence there
is always a quality of the concealed in **person** which
presents itself to us. But we have only to ask a person
to tell us about these matters and thereby express and
unconceal them for us.

To claim to be able to investigate **person** with completeness, either in terms of contemporary objectivistic
scientific models or in principle, is to commit oneself
to an abstract fictive model of **person** and to negate the
continuing, rich phenomena of **person**. This presumption
seeks to evade the veiled and concealed dimensions of
**person** as one who both is and is coming-to-be and to
belong. No doubt this negation emerges in the midst of
the frustrating difficulties and latent pitfalls, for
example, in the use of more traditional scientific
methods in the attempt at coming to know the behavior of
persons.

To interpret the 'sense' of **person** is to 'catch up'
and to see more clearly in paradigmatic form a human
be-ing as an 'I feel', as a reflexive and intentional
activity encountering itself. Thus, in its most basic

identifiable level, **person** is the seminal, originative, intentionality of human feeling, experiencing, and consciousing. The 'I feel' continues. Every attempt to articulate it alters it. Every expression used transforms this feeling; hence we are faced in our programs and research in adult education with open-ended phenomena which must be captured.

This is a difficult research problem. But we are in closer touch with the phenomena on which the research is based than traditional 'quantitative' methods of research could possibly be. So the dilemma: do we keep to the more traditional quantitative methods, while granting that they are far removed from our phenomena and subject-matter. Or do we face the fullness of the phenomena of the subject-matter of adult education, adult eductions of **person,** and the quest of persons for fullest self-realization? Do we accept the very difficult and new research problems involved and set about the necessary work of conceptualizing and implementing new research in adult education?

Each attempt is also an interpretation of a 'sense' of the adult eductions of the 'I feel.' In this context, Miss Smith's paper *in toto* presents more than its own articulation. It is the undeniable presence of intersubjectivity, a presence to be explored by the method itself.

Most of the phenomenological discussion in this section has been methodological. Specifically, it has offered a suggestive epistemology of **person.** Its aim has been to suggest the rudiments of a method for exploring and investigating the phenomenon, person. I have stressed that phenomenological methods run counter to current reductionisms of various kinds (whether philosophical naturalism, idealism, behaviorism, positivism, or others). This discussion offers at least presumptive grounds for arguing that those other methods have no real value in treating certain subject-matters, for example **person,** group, crowd, society, culture, ideology, alienation, behavior, and most, if not all, of the subject-matter treated by the human sciences.[9]

Surely reductive methods offer no help in understanding the prepositioning world opened to us by Miss Smith. It is never the abstract world which reduces **person** to fictive, unitized object. It is always some personal world that answers the question, 'Who am I?' The answer each of us gives to that question is at once one's own personal world and an entry into another person's world. Unless this were so, how could we presume to understand, communicate, agree, and disagree with another person? Or how could we expect to teach well, design relevant programs, and do the highest quality of new and originative research in adult learning? In order to do the new research necessary to deal appropriately with the phenomena of adult eductions of **person** and persons' learning and education, we must have new and alternative research programs.[10]

## B. **Phenomenological Investigations and Philosophical Problems in Adult Education**

I come now to the subject of problematics and problems within adult continuing education. I have already rehearsed some of these, for example, the more general kinds of questions: **Who am I?, What can I know?, What should I do?**, and **What may I hope?**. It will help now to begin to distinguish different sorts of problems within the context of adult education. These distinctions into appropriate kinds are founded in phenomenological explorations and are rather different from some of the other classifications of problems which have been presented and discussed in much of the most relevant literature.

Jerold W. Apps, in *Problems in Continuing Education*,[11] for example, charts out broad and basic 'problem areas', identifies 'basic problems' within these, looks at these basic problems from a variety of perspectives, and offers either a 'suggested solution to the problem' or 'guidelines for developing a solution or a perspective for the problem'. The 'basic problems' he discusses in the book are adults as participants, continuing education as a field or discipline, the knowledge content of this discipline (particularly as articulated through curricula), teaching-learning procedures, and research within continuing education.[12]

Four presuppositions are clearly and admittedly operative in what Apps argues: (1) There is a *field* or discipline of adult education, or perhaps 'continuing' education. (2) There is a body of knowledge--and thus a **content**--in this discipline. (3) There are identifiable teaching-learning procedures in adult education that assist in moving the adult learner through successful continuing education. (4) There is research which is indigenous to adult education as a field. Each of these is arguable, of course, and Apps understands this to be the case.

But there are also latent or tacit presuppositions which appear to undergird Apps's discussions. I believe that at least the following three can be identified: (1) The 'adult teacher' is essentially more important (that is, morally, politically, and institutionally more important) than the 'adult learner' because this teacher is uniquely privy to a special body of knowledge which is primarily parceled out through these teachers--who are, precisely because of their importance and power, morally entrusted and empowered with the dispensation of this special knowledge and the construction of curricula institutionalizing this special knowledge, these procedures, and this research. Of course all of the teachers pay their dues: degreeing, licensing, and certifying procedures have performed their usual regulating functions of making one 'fit' to teach within special sectors of the public at large.

(2) The research done by the 'adult teacher' (and the 'adult scholar?') in adult education is 'adult education research' and generates 'adult education knowledge.' This presupposition appears to me to have a pernicious, centripetal circularity which might parasitically draw more away from adult learners than it could possibly give to them.

As I have indicated, I have approached the problematics and the problems of adult education from a quite different point of view than the one presented with admirable clarity and fairness by Apps. I try to do essentially two things: (1) There is a sense in which I try to step back and a bit away from the 'how-to-do-it' approach in a special effort to get a larger picture or to get a hold on a larger and more open-ended clustering of phenomena within the situations in which adults find themselves, within their 'everydayness' wanting, desiring, and needing to continue their education. (2) But I am also trying to fine-tune or to register in greater and greater degrees of magnification the phenomena one readily finds in exploring more intensely and minutely the adult eductions of **person** that are the lives of persons in those situations of the varied cases and problems of their wanting, their desiring, their expectations, their plans, their transformations, and their empowerments, for example, within both learning and education.

A problem is a difficult or puzzling question proposed for resolution, a riddle, an enigmatic statement. It is a doubtful or difficult question that becomes, or may become, a matter of inquiry, of thought, discussion, or action. This definition issues from the Greek etymology of the word 'problem'. This most seminal meaning of the word is 'to throw before'. A problem therefore is 'a-throwing-before' or something which 'is thrown before'.

In a manner thoroughly consistent with Sections A and B of the Introduction to this essay, we may say that (1) problems have their originations, origins and sources, and origins, and (2) problems have their beginnings. These may be distinguished even if not separated. We may say also that (3) problems are introduced to persons and (4) persons are introduced to problems. I have tried to do this progressively, with *jolts* here and there and perhaps a *crisis* or two in one's reflections. I will continue to do it in this way since it seems to me that this is a quite normal way in which significant research problems arise.

We may also distinguish a *problem* and a *problematic.*
The latter term names what it is within certain situations that creates the essential and specific nature of
a problem. It is relative to a problem in the special
sense of constituting or presenting a problem, or as
presenting something difficult to resolve, doubtful,
uncertain, or questionable. In logic, for example, a
problematic enunciates or supports what is possible but
not necessarily true in an argument.

We may say that problems are formulated, constituted,
and presented as specific problems by problematic elements within problematic situations. Problems arise
within problematic situations. Specific problems come
into focus. Some of these come to be viewed as research
problems needful of investigation within situations in
which relevancy systems are at work.[13] They arise as
distinctive and unique structures to persons within
their situations. Only in their carefully fashioned and
structured form can problems be attacked and resolved.
Surely this is the clear testimony of all of the evidence which has come to us through the most spectacular-
ly successful sciences such as physics.[14]

*Situation* now emerges as a concept of paramount
philosophical significance as we discuss adults, education, and philosophy from a phenomenological point of
view. John Dewey's characterization of the phenomena
constituting a situation is instructive:

> What is designated by the word 'situation' is
> not a *single* object or event or set of objects
> and events. For we never experience nor form
> judgments about objects and events in isolation,
> but only in connection with a contextual whole.
> This latter is what is called a 'situation.' I
> have mentioned the extent in which modern philo-
> sophy has been concerned with the problem of
> existence as perceptually and conceptually deter-
> mined. The confusions and fallacies that attend
> the discussion of this problem have a direct and
> close connection with the difference between an
> object and a situation. Psychology has paid much

attention to the question of the *process* of perception, and has for its purpose described the perceived object in terms of the results of the process.

I pass over the fact that, no matter how legitimate the virtual identification of process and product may be for the special purpose of *psychological* theory, the identification is thoroughly dubious as a generalized ground of philosophical discussion and theory. I do so in order to call attention to the fact that by the very nature of the case the psychological treatment takes a *singular* object or event for the subject-matter of its analysis. In actual experience, there is never any such isolated singular object or event; *an* object or event is always a special part, phase, or aspect, of an environing experienced world--a situation. The singular object stands out conspicuously because of its especially focal and crucial position at a given time in determination of some problem of use or enjoyment which the *total* complex environment presents. There is always a *field* in which observation of *this* or *that* object or event occurs. Observation of the latter is made for the sake of finding out what that *field* is with reference to some active adaptive response to be made in carrying forward a course of behavior. One has only to recur to animal perception, occurring by means of sense organs, to note that isolation of what is perceived from the course of life behavior would be not only futile, but obstructive, in many cases fatally so.[15]

Problems emerge in and through the medium of situations in which adults find themselves. It would be impossible to attempt to classify and categorize all of the possible situations in which individual adults find themselves. Yet this impossible task is precisely what many professional adult educators in fact attempt in their 'how-to-do-it' approaches. Manuals of 'how-to-do-it' for specific persons engaged in specific situations with sufficient orderliness and similarity of tasks obviously are useful to have. The development of these may even be appropriate to professional adult educators perceived to be practitioners within a very broad range of professional activities taken as a field or discipline of adult education. But adult education is not a discipline, although it has a subject-matter. Manuals for specific situations or specific tasks or specific skills cannot fully perform what is promised when they are given authoritative status and significance as principal textbooks within that very broad range of professional activities taken as a professional and vocational discipline. They cannot fully do so with waiting, desiring, and needy constituencies and potential audiences, that is, without being practices grounded consistently and coherently in concrete theory.[16]

To claim that there are sufficient similarities between situations in which adults find themselves in learning activities and those in which adult educators find themselves in teaching situations for such manuals to serve as texts in adult education courses and in philosophy of adult education courses only exacerbates the problem. In practice, and through our practices, we might judge that they are, but are these based on solid and consistent theoretical grounds? The exacerbation is the plain sad fact of further and further removal from many of the principal adult eductions of **person** in the concrete process of continuing to learn: for example, the phenomena of individual adults' feeling, experiencing, and consciousing; the phenomena of individual adults' habits, relevancies, and the phenomena of a given adult's 'everydayness', languages of relevancies and discipline, and the *vital lives of individually unique adults,* among many others. Discussion of the adult eductions of **person** just cited, of course, comprises much of the rest of the content of this essay.

## Part III

### Adults:
### Realizing the Adult 'Eductions' of <u>Person</u>

*A phenomenological parable of the everyday life-world . .*

> *Man reaches his full capacity when he acquires complete consciousness of his circumstances. Through them he communicates with the universe.*
> *Circumstance!* **¡Circum stantia!** *That is, the mute things which are all around us. Very close to us they raise their silent faces with an expression of humility and eagerness as if they needed our acceptance of their offering and at the same time were ashamed of the apparent simplicity of their gift. We walk blindly among them, our gaze fixed on remote enterprises, embarked upon the conquest of distant schematic cities. Few books have moved me as much as those stories in which the hero goes forward, impetuous and straight as an arrow, towards a glorious goal, without noticing the anonymous maiden who, secretly in love with him, walks beside him with a humble and suppliant look, carrying within her white body a heart which burns for him, like a red-hot coal on which incense is burned in his honor. We should like to signal to the hero for him to turn his eyes for a moment towards*

*that    passion-inflamed    flower    which    is    at    his
feet.  All  of  us  are  heroes  in  varying  degrees
and  we  all  arouse  humble  loves  around  us.  'I
have  been  a  fighter/  And  this  means  I  have  been
a  man,'  exclaims  Goethe.  We  are  heroes,  we
are  forever  struggling  for  something  far  away,
and  trample  upon  fragrant  violets  as  we  go.*

Jose Ortega y Gasset,
*Meditations on Quixote*[1]

## Introductory Remarks

Not all persons are adults, but all adults are necessarily persons. It follows that the subject-matter of
adult education is **person**, specifically the adult eductions of **person**. Research into the subject-matter of
adult education includes investigations into private,
vocational, and professional actions of persons, investigations into persons' motives and other reasons for
doing what they do (both as learner and educator), and
the ways of transmitting the results of these investigations to both individuals and groups of individuals.
Whatever the subject-matter of adult education is,
research in adult education is research into that
subject-matter. The subject-matter of adult education
is the adult eductions of **person**, therefore research in
adult education is centered in research into adult
eductions of **person**. Whereas it is true that adult
education and adult learning may be distinguished both
as philosophical concepts and as clusterings of human
activities, they cannot be separated. For example, if,
as an adult educator, I investigate the motives and
reasons staff members in an industrial plant have for
taking quality control seminars provided by the corporation's human resources and development division, I
necessarily conduct this research first of all via my
radical self-awareness and at least through thought
experiments. And what I learn from the investigation I
appraise critically in its application to my own life.
I the investigator am also an adult learner. Those
other learners with whom I work, even if they learn

through groups in classes, must also justify in their **person**, as individual persons, any insights gained.

I shall explore these and related matters in Parts III, IV, and V. Here I wish to discuss feeling, habit, and the 'everydayness' of the adult lifeworld. Only if we have at least the rudiments of an understanding of what feeling is, how habits emerge as habituations in, through, and of feelings and beyond can we see the emergence and the constitution of the everyday lifeworld of the person in those fuller and richer realizations we call the adult life. But first there is the need to clarify what an adult eduction of **person** is.

I title Part III **Adults: Realizing the Adult 'Eductions' of Persons**. The principal focus is carried by the concept of **eduction**. My emphasis throughout deliberately rests on the processes of issuing forth, of drawing forth, bringing out, or eliciting meanings and values, and the processes of clarifying these through the stages of their development from conditions of latent, rudimentary, or merely potential existence, to the full actualization of the presence of sufficient adult eductions, a **critical synthesis of eductions**[2] of adulthood. In the remainder of these introductory remarks I want to present as clearly as I can what adult eductions are.

Who or what is an adult? I do not know, nor do I believe it possible to know, who or what an adult is as expressible in the formulation of a reductive definition or model which presents in the most precise and rigorous form possible the necessary and sufficient conditions stating all and only the exact marks, properties, and characteristics of what an adult is and what **adult** means. There will always be telling counter-examples inimical to the best of such formulations. A very young child might master some skills perceived by all as clearly 'adult' skills; an 'adult' might find himself unable to do simple sums, and so on. Moreover, the formulation of 'if and only if' conditions marking the concept 'adult' finds itself on the 'slippery slope' of distinctions: Why not include a little more or a little

less of such and such characteristics in the definition
or model of 'adult'?

Adult learners and adult educators have made careful
use of a wide variety of theories of adult development
as a phase of the construction of the theoretical foundation for practices in adult education. The works of
Erik Erikson, Abraham Maslow, Daniel Levinson, Lawrence
Kohlberg, Carol Gilligan, Gail Sheehy, George Vaillant,
and many other important researchers have all become
influential in this research in adult education.[3] Conceptions such as 'generativity', 'seasons', 'life
stages', 'mentoring', and 'passages' have become leading
research concepts. Important books have presented
distinctions (and I follow Sharan Merriam's listing
here)[4] within clusters of phenomena with age spans,
phenomena such as: the need for intimacy in old age;
parenthood and disruption within the life cycle; the
identity of life from young adulthood through mid-life
assessment to the life review; the world of work from
the early career through mid-life assessment to late-
life adjustment; questions relating to physical development from the vigor of youthful adulthood through aging
processes characteristic of middle-age; and finally to
old age and the termination of 'the physical self'.
Merriam has embarked on an eminently relevant research
program here and in a number of recent books in adducing
characteristics of adulthood through literature[5] rather
than through formulating a strict hypothetico-deductive
model of 'adulthood'. I deal with a number of these
issues in Chapter 8, "Metaphorizing Life."

The research program I propose throughout this essay
includes the presupposition that the adult eductions of
**person** constitute the fundamental subject-matter of
adult education. In the remainder of these introductory
remarks I shall: (1) present examples of what I understand to be adult eductions of **person,** (2) show how
these are the kinds of things which flow from persons as
eductions (as expressions and presentations of persons
we perceive to be 'adults') which are fundamental to the
transformations and empowerments of 'adult' lives which
adult learning, and adult education, are intended to

investigate and to achieve. These are claims that almost all definitions of 'adult education' have made explicit.

## Examples of Adult Eductions of Person

Eductions of **person** include (but are not exhausted by) activities, actions and acts of agents and agencies of the following kinds: self-conscious being and activities; feeling, experiencing, and consciousing; reasoning; willing; perceiving; discussing; knowing that one knows; producing, selecting, using, and rejecting concepts, systems, theories, laws; communicating and interpersonal communicating; deliberately habituating oneself within one's circumstances, situations, and environments, and then deliberately altering these habits; purposing, planning, judging, evaluating; describing, analyzing, and defining; planning a system of actions; organizing a system of beliefs; desiring; approving; learning to learn; formulating and appraising kinds and degrees of liberation and ways of being free; transformation; empowerment . . .

These constitute but a mere beginning of a rehearsal of the degrees and kinds of eductions of **person**. **Person** is this kind of being and doing. These are among the sorts of things persons do.

Adult eductions of **person** are at least eductions of **person** like those just presented. All adult eductions of **person** are the expressions and direct presentations of persons who in the context of such eductions of **person** as the above perceive themselves to be and/or are perceived by other persons to have or to be: *more* responsible for their choices, decision making and actions; *more* accepting of personal responsibilities in general; *more* self-supporting; *more* independent of earlier peer-pressures; *more* versed in practical wisdom and prudence in the 'everyday' world; *more* self-knowledge; *more* remembrances of a longer chronological aging coupled with increasing ability to leave them behind. . . . The surveying goes on, and it is a function of adult education research, in accordance with the overall research program being presented in this essay, to continue surveying the blurred boundaries marking adulthood and charting the general contours of valleys, plains, and peaks of the adult eductions of **person**. What one is working with all the while as the fusion of the reality of person and the concept of **person** are adult eductions actualized and realized executively in the lifeworlds of persons.

The concept of **person** and the dynamic realities of living and breathing persons are fused in the adult case by the actualizing and realizing executivity within the world of what I call adult eductions of **person**. Being an 'adult', doing 'adult' things, and speaking as an 'adult' constitute more a state of mind. These constitute a state of mind in which a sufficiently rich and varied cluster of adult eductions of **person** like those in both presentations above have become instantiated concretely in a given person whose actions in the 'everydayness' of daily life manifest these as an identifiable **critical synthesis**[6] of 'adulthood'. An 'adult' therefore is what a certain degree and kind of **critical synthesis** of eductions of **person** called adult eductions of **person** are and do.

### Adult Eductions of Person as Fundamental to 'Adult Education' However Defined

Although it is impossible to separate **person** from persons, since the former is concretely what the latter express in the world, it is absolutely vital to distinguish the two. One reason is that whereas persons, via their behaviors, are susceptible to research in accordance with behavioral and statistical models, **person** clearly is not. But if **person** is *not* fundamentally the proper subject-matter of adult education practices and research, then consider below (just a small selection of) the important kinds of things necessarily excluded thereby from the practices and research programs of adult education. I say this since these are all matters of meaning for persons insofar as they are eductions of **person** and not insofar as these are mere instances of persons' overt behavior: social and cultural symbols and their meanings; issues most fundamental to literacy/ illiteracy; planning one's profession or vocation; pleasure; happiness; one's place in the environment; oppression/liberation/freedom; citizenship; creativity; created works of art such as painting, sculpture, poems, plays, novels, music; scholarly work; purposiveness; self-development; self-realization; self-actualization; deliberate effort; inspiration; ambition; richness of life; satisfaction in the use of the mind; full knowledge of the uses and abuses of the body; structures of behavior; directions in life; knowledge; feeling; experiencing; knowing . . .

Clearly these kinds of phenomena, the meaningful personal expressions (with each one taken as a **whole**) of individuals or of groups, are excluded from the practices and research programs of adult education committed to behavioristic and statistical models. Yet all of the conceptions I have listed immediately above have been randomly culled directly from a great variety of definitions of adult education that have been offered during the last several decades. Where is the consistency of practices and theory? The consistency and coherency of research-to-practice? All of the above are variously stated goals of any adult education practices which would purport to be successful. But where are the theories consistently grounding the plethora of practices purporting to achieve those goals?

I suggest that each of those goals (and more) can be the 'object' of focus and phenomenological investigation through adult education taken as the rigorous human science of the adult eductions of __person__. My claim is that this core of a definition underlies all of the relevant definitions of adult education, or all of which I am aware. It gives them all what real substance they have; that is, this core of a definition gives meaning to *any* other relevant definition of adult education which speaks of persons in some way. And how would it be possible for any reasonable definition of adult education not to speak of persons in some degree? I have offered a definition which really tells us what these other definitions mean to say or which would give them the ground on which to say it more coherently and consistently. It also makes it more possible to evaluate them critically as good or bad definitions, and practices as successful or unsuccessful, through investigating the consistency of each of them in terms of the theoretical model and practices both described and prescribed by it.

I move now to discussions of feeling, habit, and 'everydayness' in adult lives.

# Chapter 1

## Toward a Phenomenology of Feeling

### Introductory Remarks

There is an urgent need within the practices and research which constitute adult education to develop a theory of what feeling is and what *a* feeling is. If the subject-matter of adult education is the adult eductions of **person**, if the practices of adult education include what adults do to and for themselves in more con-

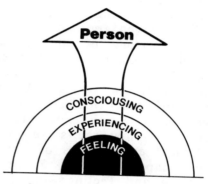

See n.3 in Notes to Table of Contents

crete and further actualizations of their **person**, and if these practices include the work of others who help to facilitate this development, then it is clear that the foundations of these practices can be identified as the feelings of persons. This means that the adult eductions of **person** as feelings constitute this foundation. Hence, adult education ultimately must have a working theory of feeling and feelings. Toward that end I offer here a brief phenomenological investigation of these phenomena.

Whereas this investigation may not yet constitute a theory, nevertheless there are certain rudimentary explorations of feeling and feelings which can provide clarificational and preparational groundwork toward the development of a theory suitable to undergird rigorous investigations in adult education. Whatever models of theory and practice may be used in adult education, no one should deny the importance of beginning with clear insight into the phenomena which are the initial focus of any given approach. Relevant[1] data must emerge from the repertory of phenomena to be investigated. This kind of exploration is precisely the work phenomenology ideally performs. Phenomenological investigations, therefore, are at least the necessary preparational work for any other methods to be used in research in adult education. Since **experiencing** and **consciousing**, respectively, follow the stage of **feeling**, I offer phenomenological explorations of these adult eductions of **person** in Chapters 4 and 7. Immediately below I consider feeling and feelings and following that, in Chapters 2 and 3, the habituations of feelings which grow into habits within the 'everydayness' of adult life.

What is feeling, and how does feeling relate to a feeling and to emotions? What relationship do these have to sensing, experiencing, cognition, and consciousness, for example? The first step is to distinguish feeling from  *a*  feeling or feelings.[2]

**Feeling as Charged Field Scanning and Sensing 'What Is' in the World**

Feeling is *both* a potentiality for contacting the world *and* the process within and through which actualizing and realizing contacts of **person** and world take place as mediated by individual persons. Feeling brings the power of **person** into the world, such that the world and 'what is' in it are enlivened and thereby realized or made real. Feeling does not 'make' the world or give it reality in any metaphysical sense, but it does bring it alive through **person**. A person (I, you) instantiates and concretizes the world through feeling the world (as episodic feelings and sensings), although feeling per se is neutral, indefinite, and indistinct, a charged scan and search without a focused object always in view.

Extended outward, as a kind of earliest scanning process, reaching out from **person** into the world within circumstances constituting specific situations, and extending itself by its very happening, feeling unfolds and offers itself to 'what is' as a field.

As both the potentiality, possibility and actualization, realization, the touch of **person** and world, feeling as field is always within a person's 'here-and-now'. As a person's 'here-and-now', in the midst of one's everyday life, feeling is presented as a *focal* region and a *penumbral* region, but without an edge. Collingwood claimed that

> The here-and-now has a *focal* region where, generally speaking, both precision and intensity are greatest, and a *penumbral* region where they decrease in every direction; until, in some outer zone of the penumbra, dimness of and confusion are such that you no longer know what it contains, nor whether it contains anything at all, nor even whether it is still going on.[3]

As a focal region, feeling is a center of greater concentration and clarity of energy and activity, as for example, the *focus* of a disease is the principal seat of its manifestation. Although being a center, as distinct from itself having a center, feeling is indistinct. As a *penumbral* region, feeling is also partial and fringe shadowings moving out from the focal region. But feeling has only blurred edges at best, or probably no real edge at all. Itself without an edge, it still 'edges' almost imperceptibly as a field always moving about as carried in the wide-awake person.

As a field, feeling (1) is a sensing of the world; it is touching, seeing, hearing, tasting, smelling the 'what is' within the world, but so far neutrally, indistinctly, without the focus of 'interest', and with no frames or systems of relevancy. In other words, feeling is not yet feelings, or *a* feeling. Feeling also (2) carries with it a 'charge'. A charge is a load placed in or upon something else. Charging something is placing in or on something else what it may be intended or be able to receive and hold, as in charging a blast furnace with ore in steelmaking. In older days, soldiers charged their muskets. A charging diffuses something throughout, or saturates it, as water is charged with carbon dioxide, or the air is charged with electricity, such that we can even say metaphorically that the air is charged with tension. Charging is carrying. Hence, we may say that in its richness and in the fullness of itself, feeling carries us along into and in the world.

When we combine these two characteristics of feeling, feeling becomes a charged field scanning and sensing 'what is' in the world. This is an early stage of **person**, something which all persons have. Without feeling, no entity or being can be claimed to be a person.

Further, feeling carries through greater and lesser strength and intensity. Its movement through the world --from potential touches to actualized touchings (as feelings), from possible contacts to realized contacts with 'what is' in the world (as feelings)--is movement toward greater strength and intensity. Another manifestation of feeling's intensity is the eduction of **person** as it more actively (rather than less actively) searches for touchings within the world. Finally, there is a way of saying that feeling comes to have no strength or intensity at all: if feeling could be purged entirely of all that constitutes feeling, nothing would be left at all. Feeling purged of its contents and 'fullness' would leave no residue.

## A Feeling as the Actualization and Realization of Feeling

In this investigation the referent of *a* feeling is present in such phrases as 'feeling the smooth silk', 'feeling angry', 'feeling ready to go to work', 'feeling the desire to change my life'. These are the kinds of linguistic ways we use to express and present degrees and kinds of feelings, as a particular sensing something, calling attention to the ways in which we become stirred, charged, and excited.

*A* feeling should not immediately be identified with, or confused with, a sensation or an emotion, and surely not with a perception. Each of the first two notions is perhaps a way of referring to distinguishable layers of a feeling, and whereas perceiving in its rudimentary stages emerges from a feeling as intended in this discussion, perceiving is neither a feeling per se nor 'causally' derived from it. Nor are feelings 'caused' or 'causal'; at least these questions of 'causality' should be put aside for the purposes of this investigation.

*A* feeling has an explorable structure, although not a spatial or temporal structure. We say, 'I feel a sharp point *now,*' or 'I felt one *then*' and 'I feel a pain *here,*' 'although earlier I had a pain over *there*'. These examples might appear to provide us with temporal and spatial references and contexts through which to locate feelings, but these idealities are not *a* feeling's own spatial and temporal structures. Nor is it necessary to a feeling, or of its essence, that a feeling move over time through spatial locations.

This structure of a feeling can be analyzed and described phenomenologically. A feeling is, first of all, feeling as sensing something, an identifiable stage of contacting, or of touching-with, the world in which I live and move and have my being. Within the relevancy system termed 'physiology' one calls attention to the senses as receptors, or as groups of receptors, specialized toward the goal of apprehending 'external objects'. But here I simply present sensing as a sensing-that I, a person, contact-with the world, am in contact with my everyday world. Perhaps sensings are originations within my own world, relatively indistinct marks, steps, and stages of the charged and scanning field of feeling graduating toward nodules of feelings more identifiable and richer, more actualizing and realizing of the world. But sensing something in particular in this world is the beginning of meaningfulness that there is something which I both am as **person** and have as a person.

And we may go further. It seems possible to identify something more of each feeling. This is the special kind of charging and energizing thrust which a feeling is. Collingwood claimed that

> a feeling consists of two things closely connected: first, a *sensuous* element such as a colour seen, a second heard, an odour smelt; secondly, what I call the *emotional* charge on this sensation: the cheerfulness with which you see the colour, the fear with which you hear the noise, the disgust with which you smell the odour.[4]

A person may see a color cheerfully or smell an odor pleasantly. The feeling, the sensing (a feeling, a sensing) has such a close connection with the emotional charge that the latter modifies and qualifies the feeling (and not the 'object' felt), hence the feeling is adverbially disclosed, modified as cheerful or pleasant. One does not have to claim that a particular color seen is a cheerful color, or a smelled odor is a pleasant odor; the feeling as a seeing or a smelling is this sensing in each case together with the emotional charge adverbially portrayed. The felt or sensed is cheerfully seen, or pleasingly smelled.

A feeling is a here-and-now. What I feel is something which is colored when, as, and how I feel or sense it. And as it is the case with the field of feeling so it is with *a* feeling. There is indeed the cheerfulness with which I see the color, the fear with which I hear the noise ('fear' if I know what it is and have good reason to expect pain to follow it, for example; 'anxiety', if I do not know what the noise comes from or what it is). But this charging is not merely an emotional ingredient, nor is it 'on' the feeling. A feeling itself more fully analyzed and described is a sensing, a stirring, an exciting, and a charging, and not merely a sensuous element 'with' an emotional charge on this, as Collingwood claimed.

Whereas Collingwood distinguished the sensuous element, I have pointed to sensing, stirring, and exciting phases of feeling per se. And whereas he identifies an 'emotional charge' as being 'on' this sensation, it seems to me that we should distinguish between an 'emotion' and a charge or charging as yet another identifiable wave or rippling within the wave of **person** which feeling is.

From an analysis of a feeling as a sensing in one stage it is possible to move to what might be termed the 'stirring' which a feeling is. It is an agitation, a perturbation, at least a slight irregularity (or much more), a disturbance, an inciting thrust, within **person** in the midst of the general and neutral reaching out and ordering of the world which the field of feeling is.

Then we can identify the 'exciting' layer of a feeling, a degree of arousal, which is a movement of the field of feeling which has centered itself as *a* feeling, swollen with the fullness and clarity of a touch. And literally *a* feeling is feeling as field moving out, back, or away from its previous stages, layers, or waves as sensing and striving. Possibly we may speak of the tenor, pitch, and additional range which a feeling is and has.

At first, it might seem that the 'exciting' layer is not a stage in any feeling, but more properly what is called an 'emotion'. William P. Alston, in "Emotion and Feeling," in *The Encyclopedia of Philosophy*, lists a number of factors which have been considered by many thinkers to be essential to emotions:

(1) A cognition of something as in some way desirable or undesirable.
(2) Feelings of certain kinds.
(3) Marked bodily sensations of certain kinds.
(4) Involuntary bodily processes and overt expressions of certain kinds.

(5) Tendencies to act in certain ways.
(6) An upset or disturbed condition of mind or body.[5]

Theories of emotion differ widely as to which of these characteristics constitute(s) emotion itself and which they take to be 'cause(s)' or 'effect(s)', or concomitants of emotion. I do not see that emotions are merely reducible to feeling, or that feeling is necessarily the most essential ingredient in emotion. I simply focus here primarily on feelings as at least essential to emotions, as fundamental moving forces, eductions, of **person**. True, an emotion is also a moving-out, a kind of migration and transferring, and although this usage of the term is obsolete, it does carry the etymology of the term as feeling but not as feelings. All emotions at least arise within feeling, but not all feelings are emotions. Hence, it would be improper analysis and description of both feeling and feelings to say that they are emotions or that they are what emotions reducibly are. Even if we speak of the emotions of pity, wonder, and sternness, can we say that each is at least a feeling, or feeling actualized, in an episode of sensing? But what then is feeling?

Finally, there are additional characteristics of a feeling that may be noted briefly for our purposes. A feeling is evanescent. Upon its very appearance it begins to perish. For its duration, however, it manifests at least two kinds of strength. These are (1) vividness, or compressive strength, and (2) tenacity, or tensile strength. As vivid, a feeling is striking--if not entirely clear and well-formed--it has intensity, the strength of life, aliveness, and liveliness. As tenacious, a feeling 'holds together'; it is cohesive enough to retain, preserve, and maintain the grasped and thereby sensed 'object'. Feelings are not so much lifelike as they are giving of the life of **person** vividly and tenaciously to 'what is' in the world.

But these are strengths with no discernible boundaries, since feelings are without edges, and if they have no edges, no precise deliminations (as feelings, although they do have edges as taken up into experiencing and consciousing, since feelings may become the 'objects' of experience and thought), a feeling can never be: (1) merely a single feeling apart from any other feeling, (2) a complex whole of several distinct feelings, (3) or a whole as distinguished from other whole feelings. Hence, feelings cannot really resemble one another (at the level of feeling, remember, although this is not true at those higher levels of experiencing and consciousing) since the possibility of two feelings resembling one another would require that the feelings be separate and that both be separated from yet a third feeling which would always be required for any resemblance to be articulated. This would require that feelings have edges, but they do not. Each feeling is simple, without parts, and thus unanalyzable in strict logistic terms. A feeling is immediate and fragmentary, the fountain of originations (but not yet the beginnings) of experiencing and consciousing properly so-called. Each feeling carries with it the coloring of the field of feeling within which it is actualized and realized.

Although we can consciously generalize about our feelings, a feeling itself cannot be generalized except at higher levels of **person**, the levels of experiencing and consciousing. Feelings per se cannot be remembered, although we can, and very often do, remember *that* we had a feeling, *that* I saw that color cheerfully, but the feeling itself goes unreproduced and unremembered because it was an actualized sensing in a 'here-and-now' situation in what is *now* a 'then-and-there' situation (if it were claimed that it could be remembered).

Above feeling, consciousness attends-to the charged scanning field of feeling, distinguishes and individualizes feelings, selects them out, and continues to work away at them in countless ways: giving them edges and boundaries, articulating particular and unique feelings, clustering some of them as complex wholes, looking into possible resemblances, 'mulling' them over, reflecting on them, searching out interpretations toward the end of understanding better and better these sensings, and thereby persons and ourselves within the world.

Remember that the charged, scanning field of feeling has both a focal region and a penumbral region. Either region may slow, or hesitate. The charged field of feeling may pause. Something becomes centered upon, pinpointed. A grasping takes place. Feeling is articulated as *a* feeling. Feeling and feelings constitute the originative layer of **person** which flows into two further layers, experiencing and consciousing. **Person is feeling, experiencing, and consciousing.** But persons *have* feelings, experiences, and thoughts.

### A Feeling-With

I am located by birth in space and time. I have my placement in the world within circumstances constituting situations. 'I', 'world', 'circumstances', 'situations' . . . Each is a crucial notion which needs more phenomenological investigation. My being, my condition as **person**, are all situated. I have a site, a place within the world, a fitting and natural place, and this is the unity of my being in the world. I contact (from the Latin, **con**, with + **tactare**, to touch) the world, or am in contact with the world. This is a state or condition of touching 'what-is' in the world, with a focus on the reciprocal relation between my **person** and the world. Putting the matter in this way suggests several metaphors: a straight line touches a curved line; two curved lines touch one another; two flat surfaces touch; 'contact-points' and 'contact-binds' come to mind. But the metaphors fail since none of them give us the sense of the fluid and dynamic quality of the reciprocity relation here.

Quite literally, my contact with the world is my 'touching-with' the world. This 'touching-with' phenomenon is my feeling of, my sense-awareness of, the world and things within the world. My sensing is the first stage of any feeling. Ortega maintained that the radically decisive mode of a person's conduct or encounter with anything is actually feeling as *touching* something.[6] It is in terms of this radical mode of feelings that he could claim that feeling-with is 'the most decisive factor in the structuring of our world.'[7] Feeling things and feeling-with things constitute the model of contact (as overlap and realization of subject and object) in the world. Without feeling and feeling-with we would not be touching anything; literally we would be out of touch with the ingredients and circumstances of the world. We would be in touch with nothing.

Ortega argued that a feeling as touching is distinguishable from all of the 'other senses or modes of presences' because in all feeling two things are always present as inseparables:

> the body we feel *and* our body with which we touch it . . . a relation . . . between a foreign body *and* our body. The firmness is a presence in which we present at *once* something which resists *and* our body; for example, our hand, which is resisted. In it we feel, therefore, at the same time the object which presses us *and* our muscle pressed.[8]

In Ortega's terms a feeling has a simple structure consisting of itself and nothing more. It is private to the person who has that feeling. It is itself and cannot be reduced to anything else. A feeling cannot be investigated and analyzed in reductive ways, but it can be focused upon, explored, investigated, and described in eductive and transcendive ways. For example, the feeling, experiencing, and consciousing of **person** that become expressed as the adult eductions of adults, which lead them in doing what they do, can be studied through phenomenological methods. This is what I have tried to show throughout this essay. This is the rightful province of the *human sciences*.

Ortega's analysis is of great importance. This is the very analysis of feelings on which he bases his notion of the 'vital' life (as I also do in Chapter 9) in activity, reason, and other conceptions such as vital mission, vital occupation, and vital destiny. It is for these commitments and phenomenological investigations that he must be counted among the most important adult educators in the twentieth century, surely so in Spain and Europe generally.

It is easy to see that Ortega is no philosophical vitalist as some of his critics have claimed. He did not posit life as an irreducible and separate ontological category as they claimed. He always argued that life, *la vida,* is pragmatically and executively expressed as feeling and feeling-with. 'Life is what we do and what happens to us.'[9] Feeling is most fundamentally what **person** is, and feeling-with is most fundamentally what adults do. These are the originations of adult eductions of **person**.

### Feeling, Feelings, and 'Feeling-With' as the Subject-Matter of the Human Sciences

A note of history may be important here. It is commonly believed that feeling and feelings cannot be the subject-matter of any special discipline, field of study, or science. Surely, these all-too-personal expressions cannot be subjected to rigorous scientific investigation, it is claimed. Among the reasons adduced for this claim are propositions of various kinds about the very characteristics of feelings I have presented above through a phenomenological investigation.

Perhaps it has occurred to the reader, as it has occurred to me, that feelings as phenomena have not so much failed the tests of precision and rigor of 'programs' of scientific research fashionable in the Western world through the centuries as these kinds of research have failed their own tests when they have been used in investigations of the most basic eductions of **person**. Feelings as phenomena are simply 'there', available for study by 'sciences' (from the Latin, **scientia**, literally, as systematic investigations of any determinate subject-matters). There are many other ways of 'determining' subject-matters besides those fashionable ways which still follow Descartes's mathematicizing principles of reductionism. Persons' feelings may not easily conform to the Procrustian rack of reductionisms (remember that Procrustes was depicted as cutting or stretching his victims into the 'right' size), but they are 'there' to be studied in rigorous ways. Clearly, adult education researchers must accept this different and more difficult challenge and responsibility.

For whatever reasons, there has not been a 'science' of feelings, but Collingwood claimed that there was, in the sixteenth century, a 'proposal for a new science to be called psychology.' In very modern terms, we might say that the proposal was rather like a call for a 'research program'. This call was not issued because reflective persons were dissatisfied with logic or ethics as 'sciences of thought'.

> It arose . . . from the recognition (characteristic of the sixteenth century) that what we call feeling is not a kind of thinking, not a self-critical activity, and therefore not the possible subject-matter of a criteriological science.[10]

It had been held previously that feeling is an activity of the mind, of cognition, that in feeling cold, seeing the color red, or hearing a shrill sound, 'we are coming to know in the various ways corresponding to the various natures of the objects known that there is something cold, or red, or shrill in the world about us.' In the sixteenth century, careful observers began to see that in 'feeling a coldness or seeing a redness or hearing a shrillness' a person is not coming to know some objective state of affairs in the world but purely and simply having a feeling, the linguistic presentation of which would be adverbially stated. A person always stands amidst circumstances in a situation and feels, sees, and hears within these circumstances. Although feelings as seeings and hearings flow into experience and thereby begin to grow as meaning, they are not themselves knowledge since they are not self-critical activity.

> The business of thinking includes the observing and correction of its own errors. That is no part of the business of seeing, hearing, touching, smelling, tasting, and experiencing the emotions associated with them.[11]

But if these activities are not the activities of a 'mind', neither are they activities of a 'body' (supposing just for the moment a separation of the two).

> To use a Greek word (for the Greeks had already made important contributors to the science of feeling) they were activities of the 'psyche', and no better word could have been devised for the study of them than psychology. Thus psychology was put on the map of the sciences, to march on the one hand with physiology and on the other with logic and ethics; a science of feeling, designed to fill a gap between its existing sciences of bodily function and the existing (criteriological) sciences of mind, in no way competing with any of them.[12]

But it did not turn out that way. Psychology has become an 'empirical' science, but not the empirical science of feeling as it might have been.

Finally, it is appropriate to ask how this brief phenomenology of feeling(s) relates to research in adult education. The answer is important. (1) An understanding of what feeling and feelings are is vital to any working theory of adult education since these are foundational for understanding experiencing and consciousing, and all three (FEC) constitute the principal kinds of eductions of **person** and hence the adult eductions of **person**. All three clusterings of phenomena present themselves as candidates for research within the human sciences, the most rigorous of which can be and ought to be adult education, as committed to taking the full measure of the phenomena most relevant to its investigations. (2) A knowledge of what feeling and feelings are is necessary to the understanding of the remaining claims and arguments throughout this essay on new directions in theory, practice, and research in adult education. It provides the basis for subsequent discussions of habit, the will-to-learn, 'everydayness', eduction as education, relevancy systems and the languages of relevancy systems, 'metaphorizing' life, and the transforming and empowering liberations of persons' lives necessary to the vital life of care and service in the world.

I claim often in this essay that countless research projects can be and ought to be devoted to the study of all these issues that are of the greatest importance to adult learning and education. I try to show throughout how it is possible to pursue this research through phenomenology, even if such projects as the study of feeling(s) do not seem to be possible through the use of one or another of most of the prevailing approaches in adult education research.

# Chapter 2

## Habits and Habituating the Will-to-Learn

### Introductory Remarks

The relationships between feelings, habits, and the will-to-learn constitute an essential structure in all learning, and they present special phenomena in learning through adult eductions of **person**. From the actualized feelings within the charged field of feeling, habituations evolve and become relatively settled dispositions or tendencies to act in certain ways, particularly in ways which have become especially fitted as responses through frequent repetition of these same activities, until they become almost involuntary activities rather than the actions of free, reasoning persons. These habits (from the Greek, $\check{\varepsilon}\chi\varepsilon\iota\nu$, and the Latin, **habere**, **habitus**, to have, to be constituted, having a possession) are settled practices, customs, usages,[1] and customary ways or manners of personal actions. Habits are also conditions of being accustomed to some actions through having that special familiarity with them which comes from having constantly to do with them.

Our birth launches each of us into the already-existing coexistence of other persons. It situates us temporally and spatially in the context of our predecessors, our 'consociates'[2] (contemporaries with whom we grow older together), and all who come after us in future years, and the even more distant years of a 'further future'.[3] From our earliest years, therefore, we are already massively habituated, and this long before we have either the inclination or the ability to reflect on what is going on. Moreover, depressingly, much of the 'K-12' education of the young is mo more than their bored, plodding passage through stultifying layers of unquestioning and unquestioned habituations to information (and misinformation). The undergraduate years of the 'higher education' more often than we usually admit offer little relief. Therefore, the intersubjectivity of persons within which each of us uniquely participates as expressive of our own eductions of **person** already manifests much typicality of action, behavior, and conduct through all levels of feeling, experiencing, and consciousing.

One major question concerning adult learning and the work of adult educators thus has to do with the relationships of feelings, habits, and the nurturing of, or very often the discovery of, a person's own will-to-learn. These are the principal issues investigated in this chapter.

## Habits and Habituations

These relationships have been richly explored in detail through the highly original phenomenological investigations of Charles Sanders Pierce.[4] Consider the following passage, for example:

It has been a great, but frequent, error of writers on ethics to confound an ideal of conduct with a *motive to action*. The truth is that these two objects belong to different categories *Every action has a motive;* but an ideal only belongs to a life [of] conduct which is deliberate. To say that conduct is deliberate implies that each action, or each important action, is reviewed by the actor and that his judgment is passed upon it, as to whether he wishes his future conduct to be like that or not. His ideal is the kind of conduct which attracts him upon review. His self-criticism, followed by a more or less conscious resolution that in its turn *excites a determination of his habit,* will, with the aid of the sequelae, modify a future action; but it will not generally be a moving cause to action. It is an almost purely passive liking for a way of doing whatever he may be moved to do. Although it affects his own conduct, and nobody else's, yet the quality of **feeling** (for it is merely a quality of **feeling**) is just the same, whether his own conduct or that of another person, real or imaginary, is the object of the **feeling**; or whether it be connected with the thought of any action or not. *If conduct is to be thoroughly deliberate, the ideal must be a habit of feeling which has grown up under the influence of a course of self-criticisms and of hetero-criticisms; and the theory of the deliberate formation of such habits of feeling is what ought to be meant by esthetics.* It is true that the Germans, who invented the word, and have done the most toward developing the science, limit it to taste, that is, to the action of the Spieltrieb from which deep and earnest emotion would seem to be excluded. But in the writer's opinion the theory is the same, whether it be a question of forming a taste in bonnets or of a preference between electrocution and decapitation, or between supporting one's family by agriculture or by highway robbery. The difference of earnestness is of vast practical moment; but it has nothing to do with heuretic science.

According to this view, esthetics, practics, and logic form one distinctly marked whole, one separate department of heuretic science; and the question where precisely the lines of separation between them are to be drawn is quite secondary. *It is clear, however, that esthetics relates to feeling, practics to action, logic to thought.*[5] (My emphasis)

I  shall  try  to  trace  briefly  Pierce's  view  of  feelings  as  the  fountain  of  habits,  and  in  the  process,  I
hope,  suggest  how  Pierce's  writings  could  be  mined
generally  as  a  rich  lode  of  ideas  for  adult  education.[6]

A  variety  of  words  related  to  'disposition',  the
concept  of  carrying  the  core  characteristics  of  'habit',
convey  a  feeling  of  the  fitting,  appropriate,  relevant,
suitability,  order,  and  actions  both  excited  and  chan-
neled  by  these  phenomena.  It  is  clear  that  personal
habits  are  conceived  within  persons'  charged  fields  of
feeling  and  are  thrust  into  the  world  first  as  originative  nodules  of  the  stirring,  sensing,  grasping-on,  and
excitive  waves  which  each  feeling  carries.

Even  if  we  are  born  into  coexistence  and  the  intersubjectivity  of  persons,  William  James's  famous  statement  that  we  are  'born  into  the  booming,  buzzing  confusion  of  the  world'  suggests  some  of  the  conditions
within  which  immediate  problems  must  be  faced.  Considering  the  vicissitudes  of  this  kind  of  world,  perceived
at  the  very  least  as  life  carried  on  in  the  midst  of
unfriendly  circumstances  inimical  to  the  eductions  of
**person**,  appropriate  life-supporting  and  perpetuating
uses  of  nature  and  of  all  of  our  environments  become
absolutely  urgent.  Habituations  generally--and  specific
habits--evolve  as  expressions  of  the  directionalities  of
the  eductions  of  **person**,  ideally  serving  us  (I  say
'ideally',  since  clearly  many  habits  do  us  disservice
rather  than  service)  through  making  it  more  possible  for
us  to  act  in  ways  both  sharpened  in  appropriateness  and
less  encumbered  by  encounters  with  the  unfamiliar.
Habits  emerge  through  specific  feelings  as  habituations
by  which  we  have  rendered  our  world  more  and  more  familiar.  The  more  familiarity  we  have  with  something,  the
more  likely  we  are  to  act  in  habitual  terms  in  respect
to  it.  What  security  we  may  have  is  itself  ample  testimony  to  the  efficacy  of  our  habits.  Development  of
life-supporting,  enhancing,  and  enriching  habits  is  most
characteristic  of  the  adult  eductions  of  **person**  executively  responding  to  the  resistances  of  this  world.

Pierce  claimed  that  the  most

genuine synthetic consciousness, or the sense of
the process of learning, which is the preeminent
ingredient and quintessence of the reason, has
its physiological basis quite evidently in the
most characteristic property of the nervous
system, the *power of taking habits*. This de-
pends on five principles.[7] (My emphasis)

These five principles may be characterized briefly as
follows. (1) The excitement of cells when stirred
spreads to other cells, and from those to others, and so
on, and with greater intensity. (2) But after time,
'fatigue' sets in as (a) 'utter fatigue', with cells
losing this excitement and excitability; and as (b)
'gentler fatigue', which is important 'in adapting the
brain to serve as an organ of reason', and which consists of the discharge of a nerve-cell as moving along a
different path than previously taken, or along a path
earlier taken, but this time with a greater intensity.
(3) The excitation of the cells may subside, but 'sensation persists' (a phenomenon long noted by physiolo-
gists). (4) When a previously excited cell becomes
excited once more, its discharge is likely to move along
one or more of the routes of its previous discharges
rather than along new routes. Pierce claimed that this
is 'the central principle of habit; and the striking
contrast of its modality to that of any mechanical law
is most significant'. [7] (5) After the elapse of a
considerable period of time with no excitation, the
nerve cell becomes progressively less likely to discharge along these previous pathways. He terms this the
'principle of forgetfulness or negative habit'.
    This phenomenological analysis of both the origina-
tions and the beginnings of habits within feelings and
the investments of nerve cell discharges is strikingly
'non-causal'. It is true that 'cause-like' terms such
as 'stimulus', 'excitation', and 'irritation' are used,
but in the larger context of Pierce's views the uses and
the meanings of these concepts are much more probabil-
istic than 'causal'. And it is instructive to recall

that these are the views of one of the most important of all of the thinkers contributing to the development of the theory of probability.

Some feelings as contacts-with the world, nurtured through repetition and the strength of intensity, become our appropriate and special reliances, our dispositions, and thus the habituations we call 'habits'. There are also 'habits of experience' and 'habits of thought'. These latter two general kinds of habits are distinct but inseparable from habits per se, or those especially relevant, disposing forms of personal actions into which some feelings grow. They are *distinct* because the eductions of **person** which experiencing unfolds carry along all that experiencing is and that experiences are. The same points may be made regarding 'habits of thought' (habituated consciousings). These latter points will become clearer as I present phenomenologies of experiencing and consciousing in Chapters 4 and 7. The two latter kinds of habits are *inseparable* from habits properly so-called (as special investments of feelings) since the stirrings, sensings, graspings, excitings which habits primitively are as special feelings continue to live on. They survive and indeed feed 'habits of experience' and 'habits of thought'. Indeed, this is the only reason for calling these two latter cases 'habits' at all.

The main reason why most of us continue to think of habits primarily as intellectualizations somehow deeply embedded in our psyches is that the only way in which we finally are able to identify the sorts of characteristics which feelings and habits have is through reflection. But in this reflection 'feelings' and 'habits' become 'objects' of our reflection, and our error is to mistake the continuing effort required in this careful reflection with the 'objects' of our reflection. Our common notion of 'habit', therefore, is derived mistakenly in this way: The referent of the concept 'habit' is mistakenly identified with the continuing felt effort of the reflective thinking process that discloses what a habit is rather than with the relevant phenomena that the reflective analysis of these phenomena discloses.

The matter is even a bit more complicated. There are at least two contradictory versions of this mistaken view of what a habit is, and each one is palmed off as a 'commonsense' view: First, there is the 'mind-focused' account of habit, which claims that a habit is somehow an intellectualized disposition, and that the way to understand, or if necessary, to change or eliminate a habit, is to 'think it all the way through'. Evidently 'thinking it through' itself is supposed to provide both the motive occasion and the necessary strength of motive to initiate and to effect the successful change or elimination of a habit. Second, there is the 'body-focused' version, which claims that a habit is 'caused' by body processes and behaviors that are disclosed by careful reductive analysis of these. And the methods whereby habits are changed or eliminated is through 'behavior modification'.

Even if either one (or both) of these accounts of the development, alteration, or elimination of habits were correct, fully fleshing out the implicit theories involved would necessitate a full investigation of the phenomena of feelings and their place in either theoretical position. However, we have already shown how a phenomenological investigation of feelings and habits clearly undercuts both of those 'commonsense' versions and how both rest on an even more basic error of mistaken identification. Pierce's phenomenological analyses also provide additional evidence of those two analyses of what habits are and how one goes about changing or eliminating undesired habits.

There are major implications here for adult education theory and practices. For example, what are the proper ways by which adults can alter and eliminate unwanted habits? Or, how do they come to see some of their habituated adult eductions of **person** in this light? Another implication is this: The 'reasons why' adults do what they do, desire to change their ways and their lives, do or do not change, are enabled or not empowered to do so, and so forth, must be traced through to their foundations in feelings by phenomenological investigations. These reasons may also be traced 'outward' from the rootages of the adult eductions of **person** and the unique actions adults use in ordering their lives and their worlds. We must not forget that there are many ways and many matrices of relationships whereby these 'orderings' are effected. Not all of these are 'causal' ways. Indeed, are any of them 'causal'?

## The Will-to-Learn

Most of our learning in early years is habituated and therefore takes place without much effort. Surely the ways in which we acquire a generalized but very basic stock of knowledge--itself the foundation to subsequent skills and to our understanding of worlds--are articulated through personal activities not requiring great effort. William James claimed 'we are misled into supposing that effort is more frequent than it is by the fact that during deliberation we often have a feeling of how great an effort it would take to make a decision now'.[8]

Sometimes effort takes place in personal actions through which learning occurs. These **effortive**[9] episodes may be actions of choosing, deciding, or resolving something. A person is doing something all the while, and when these actions are performed it seems clear enough that the willing aspect of a person's life both energizes and dominates feeling, experiencing, and consciousing aspects of that person's life. It seems clear, also, that the will-to-learn is an essential structure in the process through which persons move in learning anything at all.

Whereas it is surely the case that a person's willingness to learn--the episodic expression of one's essentially structured will-to-learn--must have been functioning already in nascent, latent, and rudimentary ways prior to any obviously effortive learning taking place, I do not intend to treat this question here.[10] The problem of the essential structure of the will-to-learn arises precisely at the juncture where effort becomes clearly evident in learning. All of these matters deserve careful investigation along phenomenological lines.

I propose to do a phenomenology of the essential structure of the will-to-learn. This inquiry consists primarily in adducing appropriate phenomena constituting evidence for the presence of this structure in all effortive adult learning. If this structure is present in all effortive adult learning, then there are inescapable implications for teaching as well.

The literature principally relevant to this investigation is the lifelong work of William James, his *Principles of Psychology,* and especially the principal essay in his first book in philosophy, *The Will to Believe,* which bears the same title. In recent years James has been rediscovered as a philosopher, but this time as a philosopher of much greater originality, rigor, and magnitude than previously thought. His momentous influence on Edmund Husserl, the founder of modern phenomenology, may be cited as an example of his prototypical importance to phenomenology.

Three other sources of importance to this discussion deserve mention. These include the works of Alexander Pfänder, Nicholai Hartmann, and Alfred Schutz.[11] Together they constitute a corpus of phenomenological investigation of the greatest value for the subject-matter of adult education.

In this section, (1) after adducing some of the evidence attesting the presence of the essential structure of the will-to-learn in effortive learning, I (2) show how feeling, experiencing, and consciousing are related to will and the will-to-learn. The will is dominant in these processes of our lived bodies in originative and generative streams within effortive learning processes. The dominance of will in effortive learning is decisive in the adult years. Parenthetically, adult learning might even be defined as effortive learning in the world. (3) I discuss some of the implications of this investigation of the will-to-learn for research in adult learning and teaching. Finally (4) I conclude with certain recommendations for undertaking research projects toward the goal of assessing the claims central to this section.

## Evidence of the Phenomenon of the Will-to-Learn

Every one of us knows adults who are willing to learn. No doubt each of us is such a person. One of my claims is that there is an essential structure of the will-to-learn in the life of each and every person who is willing to learn. Consider the following evidence for this claim.

The focus of my thoughts--the object most in my mind --as I prepare these passages is the will-to-learn and the problems of its structuring within my thoughts. I search carefully through my feelings, through my own experiencings, and within my understanding, and I find (not surprisingly) that first of all *I am a lived body* engaging in this searching. My body is particular, individual, and unique. My world is my lived world, my experienced world; with my individualized body as its center of senses, interest, and action.

Moreover, as a lived body I am conscious. Or better: as a lived body, *I conscious.* All primary functions of the body are the grounds--but not the 'causes'--of my consciousing. It is not so much a question that I find the will-to-learn *in* my · consciousness as it is that I feel, I experience, I know *that* I am willing to learn. If I feel, experience, and conscious my will-to-learn there must be a will-to-learn, itself the intended object of these flowing feelings and the rest. This reflexivity, this reflexive turn, through which I discover the phenomenon of my willingness to learn is itself evidence for a structuring of the will-to-learn.

My lived body, my consciousing--all here and now-- move through temporal spans. They take time. *They express interest through time.* This individual self which I am is my center of interest. My interest is fundamentally my feeling accompanying any instance of my attending-to something, whether object, person, idea, cluster of ideas, or state of affairs. Interest is feeling's grasp of something.

The object of my interest, of my attending-to something, is *what-is-attended-to*. This *attending-to* is the lowest degree of identifiable effort. What interests me is something toward which I am directed, toward which I am pulled. My attending-to is itself my being pulled toward something. Therefore, whereas I as lived body, and as consciousing, am 'here' and 'now', *what-is-attended-to* is 'there' and 'then'. I am not pushed 'causally' toward it, but pulled toward and by it. The object of my interest has the character of something which ought to be realized in the future. It is an 'ought-to-be' in my life.

I feel, experience, and conscious *effort expended* in this pulling. It is a power, an energy, a force, exertion, efficacy touching me and grasping me. The pulling effect is experienced as an effort, and experienced in degrees, say, as a weak or strong effort. The effort is experienced within my lived body, as conscioused, within my interest, and is experienced only in relation to my attending-to something.

We are stepping within the threshold of will. I do not speak now of will as a metaphysical entity or problem, for example, as will in the jaded 'problem of free will' (as opposed to determinism and indeterminism). I do not ask 'causal' questions about it. I do not inquire whether it exists or not. I *conscious* will. Surely I conscious *my* will. Intersubjectively, and as public information, I only attempt to guide each of us by means of coming to a clearer awareness of what I see and by trying to describe it to you. This is not so much a resolution of a problem in reason and objectivity as it is a careful focusing upon phenomena each and every one of us experiences.

We may say further that my will is a fulfilled state of affairs of the future retrospectively seeking out those effortive pathways to itself. My will is a volitional inner-directedness toward something, toward a future state of affairs. But this future state of affairs now is only a present idea. It is one of many ideas in my consciousness, in my mind. Hence James could say that the 'will is a relation between the mind and its ideas'.[12] But what kind of relation is it?

My will is my attending-to one or more of my ideas respecting a future state of affairs. It is my attending-to in an effortive manner. I am pulled toward ideas about one state of affairs, say, with lesser or greater force. This force is felt, experienced, and consciused.

> We stand here exactly where we did in the case of belief. When an idea *stings* us in a certain way, makes as it were a certain electric connection with our Self, we believe that it *is* a reality. When it stings us in another way, makes another connection with our Self, we say *let it be* a reality. To the word 'is' and to the words 'let it be' there correspond peculiar attitudes of consciousness which it is vain to seek to explain. The indicative and the imperative moods are as much ultimate categories of thinking as they are of grammar. The 'quality of reality' which these moods attach to things is not like other qualities. *It is a relation to our life. It means our adoption of the things, our caring for them, our standing by them.* This at least is what it practically means for us; what it may mean beyond that we do not know. And the transition from merely considering an object as impossible, to deciding or willing it to be real; the change from the fluctuating to the stable personal attitude concerning it; from the 'don't care' state of mind to that in which 'we mean business,' is one of the most familiar things in life. We can partly enumerate its conditions; and we can partly trace its consequences, especially the momentous one that when the mental object is a movement of our own body, it realizes itself outwardly when the mental change in question has occurred. . .[13]

The *Oxford English Dictionary* observes that the most remarkable feature of 'will' when used as a verb, besides its many idiomatic and phrasal uses, centers in its use as a regular auxiliary of the future tense. It is this sense which Alfred Schutz underscores when he observed that 'in order to project my future action as it will roll on I have to place myself in my phantasy at a future time when this action *will* already *have been* accomplished, when the resulting act will already have been materialized'.[14] This significant use in our language itself suggests the manner in which will and willing dominate feelings, experiencings, and consciousings within the 'everydayness' of the lived world of the adult. Our willing holds sway over, has the ascendancy over, and is most influential in the layers of personhood within the everydayness of the adult's planning of projects. These efforts of planning are themselves crucial features of adult learning in the adult worlds.

### Feeling, Experiencing, Consciousing, Will, and the Will-to-Learn

My lived body at work. Consciousing. My interest expressed through identifiable temporal spans. Specific objects attended-to through interest expressed. My effort expended, felt, experienced, conscioused, as pulled toward some future state of affairs among others. Feelings of my lived body pushing myself toward a future state of affairs within my lived body will be located, but a future state as conceived now. These phenomena are clearly among the available evidence attesting the presence of will and willing in a person.

Yes, the will is a relation between the mind and its ideas. My will is the relation between my mind and my ideas. But the will is a special kind of relation, a relation not arrived at through introspection but through retrospection.

Retrospection. We may study the positioning of the structure of the will-to-learn in a person's life through the degrees of commissive language which (s)he uses in describing what in effect is an absence of a willingness to learn or what in fact is a willingness to learn through one or more learning projects. Commissive language is the language of commitment. In committing ourselves we consent, we intend, and we act. We may be said to commit ourselves to something when we consent to something through: agreeing, adopting, espousing, declaring for, championing, supporting, maintaining, standing up for, siding with, embracing, and favoring something.

We commit ourselves when we *intend* something through: promising, being determined, meaning, proposing, vowing, swearing, planning to do something. We commit ourselves when we *act* through: undertaking, dedicating ourselves to doing, covenanting to do, binding ourselves to, engaging, pledging ourselves to, contracting for, and betting on something.

Willing is a conscious process which begins with deliberate choice and with resolution of questions and conflicts, continues through decisions and resolution, and ends with the realization of what is willed, the execution of the willed state of affairs. This execution of the willed state of affairs is the choice of the concrete means and the successive realization of the specific means.[15]

Consider now the *structure* of the will and willing. First we may say that to structure is to build. To structure anything is to build or form an organization of parts and elements into a whole of these parts and elements. The structure is the coexistence in a whole of distinct parts having a definite manner of arrangement. The structure is what is built or constructed.

The structure of the will is the lived body at work through consciousing activities which include the following elements: These consciousing activities are specific interests moving through temporal spans, interests attending-to certain ideas selected from among others which could be attended-to and might be at another time. A specific state of affairs of the future has been *possibilized*[16] in the present. The possibilization of itself is also an expenditure of effort felt, experienced, and conscioused as a pulling toward that possibilized state of affairs.

The essential structure of the will-to-learn is in place--is positioned in one's consciousness--as an essential structure and logical antecedent to any episode of one's actual willingness to learn. A person then is said to be disposed to learn. Relevant elements have been positioned in appropriate order in one's feelings, experiencings, and consciousings. That person may be said to be disposed toward learning something through relevant distribution and arrangement of these feelings, experiencings, and consciousings toward greater effectiveness, economy, ease or conformity to a pattern of orderly but active steps in capturing an idea. The placement of the essential structure of the will-to-learn is an instance of a singular episode of the willingness to learn. It evidences one's dispositional character toward learning through an open-mindedness toward the possibilized yet-to-be-learned, a wholehearted interest toward, and responsibility for, the particular state of affairs to be actualized through a given learning project.

## The Will-to-Learn in Research in Adult Learning and Teaching

This investigation suggests certain implications for research programs in adult learning and teaching. Learning in adult stages is more in the nature of effortive learning than learning is at earlier stages. This is true since it is more likely the case that the 'everydayness' of the adult's lifeworld manifests the greatest array of resistances, obstacles, and problems and that the adult's execution of projects and realization of goals can only be successful if these are recognized and overcome. Being willing to learn, therefore, means both acquiring the efficacy and mobilizing the power necessary to executize one's place in molding something within the real world that one believes ought to be a real state of affairs. One's willing determines and creates values in the world. Willing is bringing into concreteness an idea or ideas.

Although the originations of the will-to-learn lie in feelings such as the sensing, stirring, and exciting sensing episodes, the structure of the will-to-learn is a structuring of values within our consciousings. Some of these consciousings may be promises, hopings, believings, and knowings, for example, but each and every one is a personal action. And each is activated through willing, itself in turn the attestation of the logically prior essential structure of the will-to-learn. In promising, in hoping, in believing, and in knowing, I learn something more about myself at the same time that I gear myself executively into the outer world. My actions moving from the core, from the centrality, of my lived body and my consciousness are my willings, and these are the carriers of values. Hence the structure of the will-to-learn is a structure of values.

It follows that all research into the essential structure of the will-to-learn and research into individual persons' willingness to learn is always value-laden research. How could it be otherwise for this kind of research within the context of adult learning and adult education? Recall that I just briefly characterized adult learning as effortive learning in the face of countless known resistances within the 'everydayness' of the adult lifeworld. This means among other things that the adult first of all does not so much know something as she *is* something, that is, a lived body, a consciousing being. The adult learner, first of all, *does* something, and *will* is what the adult does in this instance. She wills: 'Let it be so!' There is no time when *all* the necessary data are in for her to start a project. There can always be additional necessary information. There is not one of these, or even a collection of these data, which could be determined to be--according to any theory of learning--the necessarily 'causative' origins of the adult's episode of willingness to learn. And the 'let it be so!' which is the will-to-learn in the adult is always singularly personal:

> (For a person) there is the tendency always to
> have something personal in (one's) volition and
> action, such that no one else can will it, or
> even imitate it--the tendency in every deed,
> together with all the general claims, to be
> something 'more' than one of many, to have a
> value of one's own in life, and thereby to prove
> one's individual moral right to existence. Of
> course this tendency can never assume the form of
> a deliberate principle deliberately determining
> the will.[17]

Central problems for relevant research programs
include: descriptions of individual persons' lived
bodies through autobiographical accounts; descriptions
of individual persons' consciousings regarding deliberation and choice of their projects in the lived world;
descriptions of what individual persons conceive to be a
*possibilized* 'ought-to-be' in their lives within their
lived worlds; descriptions of what it is in individual
persons' lives which gives direction to their conduct
insofar as it lies in the power of persons to decide for
or against a felt value as an expression of the will-to-
learn. The shopping list of possible research projects
and much more portentous research programs is almost
endless. Carrying through any one of them would be
highly significant research for adult education.

## Two Recommendations Concerning Research Projects Founded in the Claims Central to this Chapter

My *first* recommendation is that investigators in
adult education should recognize that willing is neither
reducible to nor 'causally' related to wishing, wanting,
desiring, choosing, or striving. There may be orderly
and traceable relationships between all of these, but
'causal' order is not the only kind of order and ordering process available for use in systematic study of
carefully circumscribed subject-matters. Nor is reductionism the only legitimate economizing way of reflecting. There are other kinds of order for use in these

studies, and especially so for use in studies beyond
such physical sciences as physics. Examples of these
other kinds of order include varied 'non-causal' approaches in ethics (especially in ethics), logic, epistemology, and metaphysics. But whatever these 'non-
causal' approaches are can only be brought forth for use
in our studies through rigorous phenomenological descriptions of the central features of the selected
subject-matters.

'Causal' order and the economizing of investigations
facilitated through the methodological presupposition of
'causal' order in areas of study beyond the physical
sciences go directly counter to the work of adult education. Not only does its use go counter to this work,
its invocation as a principle of method directly contra-
dicts both adult learning and adult learning. Dewey
said many years ago that although motives may induce
they do not necessitate. Each person surely has motives
for this or that action, but these motives are not the
'causes' investigators often conclude too quickly that
they are. These motives will always be one or another
of two distinct kinds. Alfred Schutz called them 'in-
order-to' motives and 'because' motives:

> Motivational relevances . . . are of two
> kinds. On the one hand are the *in-order-to*
> type, which are arranged (if not integrated) with
> one another into what is commonly called a
> 'plan': plan for thought and for action, for
> work and for leisure, or the present hour or for
> the week, and so on. Each of these, in turn,
> (is) interrelated (but not necessarily inte-
> grated) into a general, paramount plan: the plan
> for a life. These in-order-to motivations,
> however, are founded on a set of genuine *be-
> cause motives* sedimented in the biographically
> determined situation of the self at a particular
> moment. Psychologists have various names for
> this set of because motives: attitudes, person-
> ality traits, and given character.[18]

Neither of these two types of ordering is 'causal'. Investigating these distinct kinds of motives involves investigations into all of the sorts of ideas and actions which are brought forward through persons' feelings, experiencings, and consciousings as expressed through their willing something and through their being willing to bring these into being in their lived worlds. Motives may induce but they do not necessitate. Our motives are our willingness, and these in turn derive from our structures of will. Hence, any motivation to learn is founded in the essential structure of the will-to-learn. Investigations of this essential structure of the will-to-learn always involve an intersubjective and cooperative method of research. Use of a common language makes it so. It is intersubjective in another sense in that although one adult may or may not have a willingness to learn in a particular instance or situation, there is somewhere in that person's consciousings an essential structure of the will-to-learn, and another adult may be in a position to help educe or bring to birth an explicit expression of this essential structure. The hope should be that each adult should learn to do it alone if possible. This would be the essential structure of 'self-help'.

Here is my *second* recommendation. Persons are involved in the research carried out within adult education. These persons taken as 'subjects' are respondents, let us say, and as respondents they should always be allowed to respond,[19] and not in forced or necessitated ways dictated by reductionistic research methods and methodologies. The subjects of investigation, the adult eductions of **person,** should not be finitized, coerced, and rendered fictive by the methods and operations. Even in investigations of persons the methods used must always emerge from the phenomena under investigation. In the special case of investigation of adults these phenomena, the adult eductions of **person,** always include phenomena relating to what and whom persons have been and to what and whom the same persons will to be. Therefore it is not so much the case that there are various schools or philosophies of adult education (even if these are never 'pure' types of philosophies, but generally heuristic distinctions among several theoretical approaches to adult education) which provide the presuppositions and methods whereby persons are enabled to do these things along diverse ways and in accord with various--and even competing--models.

The question is how an adult comes to see that it may be possible to find a dramatically different place in the lived world through learning.[20] In investigating the ways in which it may be possible for them to do so, every one of our research projects in adult education should be **reflexive**. The study should move along in two directions at the same time. If a research project must employ statistical or behavioral methods, then it should pursue two distinct kinds of investigation as equally central at the same time. We may call these *constitutive* investigation and *eductive* investigation.

*Constitutive* investigation in this sense consists in examining relevant ingredients within a person's life by exploring these ingredients 'backward' toward the more primal stages, phases, or stretches of its constitution in situations. How did each one of these come to be what it is (although not in 'causal' terms)? Constitutive investigation is the investigation of the increasingly more tacit stages of these ingredients which may be feelings, experiences, or consciousings of persons. In what ways did each relevant ingredient come to be what it is now as it becomes the 'object' of reflection in a given person's life?

*Eductive investigation* [as phenomenology] consists in examining relevant ingredients within a person's life which are issued forth or educed. Emphasis here would be placed upon the processes of drawing forth, upon the ways of appearing through which parts-of learning become wholes, or wholes-of parts are dissembling into these parts. Elicited meanings and values would be investigated. This kind of reflection would be performed by clarifying all of these ingredients and their processes through the stages, phases and stretches of their development out of conditions or their rudimentary, latent, and tacit (or even their merely potential or possible) existence within persons' lives.

# Chapter 3

## 'Everydayness' and the Natural Attitude

There are common and customary ways in which the terms 'day' and 'everyday' are used. A day is a specific period of time through which much of our lives is ordered. For example, a whole day or a fragment of a day might be set aside or appointed for some special purpose, observance or action, as a holiday, or the time for the departure on the trip. We speak of one day as a particular time span in the past or in the future. Again: a day's travel, a day's duties, a day's responsibilities, a day's work, and a day's wages, a day's needs, and a day's pleasures. All of these are fairly common expressions through which persons (1) invoke the 'day' as a temporal span for (2) measuring out our **person** as persons (3) through personal actions (4) which are carried out through determinations of what is most relevant to persons through relevancy systems in operation in these lives, and (5) which are articulated through certain goals, ends, and purposes, but (6) with certain emphases within stretches of this temporal span.

'Everydayness' is a continuing and continued succession of days just described. It is a locution for running days together, in succession, over indeterminately periods of time, as if with little discernible changes, as Lamb's letter to Coleridge (1796) seems to suggest: 'I am heartily sick of the every-day scenes of life'. There is a succession of days, as if repetitious in life-content, inspired by such phrases as an 'everyday self', or an 'everyday world'. The 'everyday' life suggests that a person's life meets with sameness, perhaps too much sameness, or similarity of action and content, of the form and matter of the world of each and every day, and possibly through all the days of that life. The term connotes the common and ordinary, the mediocre and even the inferior quality of one's life, as in the phrasing, 'the everydayness of the workaday world'. 'Everyday' is each day, all days, and the routineness of these days.

Yet 'everydayness' as a word borne in such phrases does not present itself as the atmosphere and light of day surrounding, enveloping, and inclosing us so completely as to be the full environment of the growth of the essential structures of the adult eductions. Consider: (1) 'Everyday' is all of the temporal spans of each and every day and of all days, but there is no temporal span of one day which is felt or experienced or reflected upon as exactly the same as any other day. (2) The daily measurements of our **person** through different days are themselves different. (3) Daily actions, no matter how similar in appearance in some ways, are different in other ways; there are always differences in kinds and degrees among persons' actions day by day. (4) Different relevancy systems are in operation throughout the different days of our lives, even in the midst of felt 'everydayness'. (5) There are at least differences in our goals, ends, and purposes on differing days even in the midst of mundanity. (6) Persons have differing kinds and degrees of interest and attendant actions from day to day, even within the characterizations of the 'sameness' of interests, emphases, and actions by the so-called 'everydayness' of these.

What, therefore, does 'everydayness' mean as applied to a person's life? Two different meanings immediately can be seen. 'Everydayness' may be a cluster of phenomena which become the determinate subject-matter and the special focus of a set of systematic investigations. That is, 'everydayness' may become the subject of scientific investigations. If this were to be so, the proper kinds of investigations would be those enacted by the human sciences. In fact, I urge adult educators to hold up the cluster of phenomena of the 'everydayness' of the adult lifeworld which can be adduced easily as a prism of countless refractions of surfaces and reflections of adult eductions. Each 'seen' surface is an adult eduction of **person** which becomes a research project. One obvious example of what I mean here is Erick Erickson's account of the phenomena of 'generativity' in middle adulthood. Another example, which has undergone no investigations by researchers in adult education, is Ortega's conception of the 'generations' of each person's life.[1]

There are innumerable such projects, at least a project for each 'seen' and logged refraction of the personal prism of one's 'everydayness'. All of these are possibilities for research, but much more importantly, enriched understanding of persons. These possible research projects must be counted among the many problems, projects, and programs cited or pointed to in this extended discussion of adult education and phenomenological research. This is one of the possible meanings of the term 'everydayness', and although this is one of the important thrusts of this book (that is, the discussion of the phenomena of adults, education, and a number of the principal ways in which phenomenological investigations may be performed in adult education), this particular significance of the term is not the primary one in this chapter devoted to 'everydayness' and the 'natural attitude'.

In this chapter it is important to continue to describe the phenomena of 'everydayness' from the natural attitude of the adult. Description of these is always the necessary prelude to any systematic investigation of these phenomena, whether through phenomenology or through any scientific methods. 'Day' and 'everyday', as repetitious day by day successions of routinized actions, constitute the placements and the timing of the eductions of adult lives much more clearly than they do the eductions of the lives of younger persons. Surely there is no precise demarcation between the 'youth' and the 'adult', but the latter not only has come to realize these placements and timings through larger stocks of feelings, stocks of experiences, and some reflection, but now knows, as the youth is not normally aware, that there is more--so much more--of the same to be lived through, in both body and mind. The adult has grown older, and grows older still, in ways the young generally cannot fathom, principally because they have no reason, no motive, to do so . . . yet. The stocks of age are not yet present to the young, nor are those special responsibilities sometimes guiltily lived through day by day.

No philosopher or social theorist has presented a more telling account of the adult 'everydayness' than Alfred Schutz has provided through phenomenological investigations. Consider this passage in his classic paper on 'Multiple Realities':

> The wide-awake man within the natural attitude is primarily interested in that sector of the world of his everyday life which is within his scope and which is centered in space and time around himself. The place which my body occupies within the world, my actual Here, is the starting point from which I take my bearing in space. It is, so to speak, the center O of my system of coordinates. Relatively to my body I group the elements of my surroundings under the categories of right and left, before and behind, above and below, near and far, and so on. And in a similar way my actual Now is the origin of all the time perspectives under which I organize the events within the world such as the categories of fore and aft, past and future, simultaneity and succession, etc.[2]

To illustrate: I selected this quotation at 4:30 p.m. on a Friday afternoon in late spring. I sat on the small deck jutting out from our house on the south side and into the densely-foliaged forest as I did so. There are the noises of automobiles ahead of me, but way beyond the trees, and directly to the west. I cannot see these automobiles. I hear the noises of two small aircraft, but the leafage of many varieties of oak, maple, cherry, walnut, and ironwood trees is so thick that I cannot say with certainty where the planes actually are. Birds call, our dogs have been barking now and then, and possibly some of their attention has been directed toward our neighbor's children at play, but our neighbor's house is so far away as to be unseen, so I cannot be sure that the children are in any degree the focus of the dogs' attention at the moment. A crow flies by. Other birds, and I see several woodpeckers over there. More sounds here and there, now and then, but most of all it is a quiet place, and so I have often chosen to work here. It is a good and pleasant time in which to write on 'everydayness', and I have chosen this day within my days during which to do so.

And you, reader, where are you as you read these words? And what time is it? And why are you there? What are the present circumstances of this situation in which you find yourself? Did you plan this reading? Did you leaf through and decide to read just this passage? Was it a reading for your course? Did you have to plan your day in your effort to read these passages?

I and you, dear reader, two wide-awake adults, might be expressing what Husserl termed the 'natural attitude' of simple description of circumstances, of all that stands around us at the moment. I am actually doing it now in simple terms. Your natural attitude is expressed in reading these words and in fitting their meanings quickly to the 'everydayness' of your life. But as I reflect upon what I write, and as you think about what you are reading, we both move beyond the natural attitude, and move towards, and perhaps even into, the stages of more systematic investigations of what is written here and of the phenomena to which it refers.

Space and time surround us not as technical constructs appropriate to physics, but as felt space and felt time. The chair is soft and comfortable, a desirable place to rest, and I, with the writing board on my lap, wonder what time it is. Perhaps it is already time to go to Robinson's; if not, it soon will be. This is concrete space and practical time. I *now* write, but you also *now* read, with the common sensings of the spacing and the timing of my activities. And I wonder ahead to the places and times when wide-awake adults will read (then and there) what I write (here and now). And so I write partially in accordance with plans in mind for you, reader, then and there.

This is simple description of who I am at the moment, in the midst of my 'everydayness', calling up and expressing but a fraction of this day's feelings, this day's experiencings, this day's consciousings, and this day's consciousing of things, ideas, and persons within this day. This is a beveling slice of 'everydayness', and I look forward with the hope that the here and now slice will overlap a like region of your 'everydayness' then and there (but your here and now as you feel and experience it) where you are. But where are you now, as I write now, in the midst of my 'everydayness', through the daily regimen of writing out these days? Where will you be (and I?) as you read about my here and now in your here and now in the midst of each of our 'everydaynesses'?

The 'everydayness' of the natural attitude is that I can do all of this again, and so can each of us. In fact, reader, I can also read what you write, and in some cases perhaps I will already have done so. And if we do not always do it in the same way, since each and every act of it all is unique and non-duplicable, each act may still be typical of other acts. Certain analogies, certain similarities and resemblances, are present, and all of these are near enough for us to be able to communicate in common sense terms for practical ends.

Recall Dewey's characterization of common sense as everyday, practical inquiry in these general terms: the criteria for evaluating and assessing significance, meaning, and knowledge are more arbitrary and more changing and changeable; those judgments tend to be more qualitative and highly non-quantitative; they are more concerned with immediate, or at least more daily and everyday, use and enjoyment of all things; the thinking is more teleological, and the actions generated thereby are more purposive and end-seeking; this thinking is less specialized, and employs less technical language, with much more emphasis necessarily on literal expression and the use of metaphors, especially, since this is the personal arena within which newly-arising linguistic expressions are born via metaphors. Finally, problems in everyday life are more generalized, and all of these practical kinds of knowledge are characterized by far less precise degrees of order and systemization.

Scientific inquiry, for Dewey, arises out of this 'everydayness', this feeling-with the common, or common sense, of practical knowledge. The differences between the two are not so much differences of kind as they are differences of degree, and most significantly, the latter kind of knowledge emerges from within and through the personal qualities of the former.

The 'prepredicative' life is not at issue here, the life as formed in indeterminately large numbers of ways before the predications and placements in the world provided by language; various reductions of fashionable sorts are not at issue, either. I merely attend-to the mundane activities of the moment as I write them out in accordance with my (present, here and now) natural attitude, rather than as bounded by a scientific attitude. I now express and describe. And you attend-to these particulars as well, all the while embodied (are you seated comfortably, at ease, with a full day's time ahead of--or behind--you?). You attend-to these matters, with feelings, at first unnamed, and you learn of what I write, and learn that you learn it, through your feeling and your experiencing. If this logbook-like account succeeds in its descriptions, you will *begin* to think about these moments (the *originations* are already present to you). And when you do begin to think about them you will have left behind the natural attitude of 'everydayness'.

But let us continue with the description of 'everydayness'. It seems that the phrases 'daily world', 'daily world of work', and the 'world of everydayness' do not of necessity refer to specifically negative features of personal life. The phrases intend the more routine and standard actions--especially those called 'habits'--in which we engage each day. 'Everydayness' presents a blurring of past days and 'future' days, a blurring of what we feel we have done with what we feel we expect to do, and all of this with little change, with little difference between days to look forward to. This is true even as we recognize the usual desirability of at least some important changes occurring in our lives and of really wanting these to take place.

'Everydayness' suggests few distinctions between and among our days, every day, even if we understand that the slightest reflection would bring countless distinctions to the foreground. And more reflection would bring them into clear focus. But the days of 'everydayness' also blur into days which are not yet, days of the 'future' which have not yet been felt or experienced as those days may be but have not yet been. 'Desires thus far unmet will not be met tomorrow or the next day, either; nor will my expectations, for that matter.' This is a routine part of 'everydayness', but it does move in the direction of a meaning felt as negative.

There is a negative sense in which the phrases above, and so much of the thoughts and actions within and of 'everydayness' can be articulated. 'Everydayness' is perhaps a sensing of one's 'not going anywhere' in life, or possibly just a feeling or clustering of feelings which later come to be recognized as having been feelings at the previous time that that was indeed the case. 'I now know what those feelings really were!' It is living through indecisiveness and indecision, habitually, routinely, and standardly, even with the admission that I do not know--or do not want to find out--how to change my life today, tomorrow, or during any of the days after than in the same degree that I have been unwilling or unable to do so in the past.

Within 'everydayness' persons have tasks to perform, responsibilities to carry through. Some of these things we desire to do, some we must do; but we do not want to do all of them. Other things we may expect to do, even if we have no wish to do so. Recall Alfred Cobham's wearied words: 'I know the oppression and languor of unvarying toil at uninteresting and unpleasant tasks, the jading weariness of repeating the same mechanical movements every month for fourteen hours a day, month by month, year after year.'

'Everydayness', with its heavy-laden boredom as a kind of negativity, strictly speaking carries neither desires nor expectations into the future. My daily life consists of a 'day's work', perhaps, and surely the 'day's responsibilities,' and I expect these, desiring usually to carry through on them.

But the negativity of 'everydayness', of that sense of the standard, routine, habitual daily enactments of persons as bored with their lives, is born of the felt conflict in one's life between one's desires and one's expectations day by day, and through indeterminately large numbers of days, or throughout 'every' day. It is also a conflict between an indecision, or decision not to decide, or failure to decide, to act in terms of somewhat differing, nonhabitual desires and the failure to commit oneself to attempts to reach out for the hoped-for, out beyond the expected. Hence if a person decides to act day by day, and therefore every day, in terms of desires, this kind of 'everydayness' does not present negativity of 'everydayness'. These are habituations for the good of one's life in the midst of 'everydayness'. Nor is the negative dimension of 'everydayness' presented if a person commits oneself to the fulfillment of hopes and expectations, and thus looks forward to tomorrow and to succeeding days. 'Everydayness' therefore is no necessary negation of the positive qualities of each day's living and day by day living.

'Everydayness' in its negativity is an unnamed, uncategorized feeling at first (borne primarily through habits and habituations of a person's life), of the *conflict* between the absence of a decision to act on one's desires today or tomorrow (as one has failed to do so often in the past) and the failure to commit oneself to expectations for tomorrow (again, as one has failed to do so often in the past). If there is no *conflict* between these two, there is no negativity of 'everydayness', but in its negativity 'everydayness' is continuing felt and experienced personal failure.

'Everydayness' . . . And so it goes.

'Everydayness' . . . It is fitting to end with yet another beginning. This is the cyclicalness of 'everydayness'. And at this point it is still a neutral analysis of 'everydayness'.

We begin with an analysis of the world of daily life which the wide-awake, grown-up man who acts in it and upon it amidst his fellow-men experiences within the natural attitude as a reality.

'World of daily life' shall mean the intersubjective world which existed long before our birth, experienced and interpreted by Others, our predecessors, as an organized world. Now it is given to our experience and interpretation. All interpretation of this world is based upon a stock of previous experiences of it, our own experiences and those handed down to us by our parents and teachers, which in the form of 'knowledge at hand' function as a scheme of reference.

To this stock of experiences at hand belongs our knowledge that the world we live in is a world of well circumscribed objects with definite qualities, objects among which we move, which resist us and upon which we may act. To the natural attitude the world is not and never has been a mere aggregate of colored spots, incoherent noises, centers of warmth and cold. Philosophical or psychological analysis of the constitution of our experiences may afterwards, retrospectively, describe how elements of this world affect our senses, how we passively perceive them in an indistinct and confused way, how by active apperception our mind singles our certain features from the perceptional field, conceiving them as well delineated things which stand out

over against a more or less unarticulated background or horizon. The natural attitude does not
know these problems. To it the world is from the
outset not the private world of the single individual but an intersubjective world, common to
all of us, in which we have not a theoretical but
an eminently practical interest. The world of
everyday life is the scene and also the object of
our actions and interactions. We have to dominate it and we have to change it in order to
realize the purposes which we pursue within it
among our fellow-men. We work and operate not
only within but upon the world. Our bodily
movements--kinaesthetic, locomotive, operative--
gear, so to speak, into the world, modifying or
changing its objects and their mutual relationships. On the other hand, these objects offer
resistance to our acts which we have either to
overcome or to which we have to yield. Thus, it
may be correctly said that a pragmatic motive
governs our natural attitude toward the world of
daily life. Work, in this sense, is something
that we have to modify by our actions or that
modifies our actions.

Alfred Schutz
*Collected Papers I*[3]

## PART IV

## Eduction as Education:

## Achieving Fullest Personal Growth

A phenomenological parable about truth, knowledge, education, and the mind . . .

> *The truth is not some perfect system of philosophy: it is simply the way in which all systems, however perfect, collapse into nothingness on the discovery that they are only systems, only external worlds over against the knowing mind and not that mind itself.*
>
> *This process of the creation and destruction of external worlds might appear, to superficial criticism, a mere futile weaving and unweaving of Penelope's web, a declaration of the mind's inability to produce solid assets, and thus the bankruptcy of philosophy. And this it would be if knowledge were the same thing as information, something stored in encyclopaedias and laid on like so much gas and water in school and universities. But education does not mean stuffing a mind with information; it means helping a mind to create itself, to grow into an active and vigorous contributor to the life of the world. The information given in such a process is meant to be absorbed into the life of the mind itself, and a boy leaving school with a memory full of*

facts is thereby no more educated than one who leaves the table with his hands full of food is thereby fed. At the completion of its education, if that event ever happened, a mind would step forth as naked as a newborn babe, knowing nothing, but having acquired the mastery over its own weaknesses, its own desires, its own ignorance, and able therefore to face any danger unarmed.

The collapse of a system of thought is therefore not equivalent to the cancellation of the process by which it came into being. It collapses, but it does not perish. In constructing and destroying it, the mind has learnt a permanent lesson: it has triumphed over an error and so discovered a truth. The destroyed system collapses not into bare nothingness but into immediacy, into a characteristic or attribute of the mind itself, passes as it were into the muscle and bone of the mind, becomes an element in the point of view from which the mind raises its next problem.

For the life of the mind consists of raising and solving problems, problems in art, religion, science, commerce, politics, and so forth. The solution of these problems does not leave behind it a sediment of ascertained fact, which grows and solidifies as the mind's work goes on. Such a sediment is nothing but the externality of a half-solved problem: when the problem is fully solved the sediment of information disappears and the mind is left at liberty to go on. Philosophy, therefore, is not a prerogative kind of knowledge immune from this reabsorption into the mind's being: it is nothing but the recognition that this reabsorption is necessary and is indeed the end and crown of all knowledge, the

> *self-recognition of the mind in its own mirror*
>
> R. G. Collingwood,
> *Speculum Mentis*[1]

## Introductory Remarks

Both the subjects and the phenomena of philosophy, education, and adults are intimately related. Philosophy and education cannot be conceived or explored as separate from one another except in falsifying and abstractive ways. Although they can be distinguished from one another, in the most concrete and tangible ways they are inseparable enterprises.

Philosophy as the 'love of wisdom' forcefully communicates both to the lover of wisdom and to all of those who are in contact with this lover's reflective acts. Wisdom is the personal power of true and right discernment in life and in the continuing conformity to courses of personal action laid out by this discernment. Wisdom consists both of a high degree of aptitude, learning, and achievement and good practical judgment and common sense. Wisdom is of course an ideal, and the highest kind of wisdom is the highest kind of ideal.

For many years I have defined the process of education as a continuing conversation through which I project the disciplining **person** I **consciousingly**[2] intend to become. A course of studies is a cour**sing**, as in the coursing of a stream or a river. Together, these three terms characterize the personal activities of moving onward, of flowing through time, through personal episodes and events. And in consecutive order they present to us a coursing, a bringing together of what follows in order. A **university** itself is (or was thought to be for many centuries, and ought to be thought this still!) a process of turning ideas into unity, into oneness, or ideally into a unity of all that one encounters. Only individual persons can do this. No one else can do it for them. This is the higher reaching, we say, of the educational process. But of course the university education is not necessarily the 'higher' learning, a fact well known to almost any thinking adult. Our adult eductions of **person** as feelings, experiencings, and consciousings course through higher and wider-ranging strata and structures within the 'everydayness' of our individual lifeworlds.

Courses of study, however, are among the continuing conversations through which we project the disciplining persons we consciousingly intend to become. We attend to liberal arts courses in history, rhetoric, and mathematics, for example, with the sense that these subject-matters include the concrete realizations of **person** within culture and the ways through which persons' creative activities ought to lead to civilizations rather than to barbarisms. We call them 'liberal arts' because we hold these approaches--through studies of languages, history, philosophy--to be ways worthier of free men and women in achieving these goals than are the more mechanical and servile 'how-to-do-it' approaches which have a tendency to treat persons more as objects than subjects by providing task-specific skills rather than empowerments and transformations of adult eductions of **person**.

The coursing of the liberal arts is grounded in openness and receptiveness to new actions and new ideas. There are the disciplines of the liberal arts, or the intellectual bases for more advanced studies, or even for life-**praxis**, the special *doings* in our lives which we call experiences. These habituating disciplines of study are vital manifestations of discriminations and discretionary activities in relation to special circumstances, disciplined knowing and understanding of what is reasonable, proper, right, or just. Through the liberal arts we discover, explore and evaluate reasons, motives, grounds of **person** and persons within cultures, and the directions of the flow of cultures partially through the medium, and in the face, of violence and its special expressions as terrorism, for example.

Collingwood characterized a liberal arts education at the end of his *Speculum Mentis*. It bears repeating:

At the completion of its education, if that event ever happened, a mind would step forth as naked as a new-born babe, knowing nothing, but having acquired the mastery over its weaknesses, its own desires, its own ignorance, and able therefore to face any danger unarmed.[3]

And he also claimed 'All thought exists for the sake of action. We try to understand ourselves and our world only in order that we may learn how to live.'[4] Our lifeworld, normally structured mundanely and lived in desperate routineness, is the ground of the subject-matter of all adult education, of all authentic courses of study, the most originatively concrete of which may well be the liberal arts. These studies are differing, sometimes competing, avenues along the contours of our lifeworlds. We call them different perspectives or points of view. They transform our perspectives.[5] They all articulate disciplined inquiries generating unveiling, uncovering lines of the right, the fitting, the reasonable, the proper, the just, the true, according to guidelines which have undergone historical assessments, trials, and tribulations.

But all of this suggests much more a problematic situation than a problem per se. It suggests a program of inquiry and investigation, more a hope of discovery, than it does a statement of settled truths or solutions to specific problems. The problematic can be given a respectable name, as Alfred Schutz has admirably demonstrated in many of his writings. Its name is the **problematic of relevance.**[6] Of course, as all philosophers know, breathing a name onto (into?) some phenomenon gives us some power or moral force over it. The power is in the reaching out and in the 'touching-with' and grasping of this phenomenon more concretely and fully. It grows into the full power to explore the textures of the phenomena of the problematic of relevance. The 'moral force' I speak of is that strength and personal authority with which we move into our lifeworld more decisively and executively, capture more territory in and through what and whom we create and construct in our being and our becoming. In these ways we come to belong.[7] I discuss this problematic and some of its problems fully in Chapters 5 and 6 below.

It seems to me that there are two general, but contradictory, theoretical approaches to education and that these two senses lead directly to two distinct avenues of learning/teaching within the context of adult continuing education. These two ways are modeled after concepts characterized back-to-back in the *Oxford English Dictionary*. We turn to a discussion of each of them in the order in which they appear there. The relevant words are 'educate/education' and 'educe/eduction.'

## A. Educate/Education: Denial of Practice as Negation of Learning

The customary, and indeed most venerable avenue of learning/teaching not only in adult education, is that sense in which we rear or bring up children, and subsequently adults, who are taken as children to all intents and purposes, or who are treated in disciplining ways little different in principle from the ways in which children are treated. It is a **pedagogy** applied to all, regardless of age and distinctions between various degrees and kinds of eductions of **person**.

In this sense education is classificatory theory and practice in search of mind, body, and spirit substances as ready clay to be moulded, reared, trained, 'informed', 'formed', and 'schooled' irretrievably and irreproachably in the ways of 'right' and righteousness. And within this model or paradigm of learning/teaching many dispensers of a plethora of issue-specific certitudes of right and righteousness emerge from the cultural wood-work with their recipes and shopping lists of what must be done for all as 'right', righteous, and 'certain'. It truly is casuistry of the most reductionist kind. In this sense education is very much akin to, and sometimes even reducible to, the ways in which animals generally have been trained. One fashionable name for it is 'behaviorism'. Another kind of name is a sophisticated 'behavior modification'.

With a system of presuppositions easily generated from this sense, way, avenue, or definition of educate/education it is reasonably easy to focus on a number of serious problems in adult continuing education. We can now see more clearly how the problems discussed in Part II. B. have arisen as problematic, and we can further discern the cul-de-sac each one of these problems finally ends up 'looping'.[8]

Ultimately this is what education is and does from that perspective (educate/education), whatever generic and generalized definition might be given for it, as in, for example, Jerold Apps' definition of education as: '. . . organized and planned activity with the intent that learning will result. This activity may be available to individuals, groups, or communities.'[9]

I say 'ultimately' since a particular person--I, you, someone else--must always be in that perspective the educatee and someone else the educator. Phenomenologically there are at least three foci of phenomena central to this model: education, the educatee, and the educator. The recognition of these phenomena, in the light of my characterization above, suggests that one of the philosophically significant features which has led adult and continuing education astray is the emphasis upon education as a process, field, and discipline rather than upon the phenomenological significance of the adult eductions of **person** of both educatees and educators and upon further investigations and analyses of these and their relatedness. I have tried to show how this might be carried out phenomenologically in Part II. A. ("Phenomenology and the Personal World of an Adult").

The educate/education way is the way of supplying the needs and wants of children, especially in such fashion as to bring them up from childhood through the formulation of specific habits, manners, intellectual and physical aptitudes, and so forth, through 'schooling' and instructing them. This way generates training procedures generally developing the intellectual and moral powers of these children. The OED also characterizes educate/education as training and disciplining persons through particular inculcations and nourishment of mental or physical faculties or organs so as to develop some special aptitude, taste, or disposition. It is difficult to resist remarking that education in this sense leads directly, unerringly, and necessarily to the entire possible, and indeterminately large, range of 'how-to-do-it' and 'nuts-and-bolts' approaches which on the whole pass task-specific skills over to persons conceived more as 'objects' rather than as 'subjects'. In this case education and its 'how-to-do-it' casuistry could eventually become very nearly identical because of a false, but still presupposed, parsimoniousness in theory, thinking, and practice. Education in principle would 'cover' (that is, both connote and denote) exhaustively the range of all things that either adult learners or teachers, or both, would do by way of learning and teaching through more and more specific and specialized instruction, for example. This and this and this and. . . . These are not so much the products of thought as they constitute the flight from thought and thinking. This fleeing from thinking--with its attendant immersions in 'how-to-do' problem-solving--can only produce greater alienation in persons and close off the desired growth and realization of adult eductions of **person**. Greater alienation in persons means: less meaningfulness, much greater normlessness, less purposefulness, an increase in social isolation and self-estrangement in these lives. These characteristics surely are not desirable in the continuing education of free adults--free men and women each with unleashable potentials of vital lives.

The most general case at the very best is that education in this sense is too generalized and abstractive. It has thereby easily and irrevocably become reduced and reductionistic in its commitments to theory and practice by those who theorize about it and who practice it. In this sense 'education' is tool-oriented technique-ridden, largely stultifying and deadening to mind, body and spirit (and to soul, according to Alfred Cobham). Remember him?

The worst evils thereby are visited upon hapless adults in their attempts at continuing their education through the ministrations of their adult educators. The latter are not nearly so innocent as their victims in the certified and certifying programs, although they quite probably have been 'brought up' in the same way. The remedy, the antidote, the answer, is both absurdly simple and inordinately difficult. And what is it? The answer is: Reflect on what one really is to do, and upon who one really is. **Who am I?** Yes indeed! **What ought I to do?** Oh, yes indeed! Hence, the subtitle of this book: 'New Directions in Theory, Practice, and Research.' And the reflection is phenomenological reflection.

## B. Educe/Eduction: The Practice of Learning as Empowerment and Transformation

'Educe' and 'eduction' are akin to 'educate' and 'education,' and are sometimes used in nearly the same sense. But to use them as if they were virtually synonymous is surely to obliterate their great differences. Phenomenological explorations of some of these differences provide the groundwork for another way for a phenomenological grounding of adult education.

To *educe* something, as we have seen, is to bring out, to elicit, develop it from a condition of latent, rudimentary or merely potential existence. It is to draw forth, to evoke, give rise to actions and manifestations, for example. Already it is possible to see that a major difference between **education** and **eduction** is that the principal metaphor of the former in theory and practice is the process of *putting-in* something. Something is put-in the minds (ideas) and the bodies (habits) of children, and (because according to this model adults are treated little differently from children), into the minds and bodies of adults as well. I call this the 'PI' model of adult learning. Paolo Freire calls it the 'banking approach to adult education.'[10]

The way of educe/eduction in adult learning is understood through a quite different metaphor. This metaphor is that of *drawing-out*. Call it the 'DO' Model of adult learning. DO is a felicitous acronym because it already carries the force of action; it is the imperative, commandive, insistent performative to which the adult learner must be committed in order to learn. The adult learner must be committed to DOing what must be done in order to executize one's life in the necessary directions toward meeting one's felt needs. Only through these kinds of acts--DOings--will you be able to change your life in the directions in which it must go.

What are drawn-out are ideas, thoughts, impressions, percepts, concepts, feelings, experiences, hopes, aspirations, beliefs, purposes, goals. These constitute very much of what must be our **person** ('self', and 'I') and the unique person each one of us is. In fact, if this listing were to be extended further in analogous ways it would be difficult at some point to see what might be left out (in principle) of the drawing-out process which could still be characterizable as an adult eduction of **person**, and expressions of persons.

Hence we may claim that it is not a question of *what* is educed or drawn-out. It is a question of *who* and *whom*. Eduction as the process of adult learning is the emphasis upon persons as issuing forth and upon still other adult learners as being engaged in helping others (and thus honored as 'teachers') to learn how it is possible to allow oneself to issue forth, as it were.

Now, which metaphor--the PI Model or the DO Model--seems to be more obviously and readily applicable to the continuing learning in which adults engage? Which metaphor and model most genuinely fits adult learning?

The PI Model requires that decisions regarding the relevancy of training and schooling made available to adult learners are to be left largely to the choices made by adult educators as administrators, facilitators, mentors, and empowerers; but knowledge is still dispensed and distributed by persons, agencies, and institutions outside, beyond, and transcendent to the adult learner. Genuine choices are already pre-empted by these 'Others' or not readily available to the adult learner. And licensing and certifying procedures are left largely in their power.

The DO Model phenomenologically is closer to what is more naturally taking place in the continuing learning characteristic of adults. It articulates carefully the adult feelings, experiencings, and consciousings which emerge. It is closer to the phenomena of adult life and to the adult lifeworld.

The adult learner according to this model already knows *in some degree* what he or she must begin to do. It is primarily a matter of degree and kind of 'ought-to-do' (and 'ought-to-be') as we have already seen depicted in the reflexive turns which actions of thinking take as inquiry and philosophy are presented by Plato and Dewey.[11] The purposes and reasons--the originations and beginnings--for and of the adult's continued learning in all the informal and formal ways are surely known best of all by the adult learner herself. This does not suggest that these purposes might not become better known, or better and better known. They become better known precisely as learning continues; there is in principle no end--no final knowledge--of these purposes, these goals, or these actions of the 'ought-to-be' and the 'ought-to-do' in one's life.

## Power and Empowerment

Adult educators often claim that empowerments of persons and transformations of personal lives are two vital goals of adult learning. It is important to understand what these claims really mean. For example, precisely what is an empowerment in a person's life? What is a transformation of a person and personal behavior in adult lives in the most essential sense?

If empowerment and transformation in adult lives can be clarified then avenues leading toward their achievement can be created through adult education. We all know of striking examples of these programs, but what are the underlying structures which are essential to each?

If claims about the importance of empowerment and transformation are valid then fundamental research should attest this fact. This research should also be central to the construction of processes and programs which lead toward those goals.

The most essential steps in this research are always the reflective moves clarifying the basic concepts used in testing out the foundations and commitments of the research problems and programs. This, too, is vital experimentation. I propose to perform this kind of experiment through a phenomenological model of research. I shall do it below in the manner of a first person account in the firm and tested belief that other persons may move through the essential foundational structures of his or her own research programs and problems in closely similar ways.

*First,* I clarify what 'power' and 'empowerment' mean in most essential terms for adults. *Second,* I clarify what transformation means in the most essential terms for adults. *Finally,* I show how these two concepts are uniquely bound together, how they can be used toward a richer understanding of what adult personhood is and can be, and how research problems and programs grounded in this renewed understanding can be developed.

There may be many kinds of power. Surely the term 'power' is used in quite different ways. When the term is used in special reference to persons, however, power is one's ability to do something, or to act upon a person, an object, or in terms of some idea. My power is my physical, mental, or moral strength, might, or vigor. It is a process through which my energy and character are expressed. My power is an enabling process, the activating and originating process in my animate being. My power is a kind of control I have, or my command over something, such as specific activities in my everyday world. It is a kind of domination, rule, influence, and authority which I have. It might be political ascendancy as in exercising influence in the government of a city or country. My power may be legal ability, capacity, or authority to act, especially in the sense of delegated authority, commission, or faculty.

To empower me is to invest me formally or even legally with power or authority, or to authorize me as having a certain power or powers. It is to impart or to bestow power on me toward some end or for some specific purpose. To empower me is to enable me, to make me powerful, or more powerful, in some respect. My empowerment is either (or both) an action which gives some power to me, or it is my state of having a specifiable power of some kind and in some degree.

Knowing how to read and write are empowerments, for example. When my teachers assisted me toward knowledge and understanding in some degree they led me toward the possession of degrees and kinds of powers. My baccalaureate degree attests that I have completed successfully a prescribed course of study within an institution, and it presents me to the world as one who is entitled to all the rights and privileges appertaining to that degree. This is a paradigm case of a community's empowerment of one of its own.

Some persons within any community of persons are said to be professionals, skilled persons, and experts especially competent in their performances. *Professional*s have a determinate occupation within which they profess and practice their special skills, and they apply their arts, crafts, sciences, techniques and technologies in their own lives and in the lives of others. Even if some professionals have not received certifying and licensing attestations they may still be seen as *competent*, as persons with special powers, fit, appropriate, and proper to the performance of circumscribed activities and tasks. Their powers are suitable to these tasks, sufficient to their performance. Even if not formally licensed, these persons are competent or skilled in their powers of performance. They are capable of accomplishing something with sufficient precision, practical knowledge, ability, cleverness, and expertness. They are *skilled*. And some are *experts*, or persons with special powers within their community.

The knowledge they have is their power within the community. How did they--how do I--move through the stages of possessing power(s) to the stage of having power(s) at hand?

## Possessing Power and Having Power at Hand

Francis Bacon claimed that knowledge *is* power. But this claim is ambiguous. Are the two absolutely equal? Are the two in fact one? They appear to be neither equal nor one. My powers to see, hear, smell, taste, and touch are not knowledge per se, but my seeing objects, hearing sounds, smelling pleasant odors, tasting sour qualities, and touching rough surfaces clearly invoke my perceptions, my processes of knowing, and my states of knowledge. My power is not exactly my knowledge, although my knowledge is at least a kind of power. Knowledge is essentially power, whatever else it may be. A certain kind of power is the essence of my knowledge. Therefore, investigation of knowledge and of processes of coming to know anything at all is necessarily investigation of a certain process of gaining certain powers and of thereby coming into certain empowerments.

The act of knowing is an enabling act. My knowing something enables me to do something. It is entirely appropriate in the context of adult education to discuss knowing and knowledge and their relevance to the empowerment of persons and the transformations of personal lives. One of the richest discussions of the problem of knowledge in Western epistemology is found in the passages of Plato's *Theaetetus* which are known as the 'simile of the aviary'. These passages (and indeed the *Theaetetus* as a whole) should be mastered by all adult educators who claim to do both the practice and the theory of adult education. These passages are also a tutorial in self-learning, self-knowledge, and self-empowerment. Insofar as research into any subject, any cluster of research problems and programs, requires that persons come to know ever more reflectively, and through radical self-reflection and self-knowledge, the contributions of the *Theaetetus* are unsurpassed in perspicuity.

I now concentrate upon these passages with important changes in the text as italicized and as indicated. The changes are effected toward the imaginative end of focusing upon the special power which knowledge essentially is.[12] The move from that power which knowledge is to that power held in hand by persons whom knowledge has transformed should become clear.

SOCRATES. Well, you have heard what *empowering* is commonly said to be?

THEAETETUS. Possibly; but I don't remember at the moment.

SOCR. They say it is 'having *power*'.

THEAET. True.

SOCR. Let us make a slight amendment and say: 'possessing *power*'.

THEAET. What difference would you say that makes?

SOCR. None, perhaps; but let me tell you my idea and you shall help me test it.

THEAET. I will if I can.

SOCR. 'Having' seems to me different from 'possessing'. If a man has bought a coat and owns it, but is not wearing it, we should say he possesses it without having it about him.

THEAET. True.

SOCR. Now consider whether *power* is a thing you can possess in that way without having it about you, like a man who has caught some wild birds--pigeons or what not--and keeps them in an aviary he has made for them at home. In a sense, of course, we might say he 'has' them all the time inasmuch as he possesses them, mightn't we?

THEAET. Yes.

SOCR. But in another sense he 'has' none of them, though he has got control of them, now that he has made them captive in an enclosure of his own; he can take and have hold of them whenever he likes by catching any bird he chooses, and let them go again;

and it is open to him to do that as often as he
pleases.

THEAET. That is so.

SOCR. Once more then, just as a while ago we imagined a
sort of waxen block in our minds, so now let us
suppose that every mind contains a kind of aviary
stocked with birds of every sort, some in flocks
apart from the rest, some in small groups, and some
solitary, flying in any direction among them all.

THEAET. Be it so. What follows?

SOCR. When we are babies we must suppose this recep-
tacle empty, and take the birds to stand for pieces
of *power*. Whenever a person acquires any piece of
*power* and shuts it up in his enclosure, we must say
he has learnt or discovered the thing of which that
is the *power,* and that is what *empowering* means.

THEAET. Be it so.

SOCR. Now think of him hunting once more for any piece
of *power* that he wants, catching and holding it, and
letting it go again. In what terms are we to describe that--the same that we used of the original
process of acquisition, or different ones? An illustration may help you to see what I mean. There is a
science you call 'arithemetic'.

THEAET. Yes.

SOCR. Conceive that, then, as a chase after pieces of
*power* about all the numbers, odd or even.

THEAET. I will.

SOCR. That, I take it, is the science in virtue of
which a man has in his control pieces of *power* about
numbers and can hand them over to someone else.

THEAET. Yes.

SOCR. And when he hands them over, we call it 'teaching', and when the other takes them from him, that is
'learning', and when he has them in the sense of
possessing them in that aviary of his, that is
*empowering*.

THEAET. Certainly.

SOCR. Now observe what follows. The finished arithmetician *empowers* all numbers, doesn't he? There is no
number the *power* of which is not in his mind.

THEAET. Naturally.

SOCR. And such a person may sometimes count either the numbers themselves in his own head or some set of external things that have a number.

THEAET. Of course.

SOCR. And by counting we shall mean simply trying to find out what some particular number amounts to?

THEAET. Yes.

SOCR. It appears, then, that the man who, as we admitted, *empowers* every number, is trying to find out what he *empowers* as if he had no *power* of it. No doubt you sometimes hear puzzles of that sort debated.

THEAET. Indeed I do.

SOCR. Well, our illustration from hunting pigeons and getting possession of them will enable us to explain that the hunting occurs in two ways: first, before you possess your pigeon in order to have possession of it; secondly, after getting possession of it, in order to catch and hold in your hand what you have already possessed for some time. In the same way, if you have long possessed pieces of *power* about things you have learnt and *empowered*, it is still possible to get to *empower* the same things again, by the process of recovering the *power* of some particular thing and getting hold of it. It is *power* you have possessed for some time, but you had not got it handy in your mind.

THEAET. True.

SOCR. That, then, was the drift of my question, what terms should be used to describe the arithmetician who sets about counting or the literate person who sets about reading; because it seemed as if, in such a case, the man was setting about learning again from himself what he already *empowered*.

THEAET. That sounds odd, Socrates.

SOCR. Well, but can we say he is going to read or count something he does not *empower*, when we have already granted that he *empowers* all the letters or all the numbers?

THEAET. No, that is absurd too.

SOCR. Shall we say, then, that we care nothing about words, if it amuses anyone to turn and twist the expressions *'empowering'* and 'learning'? Having drawn a distinction between possessing *power* and having it about one, we agree that it is impossible not to possess what one does possess, and so we avoid the result that a man should not *empower* what he does *empower,* but we say that it is possible for him to get hold of a false judgment about it. For he may not have about him the *power* of that thing, but a different piece of *power* instead, if it so happens that, in hunting for some particular piece of *power* among those that are fluttering about, he misses it and catches hold of a different one. In that case, you see, he mistakes 11 or 12, because he has caught hold of the *power* of 11 that is inside him, instead of his *power* of 12, as he might catch a dove in place of a pigeon.

THEAET. That seems reasonable.

SOCR. Whereas, when he catches the piece of *power* he is trying to catch, he is not mistaken but thinks what is true. In this way both true and false judgments can exist, and the obstacles that were troubling us are removed. You will agree to this, perhaps? Or will you not?

THEAET. I will.

SOCR. Yes; for now we are rid of the contradiction about people not *empowering* what they do *empower.* That no longer implies our not possessing what we do possess, whether we are mistaken about something or not.

## The Transformation of a Person

My life is and has a shape and a structure of contours. I present my life in various ways. The 'everydayness' of my life is known through its forms, through the manner in which I perform and express my competencies. In philosophy, especially in traditions stemming principally from Plato (and in others[13]), the form of my life may be seen as the more intrinsic and essential nature of who I really am and what I really do, as distinct from what I only appear to be and the ways in which I am seen by others.

To transform my life is to move me from a certain clustering form and structure of contours of the essential form of my life through to another structure of contours, to move beyond the former. The latter then is said to transcend and surpass the former.

I, a solitary person, owe much to others, but what they offer me through their specializations and their competencies--what they offer me through their own empowerments--as established by their insights, and their tests of my competencies and performance, is for me at first only something they claim will empower me as well. If I am to accept these powers as empowerments, I must justify each of them by a perfect insight on my part.[14] My justification of my powers, my own enabling processes in my everyday world, concretizes my empowerments. I have moved from an indeterminate situation of not knowing that I did not have the power which knowing something could give me to knowing that I did not have this special power. But I have moved further, from knowing that I possessed the power to actually having it and holding it in hand. These stages mark the articulation of my radicalizing self-empowerment and thereby some of the stages of my transformation as a person.

## Empowerment and Transformation: The Research Program

Phenomenology is fundamentally a way of criticism in any discipline. The criticism may be of fundamental assumptions and presuppositions, of scientific models of observation and perception, of hypotheses, of verificational and falsificational testing and processes, and of conclusions and applications of specific research. This criticism is founded in one's own radical self-criticism, wherein--as both Descartes and Husserl claimed[15]--one's own perfecting insights must ultimately be sought and discovered.

The most relevant research programs uniquely presented by this phenomenology of empowerment and transformation of persons' accounts of individual persons' felt and experienced autobiographical accounts focus on these kinds of phenomena: (1) the indeterminateness of their situation of not (or not yet) knowing that they do not (or did not) have the essential power(s) which specific and relevant knowledge might give them; (2) the originating, motivating, and shaping tentative moves toward gaining these powers through relevant knowledge; (3) empowerments which emerge as states of personal being and new being as emergent from knowing that I know that I have these powers. These stages can be exfoliated as needed for specific and more detailed research.[16]

As these kinds of narrative accounts come in, those adults presenting them will have become radically self-aware and thereby transformed in and through relevant empowerments. Two additional kinds of research have thus emerged: (1) one's own personal criticisms of previous selves now becoming transformed and (2) the more 'objectifying' kinds of search performed by others working both on their own felt and experienced autobiographical accounts *and* on those of many other persons as well. What emerges from these fundamental phenomenological critiques of 'where I once stood but now stand' is almost any one of the kinds of specific research programs of critical interest to adult educators generally, but carried through as fundamental phenomenological explorations along the lines of those exemplified in Parts I and II above, and in Part VI below.

## C. Learning How to Learn: A Phenomenological Analysis of Adult 'Eductive' Learning

### Introductory Remarks

Learning how to learn is a process which has become the focus of increasing attention in adult education

literature. Two accounts may serve as excellent examples of this interest. For Robert M. Smith, 'learning
how to learn involves possessing, or acquiring, the
knowledge and skill to learn effectively in whatever
learning situation one encounters. If you possess the
necessary knowledge and skill, you've learned how to
learn . . .'[17] Edward Cell claims that 'all significant
experiential learning is a *change* in behavior, in
interpretation, in autonomy, or in creativity, or a
combination of these changes'.[18]

I believe that a full understanding of the accounts
of the process of learning how to learn which are presented in adult education literature can be seen to rest
on conceptual foundations which can be brought into
clear focus. Learning requires both the recognition
that something is already known and that something more
can be known. Philosophers have long claimed that knowing anything at all requires deliberate conscious acts
involving in knowing *that* we know something. Analogously, I claim that a person's learning anything at all
requires that person's personal knowledge *that* (s)he
learned it.

But learning *that* we learned something requires
that we know how we did it. What reflective moves did
we make during the process of learning within a concrete
learning project? If the reflective moves involved in
one learning project can be discovered, is it possible
to generalize in some degree from these moves to analogous reflections in other concrete learning projects?
How is it possible that these generalizations enact a
change, a move, in learning in one concrete situation to
learning in another concrete situation?

The conceptual analysis of learning how to learn
requires carefully formed answers to these three questions. If this kind of generalization and movement in
learning is not possible, then it is not possible to
provide the conceptual framework for showing that a
person indeed can learn how to learn. If this generali-

zation is possible it is a personal process, and there must be one or more *essential structures* in the process of learning to learn constituted of relevant phenomena which provide the grounds for this generalization. Learning *how* to learn therefore may be understood as *and* through a careful phenomenological auditing of the *ways* through which a person learns *that* (s)he learns. Each way is a special instance of how a person discovered the reflective moves in learning *that* (s)he learned something in one concrete case and that these moves were transferred to other concrete cases.

This section offers a thought experiment which consists of a brief phenomenological investigation in which I (1) clarify relationships between 'knowing *that* I know' and 'learning *that* I learn'; (2) identify phenomena constituting several *essential structures* in learning how to learn; and (3) point briefly to some important implications of these ideas about adult 'eductive' learning for both practice and research in matters of great moment for the subject-matter of adult education.

## 'Knowing that I Know' and 'Learning that I Learn'

We may begin this experiment by asking what the relationship is between 'knowing' something and 'learning' something. For example, does learning algebra or word processing precede knowing either of these? Or, paradoxically, must we first know something before we can learn it? The 'common sense' response is that learning something logically precedes knowing it. But consider the customary meanings of these two terms which are found in *The Oxford English Dictionary*. 'Knowing' something means (a) apprehending or perceiving something, or (b) comprehending or understanding something. 'Learning' a focused subject-matter means (c) acquiring knowledge of this subject, or perhaps a skill, as a result of experience, study, or teaching. But (a) and (b) are not identical or coextensive meanings. They are not the same thing, although both are presented as the mean-

ing of 'knowing'. More aptly stated, (a) and (b), respectively, are the earlier and the later stages of a
process of entering into a knowledge of a subject and of
coming to know it more fully. In this sense I first
apprehend algebra and then later (much later, as an
algebraist) comprehend algebra. To 'prehend' is to take
hold, grasp, or seize something. Therefore, I first
reach out to grasp something and then actually hold it
'in hand' (if a skill) or in my consciousness (if the
focused subject is knowledge, or something grasped
through ideas).

Knowing something, therefore, is a process beginning
with (a) and moving through (b). But 'learning' algebra, in the sense of (c) above, that is as acquiring
knowledge of algebra, means both (a) and (b) above: I
haven't 'learned' algebra until I 'know' it both as
having apprehended and comprehended it. We are led to
conclude at this stage in the thought experiment, therefore, that whereas I can partially know algebra without
having fully learned algebra, I surely cannot have
learned algebra without fully knowing it!

The 'common sense' view is that I must learn something before I can know it, that learning data processing logically precedes knowing it. Yet, minute reflection demonstrates that learning something is only possible if this something is already known! These are contradictory positions, and yet they both appear to be
true.

There is, however, a way in which these contradictor-
ies can be reconciled, and this interpretation becomes
vital in an understanding and explanation of learning
how to learn. Suppose that 'knowing' and 'learning' are
the same *kind* of process, and that they are distinguished only as *degrees* of this same kind of process.
Hence, 'I must know in order to learn' means that I must
first perceive, or reach out and grasp some subject, as
indicated in (a) above. And 'I must learn in order to
know' means, as in (b), that I must comprehend and
understand, or actually hold in my consciousness, a
subject.

Adult educators might prefer the title of this sub-section to be 'knowing that I learn' and 'learning that I know', since this is the much more immediate rendering of major practical problems in adult learning and education than my more philosophically-oriented heading above suggests. But one of my claims is that concreteness lies not primarily in the domain of practical and every-day affairs, but in the theoretical and the philosoph-ical explorations of the problems and resolutions to these problems which persons construct for their every-day lives. This means that persons, their problems, and their learning projects in the everyday world can only be understood and resolved when the philosophical root-ages of these are excavated and laid out for everyone to see and to explore for themselves. Then it can be seen, for example, that 'knowing *that* I know' underlies 'learning *that* I learn', and that the latter is abso-lutely fundamental to learning how to learn.

Philosophers long have claimed that knowing anything at all in sense (b) requires deliberate reflective moves facilitated by the conscious acts involved in knowing *that* we know something. And we have seen above that learning something requires *both* that that subject be already known, in sense (a), as perceived, apprehended, taken hold of, or grasped, *and* that the subject be more fully known, in sense (b), as understood, compre-hended, and actually held in one's consciousness. Moreover, it seems clear from my investigation thus far that learning anything at all requires one's personal knowledge *that* (s)he learned it. Knowing *that* I know is reflexive; it is knowing and knowledge checking back upon itself, the knowing process auditing itself. Analogously, learning *that* I learn is also reflexive; it is learning turning back upon itself, cross-checking, testing out, auditing itself. Both reflexive forms focus on thinking and discourse, on the suppositions and presuppositions of the predications of knowing what is known and of learning what is learned.

## Essential Structures in Learning How to Learn

Knowing and learning constitute the same *kind* of process, but they may be distinguished as differences of *degree* within this same process. There is already a degree of knowing something, a knowledge of this same thing in lesser degree, as we begin to learn that same thing. Learning is always knowing something more than what is already known. There is an orientation and direction toward the future in learning. It is not what is (a) perceived or apprehended that is learned, but rather (b) what is conceived or comprehended. And although (a) and (b) are the same kind of process, they are distinguished as degrees of this process such that (b) is a stage much further along in this process. Therefore whereas 'knowing' and 'learning' are not identical, the 'known' and the 'learned' are identical. To unpack what a person has learned is to describe what (s)he knows, and this can be demonstrated only through reference to concrete instances of the known and the learned. A person's having knowledge of concrete subjects is identical with that person's having learned these concrete subjects in some way(s). This is one *essential structure* in learning how to learn.

An additional *essential structure* in learning how to learn can be identified. Although to know and to learn are not identical, they can be related phenomenologically in this way. 'To know' is the focus of a person's acquisitions in consciousness in their staticity, whether one says that (s)he wants to know something, or merely that x, y, and z are the sorts of subject-matters one might possibly want to know out of all of the possible sorts of things one might want to know. One describes knowing something, or *to know* something, by saying what is the case, whereas one describes learning, or 'to learn' as what (s)he is doing, or as what is yet to be done. And learning is always in some degree knowing that is still-to-be done, or always more fully to be accomplished. Learning is knowledge still-to-be enacted and gained.

To have knowledge is to have the power to do something, and a description of what this particular knowledge is is the precise description of what this particular enabling power is. Knowledge is both possessing and having this power in hand. Learning something is *both* the process of coming into the possession of knowledge *and* of having this power in hand, such that what has been learned is this knowledge *fully* possessed and *fully* in hand. A phenomenological description of the stages through which this process moves is both an identification and a description of additional *essential structures* of phenomena and clusters of phenomenon relevant in any understanding of learning how to learn. Among some easily identifiable *essential structures* are the following ones:

(1) There is a stage at which I can be said *not to know that I do not know something*. There is at least something in particular that I do not know (out of the indeterminately large number of subject-matters I might be able to learn, but as yet have not learned). In this case I do not know that I have not learned it unless I am asked the focused question of whether I know such and such or not.

(2) There is a further stage at which I can be said to *know that I do not know* what I want to know or need to know. Knowing something in particular has become for me a relevant problem. I have somehow learned *that* I have not learned what I want to know or need to know.

(3) There is a stage at which I *know that I want to know or need to know something in particular*. I have learned that I need to learn this.

(4) There is a stage at which I *begin to know this something in particular*. I perceive it or apprehend it, without comprehending it yet.

(5) There are many additional stages *in coming to comprehend what I want to know*. But in comprehending it I must know *that* I know it. And really having learned it, I must have learned *that* I learned it. But knowing *that* I know and learning *that* I learned it are

distinct processes. It is not the knowledge gained which is transferable, but the *knowledge content as felt, as transferred from one felt place to another.* This is my definition of a metaphor. Learning *that* I learned, have arrived at knowledge of something, is always a performed metaphor. Learning *that* I learned something in some context (within the circumstances in a concrete situation) at one time demonstrates that I have succeeded. It further suggests that I can do it again . . . and again . . . , although I cannot be certain of this. I must try it out in order to see whether this is really true. Trying it out in this way is experimentation, the form of experimentation which thought experiments are. Suppose I try it out. Suppose that I move through the stages above in a variety of contexts of distinct concrete subject-matters. Suppose that I do it again and again. I come to know *that* I know a variety of subject-matters in a variety of concrete cases. Again and again I learn *that* I have learned. This is enacted through metaphor. (I discuss metaphor in detail in Chapter 8, below.)

**Adult 'Eductive' Learning in Theory and in Practice**

As an adult I have already built up a stock of experiences, including repeated experiences of learning *that* I have learned something. It is possible retrospectively to describe each of these phenomenologically if I wish to do so. Each description can be the foundation for an analysis of *how* I came *both* to apprehend *and* later to comprehend something. Through these successive descriptions of *how* I learned what I finally came to know I have learned *how* I learned what I came to know. Continuing these descriptions in the most careful terms I learn how to learn. This has been made possible principally through intuiting certain stages in coming to know something and through a description of these as *essential structures.* They are *essential structures* in learning how to learn. *How* this is done thus becomes an auditing process. I have learned how to learn, and I can learn something, therefore, in a variety of ways. In Smith's terms, as an adult I can learn through such modes as self-direction, collaboration, and more formalized institutional studies. My phenomenological account also provides a conceptual foundation for Cell's study of kinds of experiential learning.

In any case, our feelings, experiencings, and reflectings are the foundations of these contexts (Smith) and kinds (Cell). They become grounds, originations, and beginnings (but are never 'causes') of our learning. But even these contexts and kinds of processes of learning to learn cannot be clarified and understood if the conceptual grounds supporting them only account for them as atomistic and discrete classifications of what persons do in practical situations. Learning how to learn cannot be grounded conceptually in these kinds of atomistic encapsulations of knowledge. Learning how to learn requires both (1) one's personal voyage through the *essential structures* I have laid out in phenomenological terms and (2) one's own audit of this personal journey. In this latter sense I, and each of us as a person learning how to learn, must be able to draw up a formal and systematic reckoning of the ways through which I learned how to learn. This must be enacted in ways both validated and verified through the evidence which I and other persons are able to provide. This evidence is immediately available through the retrospective attestations of my (and of others') feelings, experiencings, and reflectings.

All of this is made possible, I believe, in the light of adult education characterized as a human science and as the enactment of, and the systematic investigation of, the phenomena constituting the adult 'eductions' of **person**, specifically of persons' free and deliberate motives for acting. Adult 'eductions' are adults' feelings, experiencings, and reflectings. When predicated, they are metaphorizings. (See Chapter 8.)

The significance of this thought experiment should be clear for adults, adult learning, and adult education. Each of us can come to see that we can become more autonomous in our conduct. We know that we can learn how to learn to do this, but the main problem has always been to provide the theoretical foundation for saying clearly what we believe we are able to do in everyday life. I have tried to address this major conceptual problem. The more we understand how we learn to learn the more personal responsibility we reasonably are able to assume for all of our learning projects in concrete situations.

The discussions in the three sections above lead now to a consideration of what I call a phenomenology of **experiencing**, a discussion of relevancies and perspectives, and a discussion of languages of relevance, respectively, in the next three chapters in this Part IV. Each of these subjects is of the greatest significance as one reflects carefully upon phenomena central to the lives of adults as they move through their lives and decide, plan and persue learning goals in both short-term and long-term ways toward the enrichment and enhancement of their everyday practical living.

## Chapter 4

## Toward a Phenomenology of Experiencing

The 'eight compact thesis' about experience around which I shall cast this brief phenomenology of experiencing were presented in a classic paper, "Toward a Phenomenology of Experience," in the *American Philosophical Quarterly* in 1964. The author was the 'phenomenological movement's' most distinguished historian, and surely one of

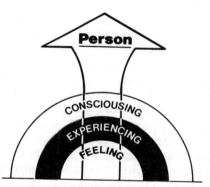

See n.3 in Notes to Table of Contents

this tradition's finest philosophers, Herbert Spiegelberg.[1]

Experiencing is the second of three principal layers of the eductions of <u>person</u>. Feeling was the first of these to be investigated phenomenologically in this essay. The third will be explored in Chapter 7. **Feeling, experiencing, and consciousing** together constitute the fullness of the eductions of <u>person</u>, and they are investigated in this essay on phenomenological research in adult education as the feelings, experiences, and consciousing of adults, and thus as the adult eductions of <u>person</u>. In Part VI, Section B., I refer to the 'FEC Structure of <u>person</u>' and present it as the ground of an answer to any person's question, 'Who Am I?' I also offer this structure there as the single most important feature of a new program of research for adult education to be conducted along the lines of a rigorous human science through phenomenological investigations.

But for the moment we move to an investigation of experiencing. This investigation will make possible the phenomenological analysis of the phenomena constituting relevance and the languages of relevancy systems. Together, these three concerns are among those most vital to any human science, and a clear understanding of them is doubly vital to the research and practices of adult education recast as the most rigorous of the human sciences.

(1) 'Experience is an "intentional" act in which an experiencer is directed toward an intentional object.'

The experiencer is a person, not a mind, consciousness, or body. In this presentation of a brief phenomenology of experiencing we do not have to be committed to one version or another of the 'solution' to the ageless 'mind/body problem' which has been the focus of so much philosophical speculation.[2] I am not invoking here (or anywhere else in this book) any view of the mind as separate from the body, nor am I offering any metaphysical or epistemological claims about these notions. I am discussing **person** as the essential structure of persons, and adults specifically, throughout the book.

A person experiences and has experiences. Experiencing is what a person is at one stage of **person**, just as feeling is what a person is at an earlier stage of **person**. Experiencing (from the Latin, **experiri**) is a person's trying in some way, and one's putting something to the test. Experiencing and experimenting have the same rootage, as the *Oxford English Dictionary* amply attests. Experience, as a substantive, is the fact of being consciously the subject of a state or condition, or of being consciously affected by some event. It is also an instance of this. An experience is a state or condition viewed 'subjectively'. It is knowledge resulting from actual observation, or from what one has undergone.

With the exception of the above citations of the properties of 'experience', the principal discussion of the etymology of the Latin **experiri** more richly characterizes the modern usage of 'experiment' than the term 'experience'. The focus is upon the active strivings of experience which are normally lost in accounts of experience as a person's passive receptivity of aspects of, or 'what is' in the world. 'Experiment' means having an experience of, or feeling, suffering, and testing something, in everyday language. An experiment is a tentative procedure, a course of action adopted in the uncertainty of whether it will answer questions at hand. It is an action or operation undertaken in *order to* discover something unknown, or perhaps the test of an hypothesis. It has to do with practice and the practical within the 'everydayness' of a person's life.

In all of these senses experiment and experience fulfill the common rootage of their etymology. In fact, a more complete phenomenological investigation of the phenomena of a genuine experiment reveals much of the core constituency of an experience in the sense that the latter, far from being merely the passive receptivity of the world which each person is sometimes claimed to be is an actual trying within the world, the concrete case of a person's putting something to the test, an intentional act which could reach the stage of articulation in speech and of subsequent predication even in logic. But these later expressions could only come through the later intentional acts of thinking and reflection. Experiencing is never passive, but always active, a striving and a testing out within the world, falling just short of consciousing or reflective actions.

The term 'intentional' (from the Latin **intendere**, stretching, straining, effort, attention, application, design, purpose) generally has been used in connection with activities of the mind or consciousness in the sense that these are actions and distinguishable ways in which the mind stretches, strains, and exerts itself in attending-to things of interest in the everyday world. These are the effortive[3] ways of the mind relating itself to the world. The term 'intentional' conveys all

of the efforts of the mind in the construction of perceptions and conceptions[4] within the world. Perceptions
are intentional in the sense that a person literally
reaches into the world and grasps certain phenomena
(which thereby become the process of perceiving and
instantiated perceptions). These are brought together,
literally 'taken altogether' through concepts (from the
Latin, **con**, together + **capere**, to take). All of these
activities are effortive activities of the mind directed
toward objects, and are therefore 'intentional'. Hence,
the thesis, 'experience is an "intentional" act in which
an experiencer is directed toward an intentional
object.' The actions of persons as experiencers include
(but do not exhaust) such activities as imagining,
thinking, remembering, and planning. These are 'intentional' activities in the special sense that they are
among the workings of the mind.

It has long been customary in philosophy to characterize mental acts as 'intentional', but phenomenologists, for example Edmund Husserl in following the lead
of his teacher, Franz Brentano, carried their analyses
of intentionality and intentional acts of the mind much
further than philosophers generally have. Their investigations have become principal cornerstones of modern
phenomenology.

(2) 'A full experience is a synthesis of several intentional acts.'

Experiencing is not merely a linear or single-series
process in a person. If it were then an apt analogy
might seem to be that experiencing is to experience as
lines are to their constituent points. But the points
are mathematical fictions necessary to account for
lines, whereas experiences are fully concrete and real
as distincts within the stream of experiencing. Surely
our personal experiences are more real to us than are
the non-existent points of a line. It might seem to be
even more fictive to hold that experiences are somehow
set within a continuity of a stream or process of experiencing. Here 'experiencing' seems less real and apparent than are the concrete and tangible experiences which

all persons have. Therefore, even if experiencing were a linear process the analogy with a line would fail.

But suppose persons engage in effortive actions, most of which consist of reaching out and into the everyday world and grasping individual phenomena and clusters of phenomena (that is, perceiving and its percepts). In this case persons intend their worlds. They intend the world through the ways--and in those times and places-- in which they attend-to and heed, or are interested in, the world. These are among the intentional acts which persons perform. These are counted among their stretch-ings, strainings, applications, designs, and purposes (all from the Latin, **intendere**), which make up the effortive activities of minds which are the work each person performs countless times during each hour of wide-awake living.

A synthesis of several of these intentional acts constitutes an experience. Since an experience is an intentional act through which a person as experiencer is directed toward an intentional object, and because a whole object, or an object in its entirety, can never be perceived or conceived through a single intentional act of the mind, a full experience is always a synthesis of more than one intentional act. Moreover, any experience properly so-called is a *full* experience, although its being a full experience does not mean that it is suffi-cient of itself to count as reflection in the process of constructing knowledge claims. An experience per se does not *ipso facto* constitute knowledge. Some eperience-based philosophers--certain empiricists-- erroneously have reduced knowledge claims to experiences while failing to see that even a full experience in the sense just characterized is not yet knowledge. Even this full experience does not 'mean' anything, although it is the just logically-prior threshold of meaning.

(3) 'The experience of an object refers beyond itself.'

Persons experience, and when they do there is always an object of each experience. This object is never fully experienced in all of its possible temporal and spatial perspectives, any more than a single glance can ever cover the entirety of another person's body. Each experience intends one perspective of the object, and since an experience does not definitely box in this particular perspective of the intended object (as a survey would do with a tract of land), no experience can be excluded exactly and precisely from another experience. This is one sense in which the experience of an object refers beyond itself. Each full experience may overlap another full experience, and thus refer beyond itself.

There is another sense in which the experience of an object refers beyond itself. Even if a 'full' experience is itself only a partial coverage of the whole object of experience, it is always the case that the actual experiencing always discloses possibilities of other experiences beyond itself.

(4) 'Experience has no temporal structure.'

A person at time 't' may experience an object, yet the experience itself has no temporal structure. An experience will always have originations and a beginning, but a beginning is not always itself a structure. It is questionable whether an experience has an identifiable end. One experience leads to another, ad infinitum. What might be mistaken for the temporal span of an experience is the span of time during which a person might attend-to or be interested in some object. A continuing interest over time in some object, however, is not the same thing as an experience of, or even having an experience of, an intended object. Further, no experience is temporally instantaneous. It has originations and a beginning, but these are **reasons** (which are not necessitated as 'causes') one might adduce for these in respect to the emerging experience. Each full experience as emergent has constituent phases which have already taken their place in time as a person experiences, but an experience per se does not have a temporal span.

(5) 'Experience extends to any type of individual objects.'

Although it might be easier to understand how persons experience material things in the world, it is not at all clear that these material things are given to us through sense-data or as sense-experience. In addition, many philosophers have argued that we experience relations, meanings, values, 'oughts-to-be' in our lives, other minds, social and cultural phenomena, and the wholeness and unity of another person's body, and even personalities, and possibly the thoughts and feelings of other persons. Careful reflection upon the more usual phenomena of hallucinations, for example, suggests that our experiences of material objects may be less easily understood than our experiences of another person's feelings and thoughts. The content of an hallucination is still an intended object of an intentional act, although the object of the intentional act does not accord with objects normally encountered in the everyday world (as measured by any reasonable theory of meaning and truth). Later, a person may judge rightly that an experience was hallucinatory, but at a given earlier time he did not 'see' it that way. In the case of experiencing another's thoughts and feelings, we may be wrong in our interpretations of what we experience or experienced, but there is no question *that* experiencing these, or knowing *that* we have experienced them in some degree is fundamental as a basis for knowing those persons.

(6)  'Experience forms the pre-predicative stage of our cognitive life.'

Direct experience is not yet thinking, but thinking must be preceded by experiencing and be founded upon a stock of experiences. Thoughts are based on experiences. In everyday language predication is the action of declaring, of setting forth (from the Latin, **prae**, forth + **dicare**, to make known, to proclaim). It is the action of asserting or affirming something. In more specific terms, to predicate is to assert or affirm a quality, property, or attribute of something. In the much more precise terms of logic the predicate is whatever is said, and affirmed or denied, of the subject in a proposition. It is the second term in a proposition which is affirmed or denied of the first term, or subject, through means of the copula, as in the sentence 'all men are **mortal.**'

Direct experience is not first of all differentiated into propositional forms which relate predicate terms to subjects, or which say something about subjects. All of this comes at a later stage. Hence, direct experience is 'prepredicative', although it is necessary to the later stage in a person's life which is called 'reflection'. Spiegelberg maintained:

> From the plain seizure of the originally given via its retentive inspection and explication for its detailed structure we gradually approach the stage of 'substratum' and 'determination' which allows for expression in logical predication.
>
> Illustrating at least something of these highly complex relationships I shall simply call attention to the situation in which we find ourselves when, after having spent some time in a room, we want to describe it. Evidently this presupposes an explicit refocussing and reorganization of the first experience.[5]

(7)   'Experience constitutes the experienced.'

To constitute (from the Latin, **con**, intensive + **statuere**, to set up, to place) is to set up, place or establish something. The constitution of anything is the makeup, form, composition, and essential elements of which anything spoken of consists. It is in all of these senses that a person's experiencing constitutes what he experiences. A person's experiences actively set up and establish the formal properties of the experienced objects or the experiences which he has. That is, the experienced object is established through experience. Just as in knowing we must always know *something,* so in experiencing we experience something, but the experiences within experiencing constitute the experienced; they make it up, they form it, and bring together the essential ingredients of the experienced ('object').

(8)   'Experience is a combination of receptive and spontaneous processes.'

There is the 'matter' of the world with which the adult works. Much of this the person receives. Some of it is the 'natural' world, some the work of other persons, the stuff of other minds, of work and marketplace, of family and larger kinship groups, of community, of culture. But a person born into this world of relationships begins to make a difference with his own network of relationships, the products of his own experiencing. Thus, a person both receives and acts. He works, and he creates things and moments of value in the world. The foundation within the person for all of this to happen is his experiencing of and in the world. Its originations may be dimly and unspecifiably emergent as the footings which feelings are. The foundation poured upon these footings is what we call experience, and as no foundation is merely reducible to the footings of it, so it is with the relationships of experiencing to feeling. And therefore experience is a 'combination' of receptive and spontaneous processes.

'Combination' is much too loose and tentative a word to express the unique relationship between reception and spontaneity in experiencing and the always novel 'togetherness' of the received and the newly creative in an experience which an adult has. This term implies little more than simple addition or the creation of a compound. But experiencing what is experienced is always more than a combination of two things. A person, a being, that is, who feels and who experiences (and 'consciouses', as shall be seen in Chapter 7) is a being who acts in the world. In doing so the person changes the network of relationships within that world.

A person is an 'executive' (Ortega's term) in the world, one who plans, follows out these plans, carries into effect intentions, purposes, places, instructions, and commands. A person fuses what is received in and from the everyday life and spontaneously reorders his own world in some way and in some degree. In doing so his reordering of the world moves over into the lifeworlds of other persons. But in the midst of the stage of **person** which experiencing is, this reordering of one's own life, with whatever impingements this may have in the lives of other persons, still falls short of the markings of predicative language.

> In sum [wrote Spiegelberg] experience is an intertwined network of receptive and spontaneous processes, of undergoing and doing, in which the active phases are in the ascendancy the closer experience approaches the predicative stage of articulated knowledge.[6]

## Adults Experiencing the World

Following the brief account of a phenomenology of experiencing above it is possible to portray some of the essential structures of the adult eductions of **person** through persons who executively realize their own life-worlds through personal experiences. As adults we encounter more identifiable resistances within the world. Resisting us, some ingredients of the world limit the spheres within which our feelings may emerge and the stagings of our experiences. Our realizations as **person** more clearly and completely are also thereby limited. Our actions are placings, situatings, orientings, within circumstances, or the things which stand around us. Actions have their special character, and the special phases, stretches, stages[7] partially by virtue of what stands around them, and of course from what stands before, during, and following any stretch of the action short of its termination. The content of any action is also related to the circumstances surrounding it at its termination. At this point a person already must be experiencing some of these ingredients and elements as similar to, like, or as resembling others. The content of the action is being brought (although not predicatively so through language, since I am still discussing the 'prepredicative' stages of **person** which both feeling and experiencing are) into felt and experienced concreteness. Its ingredients are growing together, and the fullness of the action is unfolding.

This content moves toward the level of the understanding and the understandable. But it does not thereby yet achieve the stage of the reflectively and reflexively understood.

The point immediately above may be presented differently with the use of a metaphor. It may be said that the content moves toward the level of the understanding or understandable, but only as 'feelings which have felt themselves'. This is a metaphor whose presence cannot be attended-to until the level of experiencing in **person** has been achieved, and whose meaning cannot be unpacked until the level of 'consciousing' in **person** has been arrived at within a person. 'Feeling itself' is a metaphor for 'experiencing', and 'a feeling which feels itself' is a metaphor for 'an experience'. Hence, the movement of the content of the action which is being brought into felt and experienced concreteness such that its ingredients are growing together and the fullness of the action is unfolding stops short of fully reaching the realms of the understanding, or the layer of 'consciousing' which constitutes **person** (as this is developed in Chapter 7 below).

This brief phenomenology of experiencing has laid the theoretical groundwork for the following two chapters devoted to relevancy and the languages of relevancy systems. These questions are absolutely vital to both practice and research in adult education.[8] These points should become clear as soon as the concept of relevancy is defined immediately below.

# Chapter 5

## Relevancies:  Experiencing the Creation of Meaning

In this chapter I shall sketch out the rudiments of a philosophical theory of relevance concerning the language we use *both* in fashioning our own dreams, hopes, projects and goals into living form through our motivations and willing *and* in general investigations and research into human actions and human acts. In turn, these views can be used in learning and teaching and in research and program development in adult learning and education.

*Relevance* is perspective in, of, and through the world.[1] It is literally a looking-through the world, a process taking place in time and constituted in terms of the relative priority and ordering importance of the ingredients of the world. A *system of relevance* is a way through which are presented the relative priority and ordering importance of the ingredients of the world from a fashioning and structuring point of view. This way is through the medium of a matrix of relatings manifesting themselves in degrees and kinds of phenomena in their presentation and expression from the most tacit through the most explicit constitutions. I call this matrix the *relevance matrix of personal action*. Its contents are constituted as:

(1) presenting any theme, topic, or question which becomes a specific problem within problematics in the familiar life-structuring situations of the everyday world (what I have called 'everydayness') or within the

world-as-taken-for-granted, and through the terms of which a person engages in action, or could do so;[2]

(2) presenting the webs and networks of interpretational data (feelings and experiences, for example) which have been located and situated by the theme, topic, or question which has 'jolted' a person's familiar world by arising as 'the familiar', or the problematic situation within the personal world as otherwise taken-for-granted. These data become evidence toward the construction of actual or possible enactings within the world;[3]

(3) placing a person, or persons, within the world spatially ('here' or 'there') and temporally ('now' or 'then') within situations and circumstances;[4]

(4) presenting *a* way among possible ways whereby a person or persons with a point, or points, of view may define problematic situations and problems arising within these and act in response to these, given the circumstances; and

(5) presenting *a* way among possible ways whereby a person may move through the stages and phases of the entire processes of motivating and willing the execution of actions felt, experienced, believed, or thought to be reasonable resolutions to these problems.[5]

In the remaining pages of this chapter I shall identify and characterize five relevancy systems: **etymological relevance, syntactical relevance, descriptive relevance, typal relevance, and paradigmal relevance.** *Each of these carries the same general relevancy matrix* laid out above, and which I emphasize again. Each is a system of relevance, a perspective in and of the world in terms of which are cast the appropriateness and pertinence of: the appearance and presentation of the thematic issues as problematic; the adducing and the presentation of evidential bases of possible interpretations which have been located; the descriptive reasons of how persons place themselves in situations and why persons may respond to the problems arising amidst the circumstances constituting the problematic situations within which they find themselves.

Each of the following five relevancy systems does this in its own unique fashioning and structuring ways. And each of the systems, in stamping and channeling actions within the 'everydayness' of the adult lifeworld is of the greatest importance in phenomenological investigations in adult learning and education.

In the remainder of this chapter I discuss these five relevancy systems in some detail. In Chapter 6 I try to show through a more detailed description of languages of these relevancy systems why these relevancy systems are indeed of the greatest importance in phenomenological investigations centered in the adult eductions of **person** as the subject-matter of adult learning and teaching.

## Etymological Relevance

Etymological relevance is a system of relevance, a perspective in and of the world in terms of which have been cast the appropriateness and pertinence of: the appearance and presentation of the thematic issues as problematic over long periods of time; the adducing and presentation of evidentiary bases of possible interpretations which have been located; the descriptive reasons of how persons have placed themselves in situations; and how persons have met the situations within which they have found themselves within their circumstances.

This system of relevancy carries the *relevancy matrix* fundamentally through the constitutions of the etymological structures of the concepts within the language(s), or by way of emphasizing the arrangement and interrelationships of words and groups of words which come to be joined as the concepts of the language(s) persons have used. Almost all words in use (with the obvious exceptions of newly constructed metaphors, technical terms, articles, and words of this sort) carry with them their own historicities of right and conventional uses in previous times. These are the 'etymologies' of these words. Ortega maintained

> Etymologies are not merely of linguistic interest since they permit us to bring to light situations actually 'lived' by man and which are preserved with full actual freshness, like (the) meat . . . preserved through millenia in the ice of Siberia and which men actually were able to eat.[6]

Another excellent example of the functioning of etymological relevance is found in Austin writings:

> A word never--well, hardly ever--shakes off its etymology and its formation. In spite of all changes in and extensions of and additions to its meanings, and indeed rather pervading and governing these, there will still persist the old idea. In an accident something befalls: by mistake you take the wrong one: in error you stray: when you act deliberately you act after weighing it up (**not** after thinking out ways and means). It is worth asking ourselves whether we know the etymology of 'result' or of 'spontaneously', and worth remembering that 'unwillingly' and 'involuntarily' come from very different sources.[7]

The creative functioning of etymological relevancy provides major clues in understanding the expression of the social structurings and systematizings of language. There is no question that the etymological structures of languages shape the perspectives we have within and of the world; nor is there any question that those founding shapes occur vitally through one's life.

The study of classical languages reveals obvious examples of etymological relevancy at work. An understanding, within English-speaking cultures, for example, of Greek and Latin and the influences of these languages upon English, is already a basis for understanding the generative symbolic transformations of English-speaking worlds. These have been among the most significant cultural activities of persons at certain periods along the roads to what our cultures have come to be. Etymologies carry the influences of other ethnic languages upon our culture as well. Explorations into the etymological roots adduce evidence of etymological relevancy at work, and these are necessary, in my judgment, to any philosophical investigation of any subject-matter, and hence to any phenomenological exploration within adult education.

In fact, the clearest examples of this last point are the very ways in which I have made very heavy use of the etymological traditions (and here, etymological relevance) in laying out the philosophical groundwork for adult education in these phenomenological investigations. This is true especially of such key notions as 'eduction', feeling, experiencing, consciousing, and research.

## Syntactical Relevance

It would be impossible to define one's situation, and to act meaningfully within it, without the use of language in some sense, and not only through recourse ultimately to etymologies. The system of syntactical relevancy channels its *relevancy matrix* fundamentally and primarily through the constitutions of the words and syntactical structures of the language(s), or by way of emphasizing the arrangement and interrelationships of phrases and sentences within language(s) which persons use. Different examples of this kind of relevancy system include all language activities and usages including the learning of any language from the most vernacular stages through the highest technical phases, structural grammar, descriptive grammar, ordinary language philosophies, linguistic philosophies, ideal language philosophies, and probably all approaches to deductive and inductive logic. All of these expressions of syntactical relevance express the ideas of different degrees and kinds of completeness and completability of linguistically meaningful situations in which we act.

An excellent example of the functioning of syntactical relevance is to be found, I believe, in J. L. Austin's passage:

First, words are our tools, and as a minimum, we should use clean tools; we should know what we mean and we do not, and we must forearm ourselves against the traps language sets us. Secondly, words are not (except in their own little corner) facts or things: we need therefore to prise them off the world, to hold them apart from and against it, so that we can realize their inadequacies and arbitrariness, and can relook at the world without blinkers. Thirdly, and most hopefully, *our common stock of words embodies all the distinctions men have found worth drawing, and the connections they have found worth making, in the lifetimes of many generations:* these surely are likely to be more numerous, more sound, since they have stood up to the long test of the survival of the fittest, and more subtle, at least in all ordinary and reasonably practical matters, than any that you or I are likely to think up in our arm-chairs of an afternoon--the most favoured alternative method.[8] (My emphasis)

This is one expression of the social structurings and systematizings of language. The OED presents one definition of 'syntax' (the first one, but as obsolete) as the 'orderly or systematic arrangement (of body), or a connected order or system of things'. There is no question that the full repertoire of words within syntactical structures of given languages fashion the perspectives which its users have within, and of, the world;[9] nor is there any question that this shaping continues throughout a person's life. The only issue--and an all-important one for our purposes--is the degree and kind of occurrence within a given situation. Ascertaining these would be among the goals of the investigation of the influence of syntactical relevance within a determinate situation, for example, as adults attempt to work through the more specific problems of their 'everydayness'. Surely, for example, the recent history of English and American philosophy (say, from about 1900 to the present) suggests that this system of relevancy has been operative in it. The contributions of 'analytic' philosophy to philosophical foundations of adult education flow very much along the lines of syntactical relevancy systems. Moreover, Paulo Freire's approaches to learning language(s) in large-scale literacy programs[10] are excellent examples of syntactical relevancy at work. For him, the ordering of one's language and the order of one's world are inseparable, although phenomenologically they can become distinguishable 'objects' of distinct studies.

## Descriptive Relevance

The system of descriptive relevancy carries the *relevancy matrix* fundamentally through the course of tracing out the contours of the lifeworld by means of descriptions of the phenomena of human activities, of human actions and acts. Examples of this kind of relevancy are each and all of the scientific disciplines which offer information, and provide knowledge concerning the nature and description of human activities, for example basic biology, physiology and psychology, many medical sciences, and jurisprudence. Another, and very fundamental and rigorous, example is the descriptive phenomenology presented in Husserl's *Logical Investigations.*[11]

Herbert Spiegelberg has set forth the function of phenomenological description in brief terms as follows.

A description . . . presupposes a framework of class names, and all it can do is to determine the location of the phenomenon with regard to an already developed system of classes. This may be adequate for the more familiar phenomena. But as soon as we want to describe new phenomena or new aspects of old phenomena, we can do little more than assign them places within the wider framework of classes with whose other members they show at least some similarity or structural resemblance, being unable to indicate their distinguishing features. Of course it is possible and necessary to refine the system of coordinates for these phenomena by stipulating new class names; but these will be of little help before full acquaintance with the new phenomena has been established and communicated. In the meantime description by negation is usually the simplest way to at least indicate the uniqueness and irreducibility of such phenomena. The only other way is by metaphor and analogy, which are often suggestive, but not without dangers, particularly if presented without the necessary cautions. What must be borne in mind is that *the main function of a phenomenological description is to serve as a reliable guide to the listener's own actual or potential experience of the phenomena.* It is in this sense never more than ostensive, or better, directive. *Its essential function is to provide unmistakable guideposts to the phenomena themselves.* Another feature of description which deserves mentioning in the context is that description, and phenomenological description in particular, can never be more than selective; it is impossible to exhaust all the properties, especially the relational properties, of any object or phenomenon. But selection may be a virtue as well as a necessity. It forces us to concentrate on the central or decisive characteristics of the phenomenon and to abstract from its accidentals. To this extent description already involves a consideration of essences . . .[12] (My emphasis)

## Typal Relevance

The relevancy matrix as shaped by this system of relevance builds structures of types, classes, categories and kinds, and activities of thinking which formulate the similarities, likenesses, resemblances, and exemplars of phenomena of human action. Many examples include primarily non-systematic thinking within the everyday world of the taken for granted, that world in which Husserl said so much of our action is governed by the idealities (thinkings) 'and so forth and so on' and 'I can do it again.'[13] Dewey had very much to say about this kind of thinking (as found especially in common sense inquiry) as well. These typifications are of immense significance to the eduction of meanings and values through learning and teaching. They are also a rich field of research for students of adult education interested in studying Husserl's early work in phenomenology. Most of Husserl's investigations offer rich lodes to be mined by these students, in fact. Examples also include the classifying operations which are important to all scientific disciplines, including both the history and the philosophy of science.

Typal relevance with its structures of typicalities, is the perspective of phenomena within human action (activities of thinking, and actions of having thought such and such) and may be explored as self-reflective. A prime example of this form of relevance, I believe, is the discipline of history (and clearly the historical fabric of any discipline concerned with human action), surely so in Collingwood's philosophy of history. Collingwood asked:

> How, or on what conditions, can the historian know the past?. . . My historical review of the idea of history has resulted in the emergence of an answer to this question: namely, that the historian must *re-enact the past in his own mind.*

> . . . If a mind is nothing but its own activities, and if to know the mind of a person in the past--say Thomas Becket--is to re-enact his thought, surely insofar as I, the historian, do this, I simply become Becket, which seems absurd . . . I do not 'simply' become Becket, for a thinking mind is never 'simply' anything: It is its own activities of thought, and it is not these 'simply' (which, if it means 'immediately'), for thought is not mere immediate experience but always reflection or self-knowledge, the

knowledge of oneself as living in these activities . . . . An act of thought is certainly a part of the thinker's experience. It occurs at a certain time, and in a certain context of other acts of thought, emotions, sensations, and so forth. Its presence in this context I call its immediacy; for although thought is not mere immediacy, it is not devoid of immediacy. The peculiarity of thought is that, in addition to occurring here and now in this context it can sustain itself through a change of context and revive in a different one. This power to sustain and revive itself is what makes an act of thought more than a mere 'event' or 'situation,' to quote words that have been applied to it, for example by Whitehead. It is because, and so far as, the act of thought is misconceived as a mere event that the idea of *re-enacting* it seems paradoxical and a perverse way of describing the occurrence of another, similar, event. The immediate, as such, cannot be *re-enacted*. Consequently, those elements in experience whose being is just their immediacy (sensations, feelings, etc., as such) cannot be re-enacted in its immediacy. The first discovery of a truth, for example, differs from any subsequent contemplation of it, not in that the truth contemplated is a different truth, nor in that the act of contemplating it is a different act; but in that the immediacy of the first occasion can never again be experienced: the shock of its novelty, the liberation from perplexing problems, the triumph of achieving a desired result, perhaps the sense of having vanquished opponents and achieved fame, and so forth.[14]

However, the study of any one of the social sciences (and more specifically, sciences which have to be known as human or cultural sciences) should gain a great deal through an understanding of the function of typal relevance. Understanding and knowing cannot be equated with amassed facts. The truth of this claim is clearly supported by evidence drawn from the study of the system of typal relevancy as it performs its unique structuring functions on human action. Examples of this special relevancy matrix and its uses in adult education include planning learning projects for oneself and for other adults and constructing the most relevant curriculum for achieving certain ends. The functioning of typal relevancy, for example, 'obviates the need to incorporate definitive and prescriptive formulations such as coping skills curricula'.[15]

## Paradigmal Relevance

This form of relevancy carries the relevancy matrix through to the constitution of a model, and in the case of human action through to the performance of an action measured in terms of a model action, or what Austin has called the 'natural successful act.' Surely this is the hoped-for paradigm, what the adult learner, for example, aims at, in all learning producing meaning. Following a passage in which he asks what 'an action' is, Austin writes of the 'natural successful act' in this way:

> In two main ways the *study of excuses* can throw light on these fundamental matters. First, to examine excuses is to examine cases where there has been some *abnormality or failure;* and as so often, the abnormal will throw some light on the normal, will help us to penetrate the blinding veil of ease and obviousness that hides the mechanisms of the *natural successful act.* It rapidly becomes plain that the breakdowns signalized by the various excuses are of radically different kinds, affecting different parts or stages of the machinery, which excuses consequently pick out and sort out for us.[16]

In everyday situations, under quite normal circumstances, we come to know typical actions and acts. Many are paradigmal actions and acts: if performed, each of these is a natural successful act. We offer *excuses* for failing to perform them, or to perform them well, and these acts of excusing provide a plethora of examples. When we offer an excuse for having failed we understand this failure not simply as a failing to perform conformatively to the typical act in an other than similar way. We know that we have failed, and offering an excuse is to invoke a system of paradigmal relevancy. Of course, the other person to whom the excuse is offered has also invoked a paradigmal relevancy system. Are they the same? Sometimes. And when?

The natural successful action and the natural successful act have become models, or paradigms of actions and acts, and thus a system of relevance has been imposed. It has been founded upon our stock of feelings, experience, and knowledge. The relevancy matrix of this system provides the way for exploring phenomenologically the constitutions of the natural successful act, and departures and deviations from these within the everyday world. Examples of paradigmal relevancy at work are provided through the study of autobiographies of persons, and even the accounts of business corporations, whose activities mark them generally as having succeeded or failed in carrying through projects within 'everydayness.' Their reasons, excuses, and justifications are instructive to the rest of us. The originations of our goals and the beginnings of our attempts to reach these almost routinely are founded in our perceptions of those persons and their successes and failures. An excellent example of paradigmal relevancy is Husserl's claim (discussed in Part II) that no matter what the evidence is and what the experiments have shown concerning something alleged to be true, each person must finally 'justify' this truth 'by a perfect insight' of one's own.

## Summary

Each of these five systems of relevancy has been discussed briefly in its explicit expression, but each has its rootage within the primal, radical and pre-reflective constitutions of the everyday world. These are tacitly operative from the early moments of a person's life. Therefore, each has both tacit and explicit, and degrees and kinds of, constitutions which may be investigated phenomenologically.

These are already imposed in some degree and in varying forms upon a person by the social system. They are already felt and experienced early by a person. They are system-like in the earliest stages, although they are not known to be systematic by a person in those very first incipient stages.

Relevancy shifts, or shifts among the differing carriers of the matrices of relevance, occur. The movement from the most tacit to the ever more explicit comes as nodal points of actions shaped within the matrices; first one swelling, so to speak, and then another, etc. These explicitizings of the nascent stages come to be written in larger terms, and indelibly, within the life-activities of persons. And the ontological autobiography --the real and genuine story of one's life--carries with it the sedimenting layers of the stocks of feeling, experiencing, and reflecting. It goes on repeatedly in the person. We motivate our goals and they motivate us in spiral fashion. The shifts occur within the everyday world at differing times for various persons. Phenomenological descriptions of these shifts must be obtained within a phenomenology of the adult eductive actions of **person** through study of the expressions of persons. These kinds of descriptions can be provided by philosophy as phenomenology, and also by phenomenological approaches to the human, social and cultural sciences. I have discussed them here, however, for their crucial significance for adult learning and teaching.

A brief story may be helpful. I carry a flashlight to light the path as I walk through our woods of an evening. Sometimes the light bobs at random, following loosely the tentative rhythm of my gait. Light is cast upon the ground, upon the trunks of trees, foliage, brush piles, piled-up firewood, the occasional small animal, even upon Kahlua, our Chespeake Bay Retriever, as she accompanies me. At other times the light is directed intentionally. A lighted place appears. In any case the light is the matrix of relevancy which channels, fashions, and impresses my perception of the lighted places in the woods. Each directed action of the flash-light's lighting-up of a roughly determinate place is a relevancy system at work. It would be difficult (impossible?) to offer an accurate 'causal' account of why it happens precisely in the ways in which it does. Relevancy systems are focusing directionalities of the actions of persons apart from 'causally-determined' directions given somehow to or from the mind or consciousness. Perhaps it would be more accurate--and certainly more parsimonious--to say that relevancy systems are the explicit directionalities of a person's vital life through inquiry, care, and service within the world. Ortega would have preferred this less entity-laden formulation of what relevancy systems are and how we executively live, vitally move, and create our being through them. Many relevancy systems, each one laying on its own customizing version of the relevancy matrix of personal action and lying ready for use in negotiations and transactions with the world, are always with each person. They are all with each of us as part of the stock of our feeling, our experience, and our consciousing.

There are at least two ways in which phenomenology investigates relevancies, relevancy systems, and human actions. These are the ways of (a) the *constitution of structures* of human actions and (b) the *eduction of structures* of human actions. It might be more appropriate to speak not so much of two *ways* of phenomenology as of two distinct *kinds* of phenomenology, or of two distinct *functions* of any phenomenological investigation. I prefer the latter alternative.

## (a) The Constitutive Function of Phenomenology[17]

Each ingredient constituting the relevancy matrix at work in the world as directed through any system of relevancy fashioning human action(s) may be explored *backward* through the steadily more primal, radical stages--rooted stages--phases, or stretches of its constitution in the midst of circumstances in varied situations. In this way one explores back through beginnings and originations. In what ways did each ingredient come to be what it is now as it becomes the intuited and focused object of reflection? Constitutive phenomenological investigation is the investigation of the *increasingly more tacit* stages of the constitution of each ingredient at work. I believe that it was principally this kind of investigation which was the central feature of Schutz's reflections on the phenomenon of relevance. His work was based in the early Husserlian constitutive phenomenology. However, Schutz's work consisted primarily of reflections on the natural attitude of the normal wide-awake adult in the everyday world, whereas Husserl's earlier investigations were of the transcendental sort. This is the reason why Schutz's phenomenology is more quickly and easily usable in adult education as a rigorous human science. But Husserl's more fundamental investigations will prove ultimately to be more valuable.

This function of phenomenological investigation and research is fundamental to research, programming, and curricula in adult education because it articulates the ground and foundation of particularized and unique themes, subjects, problems, and structures. It investigates the ways in which unique cases came to be what they are.[18]

## (b) The Eductive Function of Phenomenology[19]

The ingredients of the relevancy matrix carried by each system of relevance at work in the course of human action may be investigated in continuing minute detail. The movement is forward movement, creative movement, willful, purposive movement. It is the forward-building movement of adults' planned projects and operations. The emphasis here would be placed upon the processes of drawing forth, upon the ways of parts becoming wholes,

upon the ways of bringing forth something out of something else; or of eliciting meanings and values. This
kind of reflection is performed by clarifying all of
these ingredients and their processes through the
stages, phases and stretches of their development out of
the varied conditions of their rudimentary, latent, and
tacit, or even their merely potential or possible existence. This is the investigation of the adult eductions
of **person**.

This other function of phenomenological investigation
and research is equally fundamental to research, programs of action and curricula in adult education in that
it may be used to explore plans, goals, purposes, ends,
hopes, aspirations--even self-help intentions--of persons. Both constitutive phenomenology and eductive
phenomenology may be used to investigate the richly
varied ways in which these formative questions come
through the 'everydayness' of our lifeworlds and the
ways in which we come to meaningful answers to them:

**Who Am I?**
>**What Can I Know?**
>>**What Should I Do?**
>>>**What May I Hope?**

There are additional reasons why these relevancy
systems are of great importance in adult learning and
teaching. I discuss some of these reasons in the next
chapter.

# Chapter 6

## Languages of Relevancies and
## Disciplines of Practice

I have stated that relevance is perspective in and of
the world. It both emerges from and in turn fashions
our selections from within the 'everydayness' of our
lifeworld. Relevance is literally a looking-through the
'everydayness' of our lifeworld, a looking-through which
takes time and space, and it is constituted in terms of
the relating and ordering importance of the ingredients
of our lifeworld. A system of relevance is an articulation of the *contexture* of the relative and ordering
importance of the ingredients of our lifeworld from a
point of view.

Ortega claimed that every person is a point of view
and thereby has a perspective on life. He claimed that
everyone takes a different perspective in looking at
matters, and that everything may be looked at from an
infinite variety of perspectives, both in the sense that
an indefinite number of people will have an indefinite
number of perspectives and that each person may also
look upon any object of consciousness from an indeterminate number of perspectives.

All of this begins to suggest how complex are the
phenomena which persons--and especially adults, in the
light of their temporally more complete grasps of the
objects of their conscious lives[1]--present for investigation. These investigations, remember, may be *personal* ones like the search for ways of fulfilling

dreams and aspirations, ridding oneself of fears and destructive habits through the replacement of positive, life-regenerative goals and new habits as ways of achieving these. These investigations may also be those of *groups*. In both of these cases the investigations in some degree are likely to be planned as shared and cooperative goals. Even the most solitary lives require some degree of sharing and cooperation, whether this be primarily, or be limited to, the common use of a common language with attendant concepts and meanings.

These investigations may also be those characteristic of *research programs* and research projects, although research would have to be very carefully characterized in non-reductive, intersubjective, and non-biased ways. This is the manner in which research ought to be characterized and the manner in which I have presented it throughout this essay.[2]

In any event it seems to me that although Ortega has arched an arrow toward the proper target he has not aimed it at the center point. It is not simply the case that each person is a point of view or a particular perspective. The more accurate description, it seems to me, is that each person is a center (a centering?) of an indeterminate number of perspectives in, of, and through the world. This means that each person is a center of relevance. From time to time a person both selects (and to some degree is selected by) a system of relevancy from among many of those available, depending on what sorts of actions the person wants to perform. That is the person's point of view, and perhaps it could be said with Ortega then that a person is a point of view. But this relevance must be the relevance-of something.

A person brings relevance to bear within situations which have to some degree become problematicized--that is, situations which have become problematic to some degree and within which specific problems have arisen. This means that the structure of relevance requires that there be both a person (or persons) and something of interest or something attended-to by these persons. Our feelings, our experiencings, and our consciousings attest the presence together of these ingredients. The usual ways in which these feelings and the rest are brought to more explicit presence in our consciousness and shared with other persons, of course, are the ways of languages.

The relevancies and relevancy systems discussed in the previous chapter included, in order, etymological, syntactical, descriptive, typal, and paradigmal systems, with each of these exercising a unique structuring matrix itself uniquely bringing together a person (or persons) and an object of consciousness and thus selected ingredients within the 'everydayness' of the life-world. My identification of these systems has risen out of my studies of language especially, and the particular uses of language in relation to human action and acts. There are countless uses of language, as these classic passages in Ludwig Wittgenstein's *Philosophical Investigations* superbly suggest:

> 23. But how many kinds of sentence are there? Say assertion, question, and command?--There are *countless* kinds: countless different kinds of use of what we call 'symbols,' 'words,' 'sentences.' And this multiplicity is not something fixed, given once for all; but new types of language, new language-games, as we may say, come into existence, and others become obsolete and get forgotten. (We can get a *rough picture* of this from the changes in mathematics.)
>
> Here the term 'language-**game**' is meant to bring into prominence the fact that the *speaking* of language is part of an activity, or of a form of life.
>
> Review the multiplicity of language-games in the following examples, and in others:
>
> Giving orders, and obeying them--
>
> Describing the appearance of an object, or giving its measurements--
>
> Constructing an object from a description (a drawing)--

Reporting an event--
Speculating about an event--
Forming and testing a hypothesis--
Presenting the results of an experiment in tables and diagrams--
Making up a story; and reading it--
Play-acting--
Singing catches--
Guessing riddles--
Making a joke; telling it--
Solving a problem in practical arithmetic--
Translating from one language into another--
Asking, thanking, cursing, greeting, praying.
--It is interesting to compare the multiplicity of the tools in language and of the ways they are used, the multiplicity of kinds of word and sentence, with what logicians have said about the structure of language. (Including the author of the *Tractatus Logico-Philosophicus.*)

43. For a *large* class of cases--though not for all--in which we employ the word 'meaning' it can be defined thus: the meaning of a word is its use in the language.

And the *meaning* of a name is sometimes explained by pointing to its *bearer.*

65. Here we come up against the great question that lies behind all these considerations.--For someone might object against me: 'You take the easy way out! You talk about all sorts of language-games, but have nowhere said what the essence of a language-game, and hence of language, is: what is common to all these activities, and what makes them into language or parts of language. So you let yourself off the very part of the investigation that once gave you yourself most headache, the part about the *general form of propositions* and of language.'

And this is true.--Instead of producing something common to all that we call language, I am saying that these phenomena have no one thing in common which makes us use the same word for all,

216 / Languages and Disciplines of Practice

--but that they are *related* to one another in many different ways. And it is because of this relationship, or these relationships, that we call them all 'language.' I will try to explain this.

66. Consider for example the proceedings that we call 'games.' I mean board-games, card-games, ball-games, Olympic games, and so on. What is common to them all?--Don't say: 'There *must* be something common, or they would not be called "games"'--but *look and see* whether there is anything common to all.--For if you look at them you will not see something that is common to *all*, but similarities, relationships, and a whole series of them at that. To repeat: don't think, but look!--Look for example at board-games, with their multifarious relationships. Now pass to card-games; here you find many correspondences with the first group, but many common features drop out, and others appear. When we pass next to ball-games, much that is common is retained, but much is lost.--Are they all 'amusing'? Compare chess with noughts and crosses. Or is there always winning and losing, or competition between players? Think of patience. In ball games there is winning and losing; but when a child throws his ball at the wall and catches again, this feature has disappeared. Look at the parts played by skill and luck; and at the difference between skill in chess and skill in tennis. Think now of games like ring-a-ring-of-roses; here is the element of amusement, but how many other characteristic features have disappeared! And we can go through the many, many other groups of games in the same way; can see how similarities crop up and disappear.

And the result of this examination is: we see a complicated network of similarities overlapping and criss-crossing: sometimes overall similarities, sometimes similarities of detail.

67. I can think of no better expression to characterize these similarities than 'family resemblances'.[3]

Recall that *relevance* is perspective in, of, and through the world. It is literally a looking-through the world, a process taking place and time and constituted in terms of the relative priority and ordering importance of the ingredients of the world from a person's point of view. A *system of relevance* is a way through which the relative priority and ordering importance of the ingredients of the world are presented as fashioned and structured. Actually a system of relevancy is a point of view. Each system--each origination, beginning, and channeling effected through relevancy--is presented through the medium of a matrix of relatings manifesting themselves in degrees and kinds of phenomena in their presentation and expression from the most tacit through the most explicit constitution. I have called this matrix the relevancy matrix of human action, and have presented the contents of this matrix of relevancy, contents which are applicable in every case of relevancy as operative in our lives.

In the previous chapter I claimed that each of the five relevancy systems (and another very special instance of a relevancy system to be discussed in Chapter 8, metaphorical relevancy) is of the greatest importance in the philosophical investigation of adult learning and education. I presented a number of reasons there why this is so, and I now offer additional reasons in support of this claim.

*Etymological relevancy* functions in the case of every word, and the use of every word which carries with it its own history. This form of relevancy is in fact the historicity of conventionally useful and 'right' usages of words over a period of time, and often over very long periods of time. As Austin pointed out, '. . . our common stock of words embodies all the distinctions men have found worth drawing, and the connections they have found worth making, in the lifetimes of many generations: these surely are likely to be more numerous, more sound, since they have stood up to the long test of the survival of the fittest, and more subtle, at least in all ordinary and reasonably practical matters.' Our continuing uses of words and concepts chosen from this long-standing and well stocked reservoir is significant in our planning who we are and in our projections of the persons we hope to become. As teachers we use special words and concepts in teaching and in helping others as well, and in fact the content of what we say and our ways of saying this are modeled in terms of some concepts as root metaphors, or special guiding principles of the utmost importance, and of much greater significance than others we use.

*Syntactical relevancy* is always in position and functioning within the arrangement and interrelationships of phrases and sentences within the languages we use. Clearly, as we use our language in the great variety of ways barely touched upon even in those rich passages from Wittgenstein through the fusion of etymological histories and the myriad of possible ways of phrasing we literally do 'sentence' ourselves in concrete ways within our 'everydayness.'

Of all the possible uses of languages, probably the most pervasive is the use of language as descriptive of something. *Descriptive relevancy* is central and decisive. It is in place and functioning whenever we selectively attend-to something through our conscious life and try to say what it is. This descriptive use of language presupposes a framework of words, concepts, and rules of language (in addition to the etymologies and syntactical structures) through which less familiar or unfamiliar phenomena are positioned within familiar phenomena and structure of phenomena. Descriptive relevancy functions whenever we attempt to understand and to explain something satisfactorily 'to ourselves' or to other persons. However it is that our attention turns to some object in the world of consciousness, our descriptions can only be at best selective. But our selections in these ways also carry us forward, through specific adult eductions of our **person** and expressions of the persons we are and become.

*Typal relevancy* is the building of structures, types, classes, categories, and kinds of actions of thinking which form the basics of all similarities, likenesses, resemblances, and exemplars of human actions within the 'everydayness' of the lifeworld. These are the contours of 'everydayness'--personal measurings and plumbings of the breadth and depth of our lives--as we move through 'everydayness' and into and through our personal and professional lives hoping to make it all somehow more productive and more pleasurable.

*Paradigmal relevancy* functions as a bench mark of human actions, as what Austin termed 'the natural successful act.' We know that we succeed or fail in terms of our own structures of models of success and failure, even if other persons have their own models of success and failure and apply them to us. Accordingly, through our language (which is rich in these kinds of words) we excuse, justify, and give reasons for what we do and do not do in accordance with measures of deviation from what we feel, believe, or think we ought to do through that special point of view which paradigmal relevancy is.

In brief form I have shown how these relevancy systems are inescapably tied into language uses. The centrality of relevancy systems in language uses is one of the reasons why these relevancy systems are of the greatest importance to phenomenological investigations in adult learning and education.

One of the most fundamental adult eductions of **person** is the matrix of the degree and kind of language use in structuring and re-structuring the adult lifeworld. Examples abound. Adults are expected: to use the language more responsibly; to be more assertive to a clear purpose; to supply the justification for, and perhaps say the price exacted for, the issuance and acceptance of orders and commands; in making promises to keep them (both performatively, in the sense that 'making' and 'keeping' here are both performances of **person**) to understand with richer meaning the plethora of symbols, words, meanings, and all of the activities of language which make up Wittgenstein's 'language games'. In short, language and the speaking of language is a form of life or **person**. As Wittgenstein further claimed, 'the meaning of a word is its use in the language,' and it is possible to go on to say that the world as meaningful is pivotally dependent upon one's uses of languages, via the structurings of relevancy systems, in constructing the world of our everyday uses. Three major uses of language of special importance should be distinguished.

**Literal Expression**

The term 'literal' is derived from the Latin **litteralis**, or letter, as pertaining to the letters of the alphabet, or to the nature of letters, the alphabetical letters, or especially to the written word, e.g., to what someone actually wrote in a letter to someone else. The term was invoked to refer to the original text from which a scribe, in copying, might have departed such that misprints, or departures from the letter of the text, came to be recorded. In mathematical notation and computation, there developed a literal computation, or a text of letters, as distinct from the numerical text. In the translation of earlier texts, the literal text is always the original text, or the earliest extant version, or typescript of the letter of the text. The literal text would be the very words of the original, if possible, or the verbally exact words of the text.

A clear example can be drawn from the tradition of biblical exegesis. The literal pertains to the letter (or the scriptures); it is that sense of the interpretation of a text which is obtained by taking the words of the text in their natural or customary meaning, and by applying the ordinary rules of grammar in determining what meaning is expressed. The literal can also be obtained partially through the investigation of etymologies, or the relatively primary 'right' uses of the senses of words over many years, or to the sense expressed by the actual wording of passages as distinguished from any merely suggested meanings.

But how can a feeling be separated out of the flow of feeling which **person** is at one early stage and be named or captured conceptually, by the language of literal expression? We sometimes speak of a feeling as a 'familiar feeling', but a feeling as just-arising is always new and unnamed, and perhaps unnameable. But we keep trying to render them familiar, and principally through naming them. Moreover, the naming comes at a later stage, the consciousing stage of **person**. The first-arising and new, unfamiliar feeling, however, is a jolt to the familiarities of literal expression. It catches us, if not 'speechless', at least 'nameless.' And without the special power in the world which naming gives to the one who names, the less transformed and empowered that person is. Again, Paulo Freire's approach to literacy constitutes a clear example of this point: 'There is no true word that is not at the same time **praxis**. Thus, to speak a true word is to transform the world.'[4]

## Technical Expression

Technical expressions are used to specify particular subject-matters, and to do so within strictly limited parameters. They deal with the particular, the practical, and the procedural. Technical expressions are applied expressions, strictly applied words, terms, and senses. The technical expression makes possible the scientific precision, or it is the special language which expresses the orderly and systematic investigations of determinate subject-matter. Sciences generally are characterized not only by certain presuppositions of precise method (including their historically developing presuppositions and methods), but also by their technical symbolisms or special languages. And the technical languages of each of the special sciences are historically tempered as well. Investigations carried through without the use of technical expressions would be no science properly so-called. This was a major point in Dewey's account of scientific inquiry. But the free use of technical terms, or expressions simply not found within natural and ordinary language allows investigations to proceed with greater precision and rigor along systematic scientific lines.

The special terms of logic, of mathematics, and the expressions found on the standard periodic table in chemistry, for example, are not found normally in ordinary language usage. These have uniquely precise functions. Specialists constructed them for particular use, within given procedures and methods formulated to arrive at certain ends. These are to be employed only under very carefully defined conditions (for example, as in 'verbal' as opposed to 'real' definition circumstances in logic). The terms are useful, but rigid and artificial within the normal usage for which they were developed. It is true, however, that specialists, say a mathematician, may master and use a certain symbolism, and thus be in command of a language which is like a natural language in that it acquires the virtual emotional force of natural language for that person. Moreover, some technical symbolisms may be taken over by the natural language. Examples of this are words like 'stress' and much of the technical terminology of psychoanalysis. Technical terms drawn from computer technology already abound in our common languages.

## Figural Expression

A figure of any kind is the product of an activity of **figuring**. To figure is to form, to shape, to bring into shape, into some specifiable form, perhaps in terms of a diagram or picture. In speech or action, to figure is to portray, or represent, or perhaps to be an image, a symbol, type, or to represent typically. To figure is to display the form of; to exhibit a resemblance to; to represent as resembling, to liken one thing to another. 'Figure' has very wide uses, for example, within mathematics and in money transactions. In dancing, also, figures play an important part.

All language **figures**. Discourse figures, as does writing. The phrase, 'a figure of speech', in the light of this description of figuring activity, should be somewhat clearer. I suggest that we distinguish (1) 'figural language' to label what I have just described, and (2) 'configural language' to label what metaphors more accurately are and do. The languages of relevancies and the relevancies of languages go hand in hand. And not simply as our natural languages which we have been required to learn by the happenstance circumstances of the time and place of birth.

Much can be made of the fact that another of the adult eductions of **person**, in addition to adults' more and more responsible uses of natural languages, is that language sometimes fails the adult at the juncture of the 'jolt' of unfamiliar feelings. There is the celebrated adult loss of the innocence of childhood, especially of early childhood, when no penalty was exacted for being wrong in naming and expressing one's feelings. Adults often pay a high price for being wrong in naming their feelings inaccurately and by acting in the light of those inaccurately identified feelings.

But not being able to express one's **person** in acceptable oral and written language form exacts further tolls also. This point is clearly evidenced by the numbers of entirely illiterate, and by even larger numbers of functionally illiterate, persons throughout the world, even in the most technologically advanced nations such as the United States. Illiteracy as the inability to express in wider social and cultural ways the products of one's thoughts surely is co-related with a person's life as poorer, more solitary, more lonely, more brutish, and shorter than the successful use of literal language always should make possible. The conditions of persons occasioning the large-scale literacy programs of Paulo Freire offer clear testimony on all of these counts for both the adult learner and the adult educator.

Moreover, much of an adult's professional life consists of acquiring technical languages as disciplines fashioning successful professional and vocational lives. Persons as professionals discipline their **person**, especially in burgeoning technological lifeworlds, through the acquisition of, and their efficient and successful employment of, more and more technical languages. Is it necessary to evidence this point any further than merely to cite randomly such written (but not oral) languages as Fortran, PL1, RPG, Cobol, MBasic, Pascal, Assembler, and so on? Or the 'languages of nature' such as physics, chemistry, and biology, and the 'universal language' of mathematics?

New perspectives rarely are constructed, invented, created or discovered through the use of literal language or technical language. A technical expression, for example, provides a language for expressing what given phenomena are already considered to be, although a person might try to refer to something as newly conscioused, for example, as discovered, created, invented, or constructed. The proper function and use of technical expressions is that of serving us in deepening our capacities and our possibilities for re-experiencing the already familiar and in doing it possibly through the predication of something else of the already-discovered view. But technical language remains language whose most unique use and purpose is more precise delimitation of phenomena already discovered, not for use in naming their process of coming to birth.

## Figural and Configural Expression

New perspectives are ubiquitously bursts, jolts, suddennesses of consciousings of **person** within persons. They are notoriously metaphors at work. I discuss metaphors as bursts of new perspectives in consciousings in Chapter 8. Here I wish to note briefly the arena within which metaphors function. This stage is the work of what I term 'figural' and especially 'configural' expression. It is seminal movement for the adult learner, a veritable rite of passage into further, much richer and deeper, reaches of learning through restructuring, reordering, refashioning the everyday world through the sudden rise of new perspectives. These make possible the transformations and new empowerments of life effected via the surrender of one's **person** to the catchings of metaphor first staged as 'figural' and 'configural' language.

# PART V

## Philosophy:
## Learning and Practicing the Love of Wisdom

*After experience had taught me that all the usual surroundings of social life are vain and futile; seeing that none of the objects of my fears contained in themselves anything either good or bad, except in so far as the mind is affected by them, I finally resolved to inquire whether there might be some real good having power to communicate itself, which would affect the mind singly, to the exclusion of all else: whether, in fact, there might be anything of which the discovery and attainment would enable me to enjoy continuous, supreme, and unending happiness. I say 'I finally resolved,' for at first sight it seemed unwise willingly to lose hold on what was sure for the sake of something then uncertain. I could see the benefits which are acquired through fame and riches, and that I should be obliged to abandon the quest of such objects, if I seriously devoted myself to the search for something different and new. I perceived that if true happiness chanced to be placed in the former I should necessarily miss it; while if, on the other hand, it were not so placed, and I gave them my whole attention, I should equally fail.*

*I therefore debated whether it would not be possible to arrive at the new principle, or at any rate at a certainty concerning its existence, without changing the conduct and usual plan of my life; with this end in view I made many efforts, but in vain. For the ordinary surroundings of life which are esteemed by men (as their actions testify) to be the highest good, may be classed under the three heads-- Riches, Fame, and the Pleasures of Sense: with these three the mind is so absorbed that it has little power to reflect on any different good. By sensual pleasure the mind is enthralled to the extent of quiescence, as if the supreme good were actually attained, so that it is quite incapable of thinking of any other object; when such pleasure has been gratified it is followed by extreme melancholy, whereby the mind, though not enthralled, is disturbed and dulled.*

*The pursuit of honors and riches is likewise very absorbing, especially if such objects be sought simply for their own sake, inasmuch as they are then supposed to constitute the highest good. In the case of fame the mind is still more absorbed, for fame is conceived as always good for its own sake, and as the ultimate end to which all actions are directed. Further, the attainment of riches and fame is not followed as in the case of sensual pleasures by repentance, but, the more we acquire, the greater is our delight, and, consequently, the more are we incited to increase both the one and the other; on the other hand, if our hopes happen to be frustrated we are plunged into the deepest sadness. Fame has the further drawback that it compels its votaries to order their lives according to the opinions of their fellow-men, shunning what they usually shun, and seeking what they usually seek.*

*When I saw that all these ordinary objects of desire would be obstacles in the way of a search* for something different and new--nay, that they were so opposed thereto, that either they or it would have to be abandoned, I was forced to inquire which would prove the most useful to me: for, as I say, I seemed to be willingly losing hold on a sure good for the sake of something uncertain. However, after I had reflected on the matter, I came in the first place to the conclusion that by abandoning the ordinary objects of pursuit, and betaking myself to a new quest, I should be leaving a good, uncertain by reason of its own nature, as may be gathered from what has been said, for the sake of a good not uncertain in its nature (for I sought for a fixed good), but only in the possibility of its attainment.

Further reflection convinced me, that if I could really get to the root of the matter I should be leaving certain evils for a certain good. I thus perceived that I was in a state of great peril, and I compelled myself to seek with all my strength for a remedy, however uncertain it might be; as a sick man struggling with a deadly disease, when he sees that death will surely be upon him unless a remedy be found, is compelled to seek such a remedy with all his strength, inasmuch as his whole hope lies therein. All the objects pursued by the multitude not only bring no remedy that tends to preserve our being, but even act as hindrances, causing the death not seldom of those who possess them, and always of those who are possessed by them. There are many examples of men who have suffered persecution even to death for the sake of their riches, and of men who in pursuit of wealth have exposed themselves to so many dangers, that they have paid away their life as a penalty for their folly. Examples are no less numerous of men, who have endured the utmost wretchedness for the sake of gaining or preserving their reputation. Lastly, there are innumerable cases of men, who

> *have hastened their death through over-indulgence in sensual pleasure. All these evils seem to have arisen from the fact, that happiness or unhappiness is made wholly to depend on the quality of the object which we love. When a thing is not loved, no quarrels will arise concerning it--no sadness will be felt if it perishes--no envy if it is possessed by another--no fear, no hatred, in short no disturbances of the mind. All these arise from the love of what is perishable, such as the objects already mentioned. But love towards a thing eternal and infinite feeds the mind wholly with joy, and is itself unmingled with any sadness, wherefore it is greatly to be desired and sought for with all our strength.*

> --Benedict de Spinoza, *The Improvement of the Understanding*[1]

## Introductory Remarks

Once upon a time, through wonder, the message of love was born in the midst of chaos, confusion, and the scatterings of the un-wisdoms of the world. Wisdom was born in and through the markings left along the journeys which some persons--very few persons--have risked. These personal journeys have moved through the concrete feelings, experiencings, reflectings, and meditatings along the pathways of our routine personal lifeworlds. Routine and mundane worlds they are, yes, but worlds still so solitary, nasty, brutish, barbarian, violent, poor, and short for most of the people of the world.

I, a lover, that is, a philosopher, speak of wisdom. If you ask me what philosophy is literally, the reply properly is that *philosophy is the love of wisdom.* But to say that philosophy is the love of wisdom does not tell the story of its birth among persons or convey the full life of philosophy. The birth of philosophy as the love of wisdom is presented very fully and richly within the traditions of Greek mythive expression within the lives of the Greeks as they recorded their attempts to understand their world, to understand themselves, who they were, and what they were doing. The Greek myths were not simply stories, whether true or false, not merely superstitions. They were continuing attempts to construct and reconstruct worlds such that the lives of people might thereby be made more bearable.

We ought to take a look at some episodes within this tradition of myth and symbolism as we try to say more precisely what philosophy is and what it does within the processes of adult education. Plato, through the dramatic, charismatic person of Socrates, often explored the meaning and the values of knowledge and the adult educative process. One of the most famous dialogues in which he did this was called the *Theaetetus,* the dialogue in which Socrates-Plato analyzed a number of possible answers to the question, what is knowledge?[2] One of the persons in the dialogue, Theodorous, tells Socrates that he has become acquainted with a 'remarkable Athenian youth, one whom I commend to you as well worthy of your . . . attention . . . you must not be offended if I say that he is very like you; for he has a snub nose and projecting eyes.'[3] All Athenians knew that these features, among others, distinguished Socrates as an ugly man; so Theaetetus was described as ugly, although not quite so ugly as Socrates. Still, and much more important, Theaetetus was introduced to Socrates, and he proved to be a very bright young man.

Later in the same dialogue, Socrates says: 'I see, my dear Theaetetus, that Theodorous had a true insight into your nature when he said that you were a philosopher, for wonder is the feeling of a philosopher, and philosophy begins in wonder. He was not a bad genealogist [gatherer of roots of persons and their commitments, you may say] who said that Iris (the messenger of heaven) is the child of Thaumas (wonder).'[4]

Other sources also tell us that Iris was often the personification of philosophy, as the messenger from heaven, the personal message which is philosophy. As the personal message from the sources of deity, philosophy was born of Thaumas, was born of **wonder**.

But Iris also bore a son, according to some traditions, and the plot thickened a bit. This son was Eros. He was sometimes described as 'a wild boy who knew no respect for age or station, but flew about on golden wings shooting barbed arrows at random, or wantonly setting hearts on fire with his dreadful torches.'[5]

In our time, a time of *radical root-gathering*, a time of coming to know who we are partly through coming to know who our ancestors were, and what their times were like, we have a tradition of the roots of western philosophy. Thaumas, Iris, and Eros. Wonder, messenger, love, even erotic love. Then we note that philosophy is the love of wisdom. What do wonder, messengers, and erotic love have to do with a whole lifeworld of questions to which the personifying deities, Thaumas, Iris, and Eros, were together a coherent, meaningful, and living response answering enough of those questions for the lives of the Greeks to be a bit more bearable each day? The Greeks faced problems, and these gods constituted a structuring and meaningful answer to enough of those problems and questions for this tradition of Thaumas giving birth and life to Iris, who in turn gave birth and life to Eros, to be an answer which has remained alive and viable as a myth into our own time.

In another of his most famous dialogues, the *Symposium*, Plato has Socrates confide to his close friends during a banquet and drinking occasion (although everyone else is asleep by the time Socrates speaks) that a stranger, a woman named Diotima, had once lectured him on the nature of love. She said

> . . . what if man had eyes to see the true beauty --the divine beauty, I mean, pure and clear and unalloyed, not clogged with the pollutions of mortality and all the colors and variations of human life--thither looking, and beholding conversation with the true beauty simple and divine? Remember how in that communion only, beholding beauty with the eye of the mind, he will be

enabled to bring forth, not images of beauty, but realities (for he has hold not of an image but of a reality), and bringing forth and nourishing true virtue to become the friend of God and be immortal, if mortal man may be. Would that be an ignoble life?

Such . . . were the words of Diotima; and I am persuaded of their truth. And being persuaded of them, I try to persuade others, that in the attainment of this end human nature will not easily find a helper better than love.[6]

Through wonder, a message of love, the love of wisdom: philosophy. As you all know from the minutest acquaintance with philosophy (perhaps through an anguishing experience with your first course in philosophy), there is a very old tradition that philosophers are always in the clouds. There is the story that Thales, one of the first Greek philosophers, walked along the path one day unheeding of things around him, his head turned upward. He fell into a well, surely an embarrassment for that 'wisest of men,' as the elderly lady who helped him out of the well made clear to Thales.

Aristophanes wrote a play entitled the *Clouds*. It was a play depicting Socrates, his close friend and personal literary critic. Whenever it was performed in Athens Socrates was often in attendance. At appropriate times during the play, we are told, Socrates would stand up, bow, and receive the applause of the audience. Socrates was portrayed as always being in the clouds. The slightest acquaintance with any of Plato's dialogs proves such portrayals to be completely inaccurate, however.

Adult learners and adult educators rarely have the time, inclination, or willingness to drift within the clouds. I do want to argue, however, that when persons have their feet firmly planted on the ground as adults surely must, it is absolutely necessary that they sometimes speculate about what it all means, that they **wonder**, that they develop the message, send it by messenger, and commit themselves to it caringly--and if you will, commit themselves to it lovingly. In wonder messages are born. They are carried through in love. And love can only penetrate the lifeworlds of individual persons through the vital life of inquiry, care, and service.

## Chapter 7

## Toward a Phenomenology of Consciousing

### Introductory Remarks

Persons think primarily for the purpose of acting, or of doing something in their personal lifeworld. Their thinking and their acting together constitute the theory and the practice of their personal knowledge toward the furtherance of some relevant end or goal in their lives. All knowledge is at least some person's or persons'

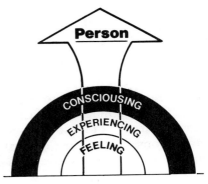

See n.3 in Notes to Table of Contents

personal knowledge, whatever additional intersubjective, and thereby public (or even, in a loose sense, 'objective') standing it may have in addition to its function as personal knowledge.[1]

I call this thinking for the purpose of achieving something in life, or thinking in order to perform any relevant action, **consciousing**. It is literally knowing-with or knowing-together. In phenomenological terms, no thought or episode of thinking is a mere thought, discrete, atomistic to itself, or apart from a continuity or stream of thinking. Moreover, every concrete act of thinking in this sense is thinking-of or thinking about. Thought always has 'thoughts' object'.[2] That is, every act of thinking has an object relevant to this act. Some of these objects, what is concretely thought, are material things which are a part of the furniture of our worlds, but most of these 'objects', each a 'thought-about,' are other than material things. They include all of mathematical thinking, most of the structurings constituting the sciences, our fabric of civility within a culture, and all personal dreams and aspirations as to what we as persons may do in order to change our lives, to name a few examples. Indeed, these non-material 'objects' comprise most of what the education of adults is all about. No doubt they include most of the more significant adult eductions of **person**. The most central ingredient of specific and unique instances of thinking-of some object of consciousness which may be the focus of investigation is the purpose, intent, resolution, and determination of a focused action of thinking.

In this chapter I shall (1) show how the neologism 'consciousing' serves to open up this process of thinking as phenomenologically described; (2) show that 'consciousing', or knowing-with, is at the same time to know something most essentially and to know it as a person who can now use this knowledge relevantly, or use it within systems of relevancy, that is to say use it purposefully, intentively, and with resolution and determination. Having this kind of knowledge is what it means to come to know something better and better and to know something in progressively clearer terms. Only then can well-informed and 'natural successful acts' (Austin) be planned and carried through. Finally, I shall show how an act of successful thinking toward the end of knowing and using something is itself a good act of conduct. The successful act of thinking and the good act of conduct have the same main ingredients which are evaluated by the same criteria.

This last claim has as much to say about logic as it does about ethics, and especially so in the context of adult education investigations. These investigations are most properly seen to constitute the most rigorous of human sciences with a special commitment to the systematic investigation of the special subject-matter of the adult eductions of **person**. In adult education, really to know is concretely to do, and to be transformed through the empowerments of personhood required in order to do still more, and this more successfully within the world.

## Being Conscious and Having a Consciousness

Consider the word 'conscious' in its etymological derivations. The Latin **conscius** means knowing something with others and knowing in oneself. In English, an obsolete usage is knowing, or sharing the knowledge of anything, together with another, or to be privy to anything with another (see Thomas Hobbes, *Leviathan*, I, vii, 'Where two, or more men, know of one and the same fact, they are said to be conscious of it one to another.'). And the phrase 'conscious to oneself' means having the witness within oneself, knowing within oneself, or being inwardly sensible, or aware. Hence it becomes possible to understand more clearly John Locke's passage (in *Essay Concerning Human Understanding*, II, i., section II): 'To be happy or miserable without being conscious of it seems to me utterly inconsistent and impossible.' Indeed so, since one's own witnessing of his being happy or miserable is at one and the same time that person's being happy, or that person's having identified a feeling as one of happiness or of misery. As Locke saw it these are not two separate and distinct acts or states of a person's being.

But there is another usage of the term 'conscious'. In this usage it refers to a person's endowment with the 'faculty' of consciousness, or to having one's 'mental faculties' actually in an active and waking state. How does this 'faculty of consciousness' slip in here in the context of a definition and characterization of the meaning of the term 'conscious'? Consciousness is supposedly a state or faculty of being conscious as a condition and concomitant of all thought, feeling, and volition, or the recognition by a thinking subject of its own acts or affections. Not surprisingly, but still illogically, the one concept is defined in terms of the other.

In attempting to render these two major usages of the term 'conscious' consistent it would appear that there is a dualism, for example, of being happy or miserable, to use Locke's example, and of either being or not being conscious of this happiness or misery. Locke denies the dualism against some philosophers who affirmed the dualism. I may be sitting in a chair which is set on the floor, without at some given instant being 'conscious' of the floor itself (although I could have become, or be, conscious of it at any time), but how would it be possible to be happy without at the same time witnessing, or being sensibly aware of, my being happy? Another person might count my behavior as 'happy', and conclude that I am happy, but another person's perception of my behavior is not at issue here.

Being happy and my consciousness *of* being happy are identical states of my **person** at one level of analysis. But being happy and being conscious *that* I am happy constitute (1) a state of my **person** and (2) an act of thinking by and about my **person**. The latter, the act of thinking, is reflexive and reflective. This analysis clarifies a central problem in adult education. In an adult's learning a new skill, for example, a form of this problem is that both the learning of the skill and the witnessing of this learning (within oneself) may take place without there being a judgment by the adult learner that this learning did in fact occur. The more definitively and exhaustively prescribed task-specific skills are, the less there will be this vital personal judgment necessary to 'learning'. Detailed 'how-to-do-it' manuals may be cases in point. Witness the adult learner's notorious (and rather surprising) reliance, in formal education contexts, upon instructors' evaluations and grades, and upon the positive reinforcements provided by the comments of professionals, experts, and specialists. The self-directed learner's case is different, of course, but the eductive processes of self-directed learning can also be clarified through the use of the notion of 'consciousing', as will be seen.

## Consciousing and the Process of Transformation

The neologism 'consciousing' is a way out of this tangle, and through the course of phenomenological analysis it provides a seminal entry into an essential structure in learning and adult education. The term 'consciousing' is constructed from the Latin, **con**, together, with + **scire**, to know. It is a present participial form which expresses a person's ongoing knowing-with, or knowing-together within the world. The use of this participial form renders it unnecessary to assume the apparent dualism of knowing something and also witnessing this knowing. The use of 'consciousing' also pre-empts any need to invoke the container notion of consciousness which is supposed to be able to 'catch up together' (what can never be caught up in fact as a unity of the moment) all of the acts of being conscious-of.

It is not the case that I am conscious-of something, although consciousing has its objects. Nor is it the case that something is *in* my consciousness. I simply *conscious*, or know-with the world. These claims are supported in the writings of philosopher José Ortega y Gasset, as the following passage clearly attests:

> The description which fits the phenomenon . . . will state that in a phenomenon of consciousness like perception we find the *coexistence of the I and the thing*, hence that this is not a matter of ideas or intentions but reality itself. So that in 'fact' perception is what there is: I, on the one hand being the thing perceived, and on the other, being myself; or, what is the same thing, that *there is no such* phenomenon as 'consciousness of . . .' as a general frame of mind. The reality is that I am reaching out and experiencing the reality of my

surroundings, and the presumed description of the phenomenon 'consciousness' resolves itself into a description of the phenomenon 'real human life,' which is the same *thing* as the coexistence of the I with surrounding things or circumstances. *The result, therefore, is that 'there is no' such thing as consciousness as a phenomenon, but that consciousness is a hypothesis, precisely the one which we inherited from Descartes.* Thus Husserl comes back to Descartes. . . .[3] (My emphasis)

The many ways in which I conscious something include, for example, purposing and planning, intending, resolving, and determining circumstances within situations in my everyday world. I conscious the world, having first felt it and then experienced it in terms of the relevantly attended-to ingredients of the world. I conscious it rather than find myself *being* conscious of it or *having* it in my consciousness. My consciousings, themselves already constituted of my feelings and my experiencings, may be expressed as descriptions of what I know, and of what I *know that I know* in progressively clearer forms. I feel the reality of my circumstances within situations. I experience these. These constitute my real and vital life, and they are, as Ortega claimed, 'the same thing as the coexistence of the I with surrounding things or circumstances.' I never do this all at once, and I never do it completely. I can only provide distinct and successive descriptions through always vital points of view, from time to time, from the perspectives of distinctive vantage points, from descriptions of circumstances in the situations in which I find myself within my lifeworld. And each of us may be said to conscious or to know-with our lifeworlds in this fashion according to our distinct operative frames of relevance.

In the light of the preceding discussion, I now want to show how any act of successful and therefore good thinking in this clarified sense of consciousing acts is at the time a good act of conduct. Recall that I said that this point has as much to say about logic as investigations into the normative thinking of persons as it does about ethics as investigations into the normative acting of persons. This is particularly so in the case of adult education when it is conceived as a rigorous human science committed to the systematic investigation of the determinate adult eductions of **person**. By both thinking and doing, adults may come both to possess and to have and hold in hand reasons which become their motives leading them into new lives.

Every person is born into already existing circumstances not yet his own. His life is born a vital life, a life coming to be executively lived through feelings, experiencings, and consciousings creating that person's unique and nonreplicable lifeworld. It is a life within community, a life of personal tastes, professions and vocations, ideals and goals, decisions rightly or wrongly constructed, successes and failures. A person's actions and conduct, founded in consciousings, are grounded in what is considered to be good and 'fine' (1.591).[4] If reflection is the basis of this conduct, then consistency of action is an ideal, and the conduct of persons is evaluated in the light of habits and of reasons which are the flesh of their goal-directed motivations and their planned activities.

Much of the substance and matter of this personal executivity in life, however, is founded in pre-existing stocks of mores, customs, and knowledge. Conformity to these already existing stocks of feelings and experiencings, for example, shapes one's evaluative moral and intellectual virtues. One 'intends' to act at least partially in respect to what one believes in the midst of the everyday personal world, and as William James maintained, beliefs themselves have emerging and motivating functions in our lives. But beliefs as ideals come to be virtual, and finally actualized, 'rules of conduct.' Perhaps they can even be labelled 'habits,' if unreflectively and uncritically so (1.592).

In the case of the particular form of consciousing which is the phenomenon of reflecting upon a specific possible course of action, one may 'consider that a special occasion is going to arise; thereupon, a certain gathering of [one's] forces will begin to work, and this working of [one's] being will cause [one] to consider how [one] will act (1.592).

One *resolves*, and looks toward a *determination* of a situation constituted through its circumstances. Feelings may be the nodules of resolution and determination of situations. But if so, they remain generally unfocused and unnamed at that nascent stage. They may be felt at this stage as generalized desire or need. At this stage they are not named this or that specific desire or need. Although themselves energizings, they are not reflectively focused upon, named or prioritized. The **consciousive**[5] actions of naming begin later.

Suppose this case. A woman in her 40s feels a desire or need to alter the main circumstances and direction of her life (1.594). Her decision to do something more with her life may evolve over a long period of time or it may be spontaneous, but it always occurs as situated, or within a situation, whether within or in a series of distinct situations, or spontaneously within a suddenly 'seen' and 'caught' situation within which she has surrendered herself.[6] But 'decision' at this stage in this case is too forceful and confining a term. It is too clearly a single stage--and this a stage of hard and fast cloiture--within a process of resolution. 'Resolve' is probably the more apt term. Her **person**, her personal being, is determined, but her determination in this moment is not causal. It is her determination. She is determined to act, although her way of ordering the alteration of circumstances within her situation is not a 'causal' ordering. Her determination is not reduced to 'causes' and effects in her past. She is adducing and evaluating reasons which either are or become (both?) her motives for changing the unique 'everydayness' of her life and her world.

'Resolving' becomes a process of actions seeking cloiture in her determination. She is thus determined. Each action within the continuity of her resolving is accompanied by a feeling or by feelings which are pleasurable. She is after all resolving to change her life with greater hope for the future, but this feeling of pleasure may not be consciousued as pleasurable at that time. It is too early in her resolution. Perhaps at a later date, as she looks back at the early stages of the resolution, she then consciouses that earlier feeling *now* as pleasurable (1.594).

This phenomenological analysis, following Charles Sanders Peirce's phenomenological account of the phenomenon of a planned action of importance, which is almost a kind of 'diagram', as he said,

> turns on the feeling of pleasure, and therefore, it is necessary, in order to judge it, to get at the facts about that feeling as accurately as we can. In beginning to perform any series of acts which had been determined upon beforehand, there is a certain sense of joy, an anticipation and a commencement of a relaxation of the tension of need which we now become more conscious of than we had been before. In the act itself taking place at any instant, it may be that we are conscious of pleasure, although that is doubtful. Before the series of acts are done, we already begin to review them, and in that review we recognize the pleasurable character of the feelings that accompanied those acts (1.595).

In the midst of her resolving, along the way and afterwards, the woman asks herself whether her determination is really what she wants, what she wants to do. Whether she judges that it is or that it is not, her judgments of her actions, her conduct toward a goal, are weighed on scales which are stipulations of her resolution (1.596). The answer to her question is 'accompanied, however, by a certain quality of feeling which is related' to these scales--a consciousced formula, as I would say--'very much as the color of the ink in which anything is printed is related to the sense of what is printed' (1.596).

> And just as we become aware of the peculiar color of the ink and afterward ask ourselves whether it is agreeable or not, so in formulating the judgment that the image of our conduct does

satisfy our previous resolution we are, in the very act of formulation, aware of a certain quality of *feeling,* the feeling of satisfaction --and directly afterward we recognize that that feeling was pleasurable (1.596).

But the housewife, who by now has labeled herself an 'adult learner' perhaps because some professional adult educator has termed her that in the midst of university extension courses, probes more deeply into her resolution and the changes being brought about in her life. Are these changes, these uniquely new determinations, in accord with her general resolution? Peirce claimed that with this kind of question 'again there will be a judgment and a feeling accompanying it, and directly afterward a recognition that that feeling was pleasurable or painful' (1.597).

The feeling accompanying this later judgment will be a lesser motivating feeling, will be less pleasure, than the outset of the resolution, 'but the feeling of satisfaction which is pleasurable will be different and, as we say, a *deeper* feeling' (1.597). But this adult learner may ask, further, 'how the image of [her] conduct accords with [her] ideals of conduct fitting to a [woman] like me' (1.598). The answer (a new judgment) will be accompanied by a 'feeling followed by a recognition of the pleasurable or painful character of that feeling' (1.598). Approval and disapproval in these judgments 'will bear fruit in the future,' and they move through the consciousings of her **person** as reasons becoming motives for her planned future conduct.

'In addition to these three self-criticisms of single series of actions' (1.599), the woman may review her ideals and beliefs, her network of beliefs as she knows them through the medium of her lifeworld within her community of 'consociates'[8] of most significance to her life. This review is a process, a reviewing over time, and these consciousing results will move first through her stock of feelings and her stock of experiencings before becoming consciousings properly so-called, or thoughts. This is meditation. Who am I really? What do I want most of all? Am I making a mistake in spending all of this time to bring acute changes into my life when I have no certainty about how it will all turn out?[9] But meditation, as Peirce claimed, 'seems to agitate a mass of tendencies and allow them more generally to settle down so as to be really more confined to what is fit for a [person]' (1.599). This is the central justification for meditation.

This personal meditation on what Peirce calls 'the fitness of one's own ideals,' however, could lead into, and have its practical nature grounded in, an assessment of the 'fitness' of her more ideal conduct. Are her resolution and its concrete determinations of the changes in her life of the kinds which they ought to have been? All of it could have been so different! Should the changes brought about by her resolve been effected to this degree? So massively? Judging this kind of question requires a more theoretical form rather than a more normally practical form of consciousing since it requires an examination of 'ideal conduct', her stipulations about the nature of 'ideal conduct' and the question of whether she did or did not conform to it in measurable ways.

## Concluding Remarks

Following Pierce's phenomenological leads I have tried to chart a somewhat typical case of some of the conscioused actions of an adult resolved to redirect her life for whatever reasons. This is a prime example of an adult eduction of **person**. Vocational and professional transformations of adults' lives obviously do not all occur in the manner I have described; many redirections erupt spontaneously and are more understandable as happenings in the midst of chance and random circumstances. But many such changes do in fact occur generally in the manner I have described. And if they occur as planned projects and projections the phenomenological description offered conforms even more closely. Even if not every case of an adult's radical transformation of perspective can be described in this way, the fact is that countless instances can still be understood in this general manner. One conclusion that can be drawn is that an arising feeling qua feeling merely appears and of itself produces no result, even indirectly (1.601).

I have woven together the phenomena of feelings and experiencings manifested in a fairly typical case among adult learners as they move through the transformations brought about by their newly acquired empowerments. And of course new empowerments are also brought about by transformations or changes in adult perspectives. I have made use of Charles Sanders Peirce's general phenomenological description of 'the typical phenomena of controlled action' (1.601). But his is not the end of it. Not only is it the case that the mere appearance of a feeling at one or another time does not of itself produce a result of any kind (since it just appears). Consciousings themselves--reasons on the way to becoming motives--are the foundations of persons' actions in order to achieve goals and ends in their lives. We are not 'caused' to do these things, a fact easily recognized by adult educators who reflect carefully on their work. We conscious these goals, we resolve, we determine them, and we act to achieve them in our lives. And frequently we need assistance in doing so.

This brief phenomenology of consciousing, however, clarifies a central structure for inclusion within the foundation of any philosophy of adult education committed to the investigation of phenomena of **person**. For a person to reason, really to reason--or to conscious, as I would prefer it--is for that person's life to change. And remember Feire's claim: 'Within the word we find two dimensions, reflection and action, in such radical interaction that if one is sacrificed--even in part--the other immediately suffers. There is no true word that is not at the same time a **praxis**. Thus, to speak a true word is to transform the world.' This genuine reasoning, this thinking and acting together with consistency--this consciousing or knowing-with--is in complete conformity with the central ingredients of one's moral conduct. All thinking goes on for the sake of acting. Peirce claimed that any act of good reasoning meant successful reasoning. In genuine reasoning which constructs possible avenues of actions, with some of them selected, all of the main elements of moral conduct are present.

> You see at once that we have here all the main elements of moral conduct; the general standards mentally conceived beforehand, the efficient agency in the inward nature, the act, the subsequent comparison of the act with the standard. Examining the phenomena more closely we should find that not a single element of moral conduct is unrepresented in reason (1.607).

Surely adult educators premise their vocational and professional lives on (among many things, doubtless) a commitment to adults becoming aware of what their lives could be like. What they 'could' become, however, is never strong enough to support the work of either the adult learner or the adult educator. Thus, an awareness of possibilities must give way through whatever agency to a person's felt and experienced values of what 'ought-to-be-in-my-life'. Even the possible or the 'could-be' is positioned for its meaning in the midst of an 'ought-to-be-in-my-life'. Thus the latter essential structure within **person** becomes a pulling rational force in an adult's life. Thinking well and acting well go irrevocably together, Pierce claimed. They are both assessed by the same cannons of evaluation. They fuse together in the consciousing processes. I know of no other mode of systematic investigation of the determinate adult eductions of **person** through which this might take place (and surely ought to!) than through adult education as a rigorous human science.

# Chapter 8

## 'Metaphorizing' Life: Felt Meanings and the Originative Language of Active Judgment

The time has come to bring together many of the points which have been developed in the book thus far. I shall do this briefly, and then show how these points are built into the philosophical foundations of adult education such that they concretely express many of the functions of adult learning as vitally, and with as much telling force, as, let's say, the central nervous system of persons both allows and limits the systematic expression of **person**. I do not invoke either a principle of reduction or a view of 'causal' determinism in employing this analogy. I use it only in order to point out the pivotal importance of both functions in their appropriate contexts.

As I have reflected on the principal claims I have tried to present, make clear, and evidence, I have been surprised by the emerging recognition that the functions of adult eductions of **person** which must be addressed always in the work of the adult educator, parallel the function of metaphors in expression. A strange suggestion! Therefore, I shall briefly present these claims as a kind of summary, lay out the rudiments of a theory of metaphor, and show how this parallel emerges. I speak of the emergent 'parallel' in terms which tend to fuse the two lines--the claims and the function of the metaphor in expression--as the 'metaphorization of life.'

A person is at least the expression of **person**. **Person** becomes the appropriate determinate subject-matter of the systematic investigations of adult education as a rigorous human science. These investigations, in accordance with phenomenological methods, disclose certain eductions of **person** which are characteristic of adults, or of what I have called adult eductions of **person**. A sufficient clustering of these in degree and kind constitute what I have termed the 'critical synthesis' of adult eductions of **person** as adult.[1] In the general case, these eductions are clustered together into phenomena constituting (at least for the purposes of this book, and this is just the beginning of it, in my view) what I term the 'FEC Structure', the 'HRM Structure', and the 'EvLV Structure'. Remember that the 'FEC Structure' addresses the question of *who* a person is. The 'HRM Structure' is a response to the question of what a person can *know*. The 'EvLV Structure' speaks always to the issue of what a person *ought to do*.[2]

The 'FEC Structure' is the general structure of the phenomena of person as feeling, experiencing, and consciousing, with the earlier phenomena flowing both naturally and logically into the latter. The 'HRM Structure' is the phenomena of **person** as habituations flowing through relevancy systems (largely pragmatic considerations which persons express as interests in goods, ends, purposes, and the like) operative in persons' lives into the expression of metaphor in language. But in this case metaphorical expression is life expression itself. The point is that one's life as lived is not very different from language alive and living to express this very life of **person**. This is the claim principally to be laid out in this chapter. The 'EvLV Structure' is the cluster of phenomena of adult eductions of **person** which can be termed the 'everydayness' of adult life, the adult language of vocational and professional lives, and the reasons and motives (reasons as motives and as **will**) realizing and actualizing concrete, vital personal life. This concrete, vital personal life is the freedom of persons which liberties give.

This is a brief statement of the philosophical claims presented so far. The question now is how these relate to metaphor and to what I call the 'metaphorization of life'. In answer to these questions it becomes necessary to discuss what a metaphor is. In doing this, I shall not work through all of the major theories of metaphor which philosophers and others have offered, or offer judgments about strengths and weaknesses of these theories as explanations of what metaphors are and do. I do cite a number of these theories in passing.

Before I move to a discussion of metaphor, however, I wish to discuss briefly the place of the 'role' theory of human behavior which has been current in the social sciences for more than three decades. Following this discussion my account of metaphor and 'metaphorizing life' will be thrown in much greater relief.

## Excursus on Role Theory

It is not surprising to find in the social sciences that human beings have become, allegedly for reasons of order and system in research investigations, *objects*. The 'objectification' of human beings finds a typical expression in the model of role playing. Although there has been wide agreement within the social sciences on the use of the concepts of role and role behavior in describing, interpreting, and explaining human behavior, there is perhaps even more widespread disagreement on the question of the meaning of roles and their use in predicting and controlling human behavior. Before presenting additional evidence for a model[3] of **person** which, unlike role-playing, is appropriate for persons (and hence much more relevant to all areas of adult education), I will discuss the role theory and point out a number of its inadequacies.

## Role Behavior

The term 'role' is borrowed from drama with respect to the functioning of the actors in the roles they play upon a stage.

For most purposes the conceptual unit of the social system is the role. The role is a sector of the individual actor's total system of action. It is the point of contact between the system of action of the individual actor and the social system. The individual then becomes a unity in the sense that he is a composite of various action units which in turn are roles in the relationships in which he is involved. . . . In each specific situation institutionalization exists when each actor in the situation does, and believes he should do, what the other actors whom he confronts believe he should do.[4]

In this context a role is a character in a drama assigned to someone or assumed by someone. The playwright and the director of the play prescribe the patterns of behavior to be assumed by the actor, and the actor is expected to create and project the greatest possible degree of credibility in that assignment. Roles express the drama, and all of the relevant matters of class, status, etc., are built into the articulations of the roles.

The term 'person' also comes from this context. **Personae** were masks employed in Greek drama by individual actors as tangible and explicit aids in depicting and portraying a certain role. It is no surprise, therefore, to find the social sciences today borrowing both terms from drama and employing 'role' as explicative of person.[5] No doubt the two belong together. To borrow one is necessarily to borrow both.

The fallacy of this transference, however, will be exposed shortly, but consider for a moment the use of role and role-behavior in the social sciences' model. The most formal role a person plays usually turns out to be a definition of one's profession or vocation, the essential function one fulfills in society, one's performance in structured living. It is based on 'a sector of the individual actor's total system of action,' according to Talcott Parsons and Edward Shils. It states one's formal interactions with other persons. A role is a unit (or a set of units) in the organization and integration of one's shared and sharing experiences. It is evidently a person's learned behavior as response in the light of what others expect one to be and to do. Roles are an organization of a person's behavior, the person's, and other persons', more organized conceptions of what one is expected to be and to do within the bounds of predictable behavior. Roles are unitized ingredients (a 'sector' of these) in a person's 'everydayness'. Moreover, roles are isolated ingredients of a person's repertoire of thoughts and actions, a specific few or many--depending on the breadth of the model used--selected from all possible ingredients ('the individual actor's total system of action'). Each role presumably is a specific, describable phenomenon exclusive of all the others. In the initial cataloging and classification of roles, all appear to have equal claim to efficacy of explanation, for example, the 'role' of the supreme court justice and the 'role' of the housewife, university professor, or the 'facilitator' among adult learners.

Some of the obvious problems involved in this view are recognized as 'role conflicts,' where the coordinate status of specific roles cannot be tolerated by a person and where 'higher' and 'lower' roles come into direct conflict, for example, in countless intermediate administrative positions such as being chairman of a university department or in being a minister of a congregation. Other problems with this model are explained as differences in roles such that some are more informal in nature. Evidently these are simply less formal than others, less identifiable as units and separates, much more shared and indistinct. These involve less precise learned, expected behavior. These admit of more of the individual's own initiative than group-forced or culture-forced behavior and/or thought patterns.

This model, moreover, is founded on the further assumption that more and more we are defined in fact by the role we play most of the time, or by the role to which we give most of our energies, whether through economic necessity, the search for social status, or a variety of other reasons. The normal tendency then is to add up all of the most relevant roles a human being 'plays' and then present these as a unifying answer to the question, Who am I? But how falsifying this kind of answer is! You have only to ask yourself whether some 'objective observer's' imputation to you of a collection of roles has much to say about your own sense of personal identity.

The theory of roles is defended generally on the grounds that it makes possible an 'objective' classification of persons and their behavior in terms of the behaviors customary to persons and commensurate with their status and their social position in a group. As a father, husband, or son within a group one has certain prescribed and predictable behavior in which he must engage. The degree of precise participation in terms of these roles allows precision of classification of human behavior in certain groups. It is possible then to study human groups with these unitized and separate categories as the guide, for the observer can assess the rewards and punishments meted out to persons in accordance with, and in deviations from, their actions taken as prescribed and predictable behavior. Thus, predictability of human behavior in the social stage, for example, allegedly becomes possible through the use of role theory.

## Weaknesses of the Role Model

It is unlikely, however, that the possible strengths of the theory counteract the obvious weaknesses. The latter are many and varied. For example, the theory of roles is not drawn from single or individual behavior. It is drawn from observations of many human beings in their typical (but wouldn't these have to be *identical* in order for the observed phenomena to be susceptible to the rigorous treatment which the 'role' theory allegedly makes possible?) everyday activities. Evidently this identity of behavior over large numbers of persons is supposed to be the foundation from which roles are drawn. Yet which came first, human actions or the 'typical character' of their actions? Where should the focus of description be? In other words, has the observer actually *drawn* a role-playing from the actions of a human being, or has this spectator in fact *forced* these actions into the separatizing categories of a classification of roles? If the latter, have not these 'roles' been unmasked as the fictionalizing of personal actions which they really are? These remarks suggest that the concept is an empty one, and that whereas we might legitimately speak of the roles of the husband among the Trobriand Islanders and among Californians, surely we cannot say that the contents of the roles of the husbands are the same in all cases. Degrees of similarity, however, may often suffice to justify the application of the concept in several cases; yet how closely similar are the roles of the husband in the two examples?

Just because role theory is drawn from many instances of behavior which are supposed to be sufficiently similar to each other, the observer is supposed to be justified in imputing roles as unitized instances of typical human behavior. Yet we can see that roles do not pertain to concrete living, individual persons. They pertain to constructed and invented abstractions and fictions. Persons are never strictly like their portrayals by the observer. The observer's 'persons' are abstractions, and the use of role-theory purports to be objective, empirical investigation of persons. But this notion, which supposedly provides the most objective portrayal of persons available to the social sciences, upon close examination can be seen to be the weakest (because it is the emptiest) of almost all of the principal categories of these sciences. These roles are never seen by the 'role-player' person with even that degree of exactitude with which they are imputed by the external observer. Evidently the social sciences are more impressed with the phenomenon of 'role-giving' than with the phenomenon of 'role-taking.' And no one gives roles except an 'external' observer following the methodological guide of the role-model. Role-taking, on the other hand, from this point of view, becomes simply a spurious way of speaking of a person's articulation of oneself.

The notion of the role was drawn analogically from the context of drama. Analogies drawn from the areas of human activity are sometimes very fruitful, for example, field theory psychology as drawn from field theory in physics; but analogies of this kind are always suspect in some degree. Dramatic roles are deliberately placed by a playwright within the context of a given play, and the sum total of these deliberately conceived roles enacted by chosen participants plays its own part in defining the play. Drama is an interaction of these roles. When the concept of a role is taken from this understanding, and embraced as a primary means of under-standing human behavior, where is the equivalent 'role' of the playwright in the circumscribed context? In other words, these questions surely point up the fallacy not so much of the possible imaginative use of role-theory outside of its proper dramatic bailiwick as the thorough fallacy of its definitive use as a primary category so as to reduce human behavior to unitized portrayals. If human beings (who are not actors) play roles in their ordinary and everyday life, what is the play, who is the playwright, and where is the stage?

In experiencing, persons are not first experiencing a phenomenon and acting out some part already written for them by some angelic playwright. We are not dealing with actors wearing the masks of **person** on some grand stage. In short, we are not dealing with *actors* at all.

If we were keeping to the analogies drawn from drama, we would have to say that we are dealing with bona fide playwrights themselves. Persons, like playwrights, are articulating, seeing, writing; they are desiring, hop-ing, planning, expecting, etc. Playwrights very rarely play roles in their own plays. Persons are not role-players at all. Any 'scientific' model which asks us to believe, or even to assume for scientific purposes of explanation, that they are is a model which mistakes a writer *of* a play for a character *in* a play. Much more disastrously, the role model approach is a commitment to a research model which mistakes persons for **person**. The ensuing behaviorism and statistical treatment of persons' behavior become quite clear in the light of these methodological beginnings.

The role-model of human behavior for the social sciences is both a fruitless and harmful one. Not surprisingly, however, there is one possible sense in which one can understand such a model. To be sure, the model I have in mind is not one the social scientist should find entirely palatable, for it requires that the social scientist himself be the playwright, his role theory the drama itself, and all human beings merely actors on his stage. In this case what has happened to 'objectivity'? Have (all of) the relevant phenomena then been studied? And how much adult education research is carried through in accordance with this model of research?

The role-model is perhaps still a central device used by social scientists in their attempts to investigate persons. Yet we must conclude that this model: (1) necessarily presupposes the abstractive dichotomization of 'object' and 'subject'; (2) is a commitment to the 'object'-side of this dichotomy; and (3) is a commitment to the reduction of persons to object.[6] And what place could **person** and the adult eductions of **person** possibly have? There appears to be no possible way in which the role-model, by manifesting the closest attention to the 'I feel' of our personal lifeworlds can truly lay out the dynamism which lies behind our projects of fact and value.[7]

With its requirements of an 'external observer,' with the abstractive selection of role, as if separate yet still imposed upon 'agent' or actor, with its assumed dichotomy of 'object' and 'subject,'[8] and with its passive receptivity to the kind of phenomenon we ordinarily call a 'person,' the role model fails to provide the grounds for our feeling, experiencing, and our consciousing[9] of another person. It fails to provide for the grasping of another person, the allowance of another person, as speaking to us. Such a model proves a *cul de sac* in any exploration of either persons or of **person**.

## Metaphor

All scholars working at the transforming edges of their disciplines must find ways of dealing with the metaphorical uses of language alongside the literal and technical rises of the language in all of the literature relevant to their research programs. But even if all scholars have some stake in clarifying what metaphors are and what they do, philosophers usually have borne the greatest responsibility for constructing and critiquing general theories of metaphors. Likewise, they bear the greatest culpability for their failure to deal with the subject of metaphor in completely successful ways. In the midst of other projects I have been at work on a theory of metaphor for some years. I have found, for example, that some of the notorious problems involved in conceptual analysis of the concept of **person**, and of the everyday lives of persons, clearly could be alleviated somewhat not only by careful analysis of specific, rich, root metaphors used in talk about persons, but also by a more grounded understanding of what metaphors really are and what they do in expression and communication. Further, I have been able to show elsewhere that some concepts commonly thought to be synonyms for violence (for example, power, force, and strength) are in fact metaphors of violence.[10] Finally, in working on this much-needed philosophical foundation for the subject-matter of adult education--work which ideally would require phenomenological investigations of special root metaphors used in metaphysical and epistemological positions--I have found that the commonly proffered theories of metaphor normally fail to show how specific metaphors in the relevant adult education literature actually assist in the transformations and empowerments of persons in everyday life.

It is not difficult to recognize metaphors in either verbal or written discourse. Examples: 'He is a wolf', 'the cypress is a flame', 'the stream of consciousness', 'the stream of thought', 'education is banking'. It is difficult, however--and the subject of extending debate

--to explain precisely what metaphors are and what they do in language. As a provisional definition of metaphor we may use the definition offered in the *Oxford English Dictionary*. There we find that a metaphor 'is a figure of speech in which a name or descriptive term is carried over, borne over, or transferred to some object different from, but analogous to, that to which it is properly applicable.' This definition in common use is instructive, not because it provides clarification as to what a metaphor actually is (since it fails to do that), but because of the portentous errors in the accounts of metaphors which it authoritatively fosters. Any theory even tacitly invoking this definition of metaphor is rudderless in uncharted seas from the beginning.

The definition lacks a further, necessary specification of what a figure of speech is. In presenting 'name' and 'descriptive term' as the phenomena 'carried over' it seems to limit metaphor to nouns and adjectives, something it would not do had the more extensive term 'word' been presented. Since analogies are founded on resemblances, likenesses, and similarities (but are not identical with these) the fundamental presupposition upon which this definition is based remains unexpressed, i.e., the pivotal notion of 'resemblance' goes unmentioned. And of course, 'proper applicability' in the OED definition can only be understood in the light of what literal expression and technical expression are. This necessarily makes those kinds of expression determine the meaning and function of metaphors, when in fact the reverse is more likely the case. This definition, in short, abscures and obfuscates much more than it could possibly uncover and clarify about metaphor, and remains a surprisingly inept definition of an important subject.

Two extreme views of metaphor are readily identified.[11] The classical view (Aristotle, Cicero, Horace, Longinus) primarily consisted of formalizing the identification of the function of metaphor and prescriptions concerning the uses and abuses of metaphors. It seems to suggest that metaphors can be cut out of the common

language and then be forced back in for specific effects. The romantic view of metaphor (Plato, Shelley,
Herder, Vico, Wordsworth, Coleridge) held metaphor to
be inseparable from common language. Metaphor is in
this view language alive, intensifying and creative of
new reality.

Between these older views of metaphor lie most twentieth century views. Some of these modern theories
include the emotive theory, the comparison theory, the
iconic signification theory, and the verbal signification theory. Other names of the theories, and some
variations, include the supervenient theory, the contro-
version theory and the substitution theory.

My thesis is that **a metaphor is originative language
of active judgment.** In fleshing out this main thesis I
argue that the word 'metaphor' (from the Greek, **meta**,
change of place, order, condition, or nature, + **pherein**,
to bear, carry), transference and transposition, indi-
cates etymologically the position of one thing in the
place of another. But the transference is always mutual
and reciprocal, and this suggests that the place where
each of the conscioused 'objects' party to the metaphor
is placed is not that of one *or* the other parts of the
metaphor, but a **felt place** which is the same for both
parts of the metaphor. Metaphor, therefore, consists in
the transposition of a conscioused 'object' from its
real felt placement to a new **felt place.**[12] It seems to
me that this recognition must be accepted by any
successful theory of metaphor.

What is a metaphor, and what does a metaphor do? In
order to answer these questions it may be helpful to
return to a discussion in a section ("Figural and Configural Expression") in the latter part of Chapter 6.
There I said that new perspectives rarely are constructed, invented, created, or discovered through the use of
literal or technical expressions. These are rarely, if
ever, enacted through these uses of language within the
'everydayness' of persons' lives. A technical language
expression, for example, provides language for describing as precisely as possible what selected phenomena are
as already present in some form.

New perspectives in and of the world (with their frequently attending joltings, shocks, and surprises are rarely, if ever, disclosed or unveiled in these ways. Moreover, quick movements from one relevancy system to another normally enact new metaphors at first. And the literal uses of language fare no better in these matters, since they are completely fettered by the everyday and familiar phenomena. In fact, this recognition is almost the common sense understanding of the term 'literal language'.

New perspectives rarely are disclosed in these ways. They are ubiquitously bursts, jolts, shocks, suddennesses of the feelings, experiencings, and consciousings of **person** within persons. These are ubiquitously the work of metaphors. The ground upon which metaphors function and in terms of which they live and move and have their being is what I have called 'figural' expression and 'configural' expression, although only the latter form of expression flows into metaphor properly so-called. This kind of expression is seminal movement through feelings, experiences, and consciousings of the adult learner, and is truly the richest constitution of the genuine stock of adult eductions of **person**. These are personal expressive passages into further, much richer and deeper, reaches of learning through restructuring, reordering, refashioning the everyday life of adults through the sudden rise of new perspectives. 'Configural' expressions make possible the transformations and new empowerments of adult life via the surrender of one's **person** to the catchings of metaphor first staged as 'figural' and 'configural' language.

But this analysis of a special relationship between metaphor and the adult learner may be carried much further. This is the relationship between what a metaphor is and does and who **person** is which I shall discuss below.

According to the view that metaphor is the originative language of active judgment, a metaphor is: (1) A language expression (2) through which one conscioused 'object' (3) situated as it is felt in one place (4) is transferred or carried over to another situation as it is felt; and (5) the conscioused 'object' as already felt in that second situation is also (6) transferred or carried back to the felt situation of the first con-scioused 'object'. Each of these steps or stretches of transferring and transpositional process is an action, which can be investigated phenomenologically.

Transference is always mutual and reciprocal, and this suggests that the place where each of the con-scioused 'objects' party to the two moments of the metaphor is placed is not one *or* the other parts of the metaphor, but a *felt place* which is the same for both parts of the metaphor. This is what a metaphor does, and what a metaphor does is precisely what it is. Thus, it is not necessary, for example, to say that the two parts of a metaphor resemble one another in some way, as some theories of metaphor claim; nor is it accurate to argue that the metaphorical expression is some deviant or aberrant form of literal expression which fails as literal language but succeeds as a figure of speech of a special kind, as other theories of meta-phor have long claimed.

A metaphor expresses specific actions performatively, that is, in the very action of performing these actions. And what a metaphor does is what a metaphor is. A metaphor is the actual linguistic expression of the performance of the six stages or stretches of action described above. It is instructive here to look briefly at what 'expressing' something really means. The term derives from the Latin, **ex**, out + **pressare**, to press, and as a verb it is the action of pressing, squeezing, or wringing the contents out of something. It also means to portray or represent some notion through sculp-ture, drawing, painting (cf., the theory of art, and the phrase carrying this theory, 'art is expression'), or in generally symbolic ways. Finally, its uses move into representations of the world through language by means of which meanings, thoughts, and states of things are given utterance and a place in the world.

I move now to a consideration of the phrases which are central to this entire chapter, '"metaphorizing life': felt meanings as the originative language of active judgment." Begin by considering that every adult is enmeshed in 'everydayness', in familiar, habitual, standard, and routine daily actions, with or without that special kind of conflict which I earlier characterized as the 'negativity of everydayness'.

Suppose that we are dealing once again with the case of the housewife discussed in Chapter 7 who has begun, through whatever originations, to consider drastic changes in her life. Who and what she is is her **person** (1) as expressed most of all in what she is in the here and now of the 'everydayness' of her life. Any kind of thinking at all in the midst of this 'everydayness' is what I term 'consciousing', and there can be no consciousing at all without there being an object, or objects, of this consciousing. Therefore, if she thinks about making changes in her life, her thinking (2) is through conscioused 'objects' (such as a desire, a hope, a plan, an expectation); and these are, as I argued in Chapter 7, founded on feelings, and (3) a feeling is always situated in a 'here and now', or within a given situation in a person's world. If she formulates a plan, the housewife 'sees' herself in another situation, in a 'then and there' at the very same time that she 'here and now' feels herself to be a person-who-is-planning (or desiring, hoping, expecting, etc.) in the 'here and now' of her present consciousing of the 'object' (the planning, desiring, etc.). 'Seeing' what her life could be, or perhaps ought-to-be within the circumstances of another situation may mean either 'seeing' as feeling, or as experiencing, or as consciousing herself in this other (desired, hoped-for, planned, expected . . .) situation of 'everydayness'. And she does not have to have a sense of the 'negativity of everydayness' born of a conflict in this case. (4) Therefore, she has transferred, transposed, and carried herself over to that other expression of 'everydayness' as a person. This is made possible fundamentally not as something which she does as a person, but as something which her **person** does, and as another adult eduction. (5) From that other expression of felt 'everydayness', however, (6) she can transfer or carry

herself back again feelingly to her more routine and
habitual felt (and experienced and conscioused) 'everydayness'. Each of these six steps and stretches of
action can be termed an eduction of **person**, and in this
case all may be termed adult eductions of **person**.

Each of the six stages of this person's action, with
each stretch being an adult eduction of **person**, coin-
cides exactly with the six stretches of the performative
action and function of a live metaphor which I laid out
in phenomenological terms above. Hence the origination
of my phrase, 'metaphorizing life'.

Poetry, drama, novels, and short stories are essentially 'metaphorizations' of personal life. This means
that they are expressions of persons, and insofar as
they treat problems ubiquitously present to adults,
these eductions are adult eductions of **person**. Sharon
B. Merriam[13] has been one of those prominent researchers
in adult education who has been most successful in
bringing literature to the forefront in the study of
adult learning and development. One of her principal
claims has been that

> Literature offers a mode for understanding
> adult development not readily accessible through
> conventional social science materials. Sensitive
> and perceptive literary artists portray themes of
> human experience in ways that allow us to under-
> stand, to see our own lives with greater clarity
> and order. . . .

> Thus literary works can bring to life the
> knowledge uncovered to date by developmental
> psychologists, and social science findings can
> provide a framework for understanding the human
> truths depicted in literature. Both sources
> comment on human behavior, both borrow from 'the
> stock of knowledge that human beings have about
> their own behavior,' and 'both the novel and
> social science use familiar notions, rephrase
> them, and try to add to one's understanding'.[14]
> A young adult can be told as a fact that a shift

in time perspective occurs in mid-life or that coping with the death of a spouse in old age is a difficult adjustment. But to be in the mind of a middle-aged protagonist as he or she experiences the shift, notices the body aging, and feels time running out, or to follow an elderly person through the grieving process is to more fully appreciate the impact of such occurrences on the lives of those who experience them. Literary works thus become a valuable teaching aid in facilitating an in-depth understanding of adult developmental processes.[15]

Finally, Merriam cites with favor, as I do, the following claim:

The best stories, as far back as we can trace the tales, myths, and dramas of man, sweep us out of our world into a new, intriguing setting, yet in the final analysis they return us to our present lives by reminding us of truths, character types and patterns of experience we already recognize in our own existence.[16]

I shall close this chapter by showing in phenomenological terms why and how literature, especially as in poetry and drama, is of fundamental significance in the understanding of adult learning, and why it must be heeded closely in any research in adult education. My arguments move through discussions of 'dialog' and 'dialectic' as specific forms of the 'metaphorization' of life.

## Dialog and Dialectic

Far more promising than the alleged 'objectivity' obtained through the use of 'role' theory is an exploration of person-to-person encounter that is disclosed through a rudimentary description of what we commonly term 'dialog' and 'dialectic.' These are among the principal ways in which the 'metaphorizing' of life takes place in the arts. Dialog and dialectic are notions derived from the Greek, **dialegesthai** (**dia**, 'through,' 'across,' 'between,' + **legein**, 'to speak,' thus 'to speak across'). The use of both modes of expression is to make communication between persons possible across the chasm of separateness of persons, to provide a communicative content and structure to this 'betweenness', thus enabling one person to move through to another as a practical and everyday consequence of the methodological presupposition of intersubjectivity.

Consider **dialog** first. Its prototype is found in poetry and not initially in drama in the broad sense (as in the case of speaking of the 'dialog' of the drama). Dialog is the actual encounter, the real involvement, the full commitment. Dialog is meeting, the 'real living' Martin Buber intended in his presentation of real living as **meeting**.[17] Dialog is the rich focusing of many felt experiences, whether uttered or unexpress- ed, even the wordless silence sometimes felt as experi- enced by another, or the telling and forceful use of the single word which moves between two persons, and which is facilitated by eductions of **person**. Dialog is con- creative experience, and the full expressiveness, if not full structure, of intersubjectivity. Thus poetry is a- speaking-through of poet and listener. A poem is not made by a poet and then understood by another person not a poet. A poem is made jointly, a concreative process of one who speaks across, by, through, of, and for other persons, as the root of dialog suggests.

**Dialectic** shares the same root as dialog, but reflec- tively transcends beyond the latter, not in richness and originativeness, but in the sense of concrete dialog, dialog articulated, reinterpreted, synthesized, written, and argued. It is a reflective reconsideration of dialog, dialog known as the basis and the spring of speaking and exploratory conversation. It is conversa- tion, especially of the question-answer-question pro- cess, a-speaking-through in the sense of a play. It is interwoven, structured concrete dialog spoken across persons. Dialectic is the closest approximation of dialog as actually in process and known reflexively as being in process. It is a re-creation, re-interpretation, and transformation of dialog.

Dialectic, as the closest approximation of dialog in action, reflexively changes and transforms dialog. Dialectic is not dialog, but a speaking about, or of, dialog, and thus is a second step removed, but a necessary removal all the same. Dialectic of or about dialog is a new entering upon intersubjectivity. In dialectic, for example, symbols not only express meanings; they also transform the very meanings they are supposed to convey.

Poetry as fundamentally dialogic and drama as fundamentally dialectical are intersubjective attempts to express **person**. As concreative encounters, poetry and drama preclude a reductionist view of **person** which the role model requires, for example. They are, rather, based on a model of **person** that requires that men and women qua **person** be understood as going beyond an organismic, space-bound pivot and as transforming, re-creating, surpassing, and transcending individuality themselves. **Person** is eductive and educed, and articulated as persons thrusting themselves through vital life. Since the thrusting occurs as dialog in person-to-person encounters, the Socratic midwife metaphor is not amiss. Certainly birth as something coming into life is a more appropriate model for the being and reality of **person** than those odd fictive abstractions provided by the role model.

The work of the artist, for example, is a result of continuous dialog thrusting into life. One person gifted and skilled above others in special ways makes a poem, a painting, or music by individualizing some tissue or rubric of and within the 'everydayness' of person-to-person encounter. A person chooses a subject matter, an individualizing selection in itself, and through transformations of it through feelings and experiencings brings an 'object' to birth by expressing oneself as **person**. What a person expresses is oneself as **person** moving through to more conscious awareness. One comes to know more and more what one's **person**-to-**person** encounter is as individualized only by doing it

and by continuing to express oneself. The artist as
**person** has no prior conception of what he is about.
Thus his personal expression is never complete or finally fulfilled. Yet, one's personal expression is also
the expression of a person's audience, for a person and
a person's audience are inseparable. They partially
gave birth to this **person**, and they listen to this
prophetic voice among them. Although the audience may
be unskilled in the making of poems and paintings, for
example, the individual persons constituting this audience understand one among them to be gifted in bringing
their personal encounters and expressions to birth.
Thus they, too, come to know themselves through the
artist who is one of them and who speaks of, with, and
through them. The work of art--the **person**-to-'object'
encounter--is the public vehicle of this **person**-to-
**person** encounter. This **person**-to-'object' encounter (a
poem, a play, a novel) is an exemplar of 'metaphorized
life,' or a special noematic object, in Husserl's
sense,[18] but of a very special kind, for Collingwood:
'Art is the community's medicine for the worst disease
of the mind, the corruption of consciousness.'[19]

The artist is never merely an individual person, but
always a community of personal encounter: the collaboration of one who makes an object, one who performs it,
and one who 'sees,' 'hears,' and comprehends. Art is a
concreative encounter of persons moving from **person**-to-
subject through to **person**-to-'object' encounter. If one
asks what the artist (the poet and the dramatist) is
trying to do, the answer is: the artist is a person
trying consciously to experience **person** through encounters founded in feelings and rising up through experiencings and consciousings. Clearly then, next to persons' own articulations of their adult eductions of
**person**, literature does indeed provide one of the
richest possible lodes of the adult eductions of person
for adult education research.

## Chapter 9

## Vital Life Through 'Unrestraining' Liberty

*If I am right in my assertion that being-belong-becoming should be found at the central core of adult education, at least four tasks are needed: conceptualization, persuasion, curriculum, [and] method--to choose and organize and refine the means to learning that help men and women to be free.*

James Robbins Kidd, 1973[1]

*The plain and obvious meaning of the words* **Freedom** *and* **Liberty**, *in common speech, is power, opportunity, or advantage, that any one has, to do as he pleases. Or in other words, his being free from hinderance or impediment in the way of doing, or conducting in any respects, as he wills. . . . To be free is the property of an agent, who is possessed of powers and faculties, as much as to be cunning, valiant, bountiful, or zealous. But these qualities are the properties of men or persons and not the properties of properties. There are two things which are contrary to this which is called* **Liberty** *in common speech. One is* **constraint**; *the same is otherwise called force, compassion, and coercion; which is a person's being necessitated to do a thing contrary to his will. The other* *is restraint; which is his being hindered, and not having power to do according to his will. But that which has no will cannot be the subject of these things. I need say the less on this head, Mr. Locke having set the same thing forth, with so great clearness, in his* **Essay on Human Understanding.**

Jonathan Edwards,
*Freedom of the Will*, 1754[2]

## Introduction

Liberty may be both constrained and restrained. Constraint means that a person's powers, opportunities, or advantages to do what one wants to do on the one hand may be bundled, tied, or drawn so tightly together as to have the special compression we call force, compulsion, and coercion. But liberty may be restrained as well. Restraining liberty requires that a person's powers, opportunities, or advantages to do what one wants to do may be bound fast, or confined. The restraint of freedom is the hindering of a person's powers, opportunities, or advantages to do as one wishes to do. The etymological source of both notions is the action of an astringent on the body.

In this chapter I discuss the second case, the restraint of liberty. I note that whereas the underlying importance given to liberty within a society's scheme of values does vary over time (given enough time), it is pivotal reflection in moral, social, and political theory to ask whether this variation may be legitimated. I shall (1) try to sculpt this question into a proper form manageable within a few pages; (2) draw out a model case of the legitimation of the variance of liberty as articulated in the special form of assentive/dissentive speech through which a person feels, lives, and finally says 'yes' or 'no' in response to vital conflicts within the everyday lifeworld; (3) apply this account of legitimated 'unrestraining' liberty to the practical problems in adult education. Finally, I try to show that empowered persons are persons transformed through the power which liberty is and gives. These are persons whose valuational feelings and felt values[3] arise partially from within an already underlying scheme of values with the importance of liberty already situated and who partially restructure this scheme through their assentive/dissentive responses within their own historical circumstances and contexts.

## Society, The Scheme of Values, and Liberty

A society is a social system through which persons have formed continuing and regulating associations of their activities and customs for their mutual benefit and protection. At the core of this continuity and regularity are the training, development, and refinement of the minds, tastes, and values. And vitally coursing through these is the structure of the continuity itself which might be called a society's scheme of values.

But how is this scheme of values to be identified and investigated? It is a scheme of values located within and structuring an already existing society. Is the unity of life and tradition, a given moral consensus among all, or most, of the persons constituting a society, for example, a consensus on virtues in accordance with Aristotle's phenomenological account of those situated in his own time and place?[4] Is it the kind of moral consensus perhaps characteristic of the middle ages?[5] If a society's scheme of values is a moral consensus of this kind, how would it be possible to identify the scheme in our own time if Friedrich Nietzsche, R. G. Collingwood, and Alasdair MacIntyre are all correct in characterizing our own age as a society which lacks an authentic and bonding core of moral consensus?[6]

Whatever the answers to these questions, it is possible to show that liberty is the articulation of specific values, of felt freedoms as guaranteed, for example, by the civil liberties of freedom of religious worship, freedom of speech and press, and the right of the people to assemble, in the First Amendment within the Bill of

Rights. The liberty a person takes is the actual freedom which one has. The fullness of the content of freedom (and there never is pure, complete, or absolute freedom) is liberty. The totality of liberties which are legitimized for all persons within a society constitute the freedom within that society. Freedom remains an abstraction, a fiction, even if a normative one, without liberties which actualize and realize it within the concreteness of personal circumstances and contexts. Nicolai Hartmann pointed out that 'the profound struggle of human thought to attain a metaphysical proof of freedom of the will is a witness to [freedom's] worth,'[7] even when we grant with both Edwards and Hartmann that freedom of the will is neither liberty's content of freedom, nor freedom cast through the prism of the Bill of Rights into the spectrum of degrees and kinds of liberties we have been able to create and protect so far.

## Assentive/Dissentive Speech and Valuational Feelings of Liberty

Albert Camus asked, 'What is a rebel? A man who says "no" but whose refusal does not imply a renunciation. He is a man who says "yes," from the moment he makes his first gesture of rebellion.'[8] I believe he meant that saying 'yes' or saying 'no' when a person lives through the feeling of response which cannot but be said in this way is among the most fundamental footings of personal care and action. New occasions teach new duties. When the slave says 'no' he means 'this has been going on too long,' 'up to this point yes, beyond it, no,' 'you are going too far,' . . . 'there is a limit beyond which you cannot go.' In saying 'no' the person affirms the existence of a borderline, but at the same time one is saying 'yes' to a felt value, a concrete liberty which either is or ought to be a felt value for all within the society.

To assent to something is literally to come to it, or come together with it in feeling and thinking. To assent is to feel-with and to think-with. To dissent from something is literally to affirm one's feeling and thinking apart from something. To dissent is to feel-apart and to think-apart from something. Assenting and dissenting are conscious presentations of one's feelings and experiencings; each must be defined in juxtaposition with the other. The one has no content without the other. Dissent at the abridgement of speech necessarily assents to free speech. 'In every act of rebellion,' said Camus, 'the rebel simultaneously experiences a feeling of revulsion at the infringement of his rights and a complete and spontaneous loyalty to certain aspects of himself. Thus he implicitly brings into play a standard of values so far from being gratuitous that he is prepared to support it no matter what the risks.'[9] The exemplar of the rebel's assentive/dissentive speech offers us a clear case in which the underlying importance given to liberty within a society's scheme of values legitimately varies with historical circumstance and social context.

### Adult Education as the Transformation and Empowerment of Persons

On the one hand, we may believe that in almost every society there is an underlying importance accorded to liberty and that 'liberty can only be restricted by liberty;'[10] that this commitment is at least covertly espoused; that there is an essential unity to this grounded feeling within the diversity of circumstances (all that stands around us) and social contexts; and that any significant deviation from this belief is some form of pernicious historicism and therefore inadmissible as systematic philosophy.

On the other hand, there stand the modern practices of 'adult education,' which 'include[s] all the activities with an educational purpose that are carried on by people outside the ordinary business of life,'[11] or 'an educational program that is planned and organized to assist adults in meeting their responsibilities as individuals and members of society.'[12] All of the principal theoretical approaches to, or 'philosophies' of adult education, through the diversities of their treatments of their most relevant data, purport to ground the ways in which changes are sought in persons, whether these changes are first of all powers which individuals acquire, or powers which are acquired by community-based organizations, or through more globally oriented programs.

Most of the approaches seek to bring about transformations of persons through the empowerment of persons.[13] To empower a person is to invest one formally or even legally with power or authority, or to authorize one as having certain power or powers. It is to impart or bestow power on persons toward some end or for some specific purpose. To empower one is to enable one, to make one powerful, or more powerful in some respect. It is clear that the empowerment of persons is the liberation of persons, or what I am calling 'unrestraining' the liberty of persons.

The most prominent theoretical approaches to the practices of adult education have already been identified as 'liberal', 'progressive', 'behaviorist', 'humanist', 'radical', and 'analytical perspectives'.[14] Each of these positions presupposes that the underlying importance given to liberty within a society's scheme of values legitimately varies with historical circumstances and social situations. The vital first step in the transformation of persons effecting their empowerment (for example, literacy programs among Brazilian peasants, or job-retraining programs for unemployed workers in Chicago) consists in individual persons' recognition that their liberation from emotional, intellectual, and social bondages seen as most oppressive will vary in direct proportion to their own work at 'unrestraining' their liberty precisely within their unique circumstances.

Each of those distinct theoretical approaches, if considered as a coordinate but mutually exclusive class, has sometimes been proclaimed normatively to be the principal 'philosophy' of adult education with available resolutions to all relevant problems (at least in principle). However, all adult educators claim to be dealing with persons in one way or another, although it is not always evident what essential structures of **person** are under investigation.

Let us rehearse for a moment a portion of the argument presented in the Introduction, Section D. Suppose that 'adult education' is a generic concept (and thus with all of its theoretical approaches or 'philosophies' considered as overlapping) rather than a class concept (in which case those theoretical approaches could not overlap, and would have to stand each by itself as mutually exclusive).[15] A classification of the different classes of 'philosophical' foundations could then give way to phenomenological investigations of the thoughts and actions of persons, and these investigations would not be limited to sets of phenomena whose selections are regimented by exclusive, class-concept generating, mutually exclusive perspectives. Suppose that adult eductions of **person** constitute the essential subject-matter of adult education. Suppose that both the sense of an enduring self, the capacity for self-recognition, and the reflexive capacity for new, unfamiliar, and non-habitual actions are among (but do not exhaust) the essential structures of what we mean by adult eductions of **person**.

If these suppositions are granted for the moment, a phenomenology of the essential structures of adult education uncovers a definition of 'adult education': **adult education is the performative enactments of, and systematic investigation of, the essential structures of the phenomena constituting adult eductions of person, specifically of the deliberate liberative actions of consciousing and responsible persons whereby they become transformed and empowered with vital motives for acting.**[16] Theory and practice are brought together conformably. Gaining and affording oneself motives, which is the reason-giving process for personal action, is crucial in adult education: (1) From the adult educator's perspective a person can be offered a reason for having acted. This means that *either* a person's actions can be understood in the context of motives (reasons) supplied by the investigator, *or* that a person may be given, and accepts as his/her own, motives (reasons) for having acted. Or it may be both of these at once. Gaining motives in this sense means *reasons-why* have been afforded. (2) From the adult learner's perspective the person may be given, and accepts as one's own certain motives (reasons) for acting. Or it may mean that the person has educed his/her own motives (reasons) for acting. Affording motives (reasons) in this perspective means that *reasons-why* are being given.[17]

## Liberative Theory and Practice: Empowerment and 'Unrestraining' the Liberty of Persons

Feeling my motives, experiencing my motives, and knowing what they are, are enabling actions. Feeling them marks their presence, and later makes it possible to name them, to sort them out. Prioritizing them has already thus begun. Feeling, experiencing, and knowing them, with priorities coming more evidently into shape, all enable me to perform personal actions. Performance of personal actions is already the restructuring and the transforming of my life. These performances may be distinguished (but not separated) into degrees and kinds, and they can be investigated phenomenologically. The essential forms and contours of my life are reconstituted in accordance with a specific liberty, the removal of the restraints of which are both within my power and themselves constitute the calibrations of the stages of my own self-determination. Can this not be otherwise termed an authentic liberating process, or the 'unrestraining' of liberty?

Once again we may refer to Husserl's insight about a person's justification of truth through one's own perfect insight. I, a solitary person, owe much to others (including a scheme of values into which I am born, with the importance accorded within it). But what they offer me through their abilities and the liberties which they created and protected, as established by their insights and their tests of my competencies and performance, is for me only something which they claim will empower me as well. I must justify and legitimate the powers and the importance of liberty by a perfect insight on my part.[18] My justification, my legitimation, of my own enabling processes in my everyday world instantiates my empowerments.

Careful phenomenological reflection discloses that in this process I move (1) from an indeterminate situation of not knowing that I do not have a specific liberty which a certain enabling empowerment would give me, (2) to knowing that I do not have this specific liberty. But I have moved further, (3) from knowing that I possess this specific liberty, to (4) actually having it and holding it in hand. These stages mark my radicalizing self-empowerment. They are also among the stages of my transformation as a person. Any person who is thus transformed is a more liberated person, a person who has removed specific restraints of his/her liberty.

## Conclusion

Elsewhere I have claimed that I know of no systematic investigations in which the determinate subject-matter comes to be more enriched for personal uses whereby persons become transformatively empowered to assume greater, liberative, charge of their own destinies than within the practices of 'adult education' located within the normatively conceived scientific position I have tried to construct. I also called 'adult education' potentially the most rigorous human science.[19] I still believe it to be that.

I conclude with an additional claim which addresses the restraint of liberty. The underlying importance given to liberty within a society's scheme of values does vary legitimately with historical circumstances and social context. Not only does it happen, but it can only do so through the lives of persons living through 'everydayness'. Astringencies in our lives are no more abstract in their effects upon us than astringents are when pressed against functioning organs of the body. But as the latter can be removed, and must be removed at relevant times to allow organs to function properly, so must the former.

It may be true that liberty can only be restricted by liberty, but the restriction is facilitated by persons' beliefs in a liberty carrying through a higher degree and kind of freedom as restricting a liberty carrying through a lower degree and kind of freedom. In short, the legitimation of the importance of liberty requires adjudication between degrees and kinds of liberty, and this can only begin with investigations into valuational feelings, some of which are incipient prioritizations of values, including the values of liberties.

# PART VI

## New Beginnings:

## Phenomenology as a New Paradigm and Program of Research in Adult Education

*I attempt to guide, not to instruct, but merely to show and to describe what I see. All I claim is the right to speak according to my best lights--primarily to myself and correspondingly to others--as one who has lived through philosophical existence in all its seriousness.*

Edmund Husserl, *Die Krisis der europaischen Wissenschaften und die transzendentale Phanomenologie (Husserliana,* 1936, V. I, 17)[1]

*It is Husserl's view that the modern tragedy of Western civilization comes from halfway measures, from a failure to turn to knowledge in its genuinely universal foundations, from a naive acceptance of a limited and ultimately inadequate conception of objective science in place of rigorous science, from a refusal to recognize the meaningful status of the life-world in relation to knowledge, and from a despairing and benighted assessment of the nature of authentic subjectivity. The politics and sociology of culture are grounded on a fragmented conception of theory and a displacement of the vocation of philosophy. It may or may not be true that transcendental phenomenology alone has the power to reconstruct what unreason has demolished, but it is at least certain that Husserl has been able to present a philosophy which traces out the source of crisis in uncompromising terms. It is not his claim that sounding the alarm is equivalent to putting out the fire, but he has demonstrated what is wrong with a culture which no longer recognizes alarms. Husserl's perseverence in holding to Reason vindicates his own concern with history and brings into unity the full career of Man as a being whose roots define his destiny. Reason requires an acknowledgment of the past, just as it demands a lucid, reflective awareness of our present direction. To forget the past is to make it impossible to persist. In this sense, the future of phenomenology is allied with historical consciousness. The hope one may find in Husserl's insistence on Reason is that we are still rememberers, beings who not only become but seek to narrate that becoming. 'In the beginning' is. also the language of phenomenological genesis; it is the cry of origin.*

Maurice Natanson, *Edmund Husserl: Philosopher of Infinite Tasks,* 1973[2]

## Introductory Remarks

In previous chapters I have tried to show in various ways what phenomenology is and how it is uniquely suited for use in investigations in adult education conceived as a rigorous human science defined and characterized as systematic investigations into the determinate subject-matter of **person**, specifically of the adult eductions of **person**. I want to show now how phenomenology may be employed as a new paradigm of research in adult education in the special sense that phenomenological investigations *ought* to be deliberately established at least as another alternative model of research in adult education. And it is a model which singularly undercuts, for example, the customary dichotomies of theoretical *versus* practical research and quantitative *versus* qualitative research in current research methodologies in adult education. For example, statistical models of research of various kinds may be used in conjunction with phenomenological investigations, although the use of the former in this case must be done without the usual and standard invocation (perhaps unthinkingly and uncritically, as a 'habit' of research) of methodological principles of 'causal' order and mathematical unitizations, as if the latter constituted a virtual metaphysics and not simply a variety of systems of methods of ordering which can be usefully employed in handling large masses of data and evidence. There is no necessary reason, for example, why some mathematical models without encumbering metaphysical presuppositions of reductionisms and certain kinds of phenomenological investigations cannot be used in the *same research project* focusing on the same problem(s). Indeed, this would be one example of the kind of double-pronged research which in Part I, Section C, and Chapter 2 I called 'reflexive experimentation' and urged adult education researchers to consider using in all research projects carried out in adult education. The phenomena constituting the adult eductions of **person** are indeed very difficult to investigate fully and fairly. A focused subject-matter requires investigations directly arising from it. Adult eductions of **person** are the subject-matter of adult education as a rigorous human science. These flow from within the constituted structures of **person**. Hence both constitutive and eductive phenomenology should be used in every research project.

Phenomenology may be claimed as a paradigm of research in adult education for a number of reasons. These will include reasons which show how phenomenology is the most fundamental and rigorous kind of research and how it is a paradigm of research so conceived.

## A. Phenomenology as a New Paradigm of Research in Adult Education

Strip aside for the moment a number of your long-standing notions of 'research', and attend to the concept itself. Your long-established, tried and true, and by now habitual, presuppositions about the nature of standard and normal research in adult education might sneak back in soon enough! But hold them in abeyance, or parenthesize them, and bracket them for the moment, and in these ways put them aside.[3]

'Research' is at least a search (from the Latin, **circare**, to go around). Reflect carefully now on what a search is. A search is a seeking-out, an exploration, or the thorough examination of something. It is a personal action, act, and process which is situated within circumstances and takes place over time. A search is the ascertaining of the presence or absence of certain phenomena, or certain properties, characteristics, marks, or attributes. A search is a looking-through phenomena in order to bring to light, to discover, to un-conceal whatever might be present, particularly in the case of whether the searched-for 'object' is present or not. A person reaches out in an effort to locate, to test, and to reveal. A search might be a penetration more deeply into the 'everydayness' of the familiar lifeworlds of persons, or steps into the great vastnesses and unknowns in the light of whatever phenomena thereof can be attended-to. Fundamental to any searching as so far characterized is the examination of phenomena. Phenomena located and situated within matrices of other relevant phenomena are observed and described, and become 'data'.

When I examine (from the Latin, **examinare**) something, what do I do? I weigh that something as accurately as I can, I inquire into it, test it, try it out in terms as accurate as possible. Hence, any search has these activities built within it, and it becomes possible to capture the full sense of what research is.

Research is **re**-searching. It is to engage in all of the kinds of activity I have just detailed, and to do so both in private and in public, individually and in cooperation with others. The foundation for both of these approaches in bringing the results of research into focus is the presupposition of that intersubjectivity which is already originative within the coexistence of persons. All knowledge (or as I would prefer, all consciroused 'objects') can become public knowledge on this presupposition, under the right circumstances. But not all feelings and experiences can become public knowledge, since these are not yet 'knowledge' or fully consciroused 'objects'.

Research is **re**-search. It is a search for investigation directed to the discovery of data which become facts (if carefully structured within other facts and tested out) by careful consideration or study of a subject, or a course of critical or scientific inquiry. Research is to search again . . . again . . . and again, without any logical necessitation that it end. A research project 'ends', yes, but consider the logic of its ending as distinct from mundane 'empirical' questions of lost funding, loss of interest by the researcher(s), the politics of research, and the sociology of research, to name but a few obvious reasons why a given research project 'must' shut down. But are these reasons for ending specific research (or for beginning them) also reasons necessarily built into the processes of searching and re-searching?

Research is searching, and searching again . . . and again. It might mean that in searching again a person goes back to **originations** and to **beginnings**, back from some point arrived at, or back to or towards a starting point; it might be a form of searching which leads back, carries back, 'pulls' back, or calls back a person. Research in the form of reflection (from the Latin, **reflectere**, 'to bend back'), or thinking as bending back upon itself such that 'thoughts' become consciroused 'objects' disclosed through thinking's thus bending back upon itself is absolutely vital. Remember the discussions of Plato's 'simile of the line' and John Dewey's account of the continuum of common sense and scientific inquiry in the Introduction. The many forms of this kind of thinking as research include 'thought experiments', and research into theory as well as practical research, or literally the re-searching into any and all of our practices. All of these kinds of research are needed.

This full description of what research is also goes a good distance toward describing what phenomenological investigations are, although the latter are much more than mere research, since they include descriptive processes and ways of continuing criticism within any discipline. But phenomenology as re-search constitutes the telling force of its full powers of the continuing search into any and all phenomena which can become the sufficiently focused and determinate subject-matter (the 'intuited object' which becomes the focus of search) of systematic search and re-search. And all the while, the presuppositions utilized in phenomenological research undergo constant and continuing examination.[4]

This section, surprisingly, seems to be a partial restatement of Part I, Section A, although the focus here has been on the definition and the characterization of research, and that earlier focus was on an introductory discussion of phenomenology. The two accounts coalesce so fully as to be a rehearsal of Husserl's own evidence for his claim that phenomenology is the rigorous foundation for any science.[5] I claim here only that phenomenology is the clearest, most foundational and fullest form of investigation appropriate to adult education as a rigorous human science with the special, and by now I hope obvious, subject-matter of the adult eductions of **person**.

In the light of the discussion of the essential structures of research in the passages above, it is now possible to show how phenomenological investigations constitute *a new paradigm of research* in adult education. The literature on the subject of paradigms has grown enormously in the aftermath of Thomas Kuhn's original and brilliant (even if highly ambiguous and inconsistent) development of this concept in the first edition of his *The Structure of Scientific Revolutions.*[6] Some of the most instructive and provocative of these discussions have been offered in *Criticism and the Growth of Knowledge,* edited by Imre Lakatos and Alan Musgrave, in Harold I. Brown's *Perception, Theory, and Commitment,* and in Larry Laudan's *Progress and its Problems,* among a number of other excellent sources.[7]

It is neither possible nor necessary here to discuss fully Kuhn's and his critics' conceptions of the 'paradigm' of a science. I call attention to this tradition and to some of its most important literature, and urge readers to examine it carefully if they wish to understand fully what science, paradigms of science, and research programs are now conceived to be within the context of the 'new philosophy of science'. I mention this literature in an effort to suggest the place of the conception of a scientific paradigm even in research in the human sciences. Moreover, in this brief discussion of phenomenological investigations as a new paradigm of research in adult education as the rigorous science with adult eductions of **person** as its subject-matter, I shall try to state clearly what this new paradigm is. But first, what is a 'paradigm'?

A paradigm (from the Greek, παράδειγμα, and the Latin, **paradigma**) is a pattern, model, or example. It intends the action of exhibiting something beside something else, or of showing something side by side with something else. It has come to be a pattern, example, and exemplar. My use of the concept of the paradigm conforms to the OED's exhaustive chronicle of rich etymologies tracing the successive 'right usages' of the term 'paradigm' into the present day. I present its characteristics more fully, and discuss them in the following order:

(1) A paradigm is a pattern and patterning of the thoughts and thinking of persons. I prefer to say that a paradigm is a pattern and the patterning process of the conscioused 'objects' and consciousing 'objects' of persons. The term derives from the Middle English and

late French, **patron** (which continues to mean both 'patron' and 'pattern' in French), and still conveys some vestiges of 'patron' as protector, defender, father, or as one who stands to others as their lord, defender, master, or protector. In other words, 'paradigm' still connotes a pattern of transcendence, superiority, and protection which is overriding in its relevance and significance. These connotations already bring us rather close to the meaning(s) the concept has in the discussions in the literature of the 'new science' and the 'new philosophy of science'. A paradigm is a pattern. A pattern is to its copies as the original and 'superior' form and design are to these copies. A paradigm is a model of particular excellence, a superior model from which anything is made, or a plan, design, or outline of supreme importance. To pattern something is to make something in conformance with a model or design, or to work out or construct something according to a model.

(2) A paradigm is a principal example among a number of examples, or what is known as an exemplar (from Latin, **exemplaris**, and Old French, **exemplaire**), or a perfect specimen of some quality, pattern, or model to be imitated or followed, or in accordance with which certain actions in designing something should be taken.

(3) A paradigm is also an action, the action of exhibiting something beside something else, or side by side with something, such that descriptions of both, and comparisons, become unavoidable. It is the action of holding out, or of submitting to view, something of importance and significance, such as the delineation or an embodiment of an idea in words in such a manner that something is given existence or indicated as existing. When the unavoidable descriptions and comparisons are necessarily offered following the action of exhibiting something side by side with something else, they may take the form of comparisons in virtue of 'better' or 'worse', 'more than' or 'less than', 'of greater importance' or 'of lesser importance', and so on.

We can see clearly that the essential structure of a paradigm is a pattern of thoughts which constitute a design or model held to be superior, as an exemplar, to other designs or models and which 'ought' to be followed in systematic investigations of a determinate subject-matter, when compared with those other models, designs, and patterns of thought which could be followed in investigations into the same determinate subject-matter.

This is not yet the paradigm which phenomenological investigations uniquely constitute. The above definition is a definition of the matrix which any paradigm properly is. We can term it the 'paradigm matrix', and it can be applied as the definition of the matrix of any scientific paradigm properly so-called. Hence it can also be applied to phenomenological investigations such that these now can be seen to constitute a paradigm of research within the human sciences.

Phenomenological investigations are patterns of thoughts which constitute a design or model which can be held to be superior to other designs and models, and which ought to be followed in systematic investigations into the determinate subject-matter of the adult eductions of **person**. Among these patterns of thought are the 'steps' or 'stages' of the essentials of the phenomenological method.[8] Also included are the personal consciousing actions of suspending all judgments about the existence or non-existence of **person** and the adult eductions of **person** and the consciousing actions of suspending judgments about 'causal' processes.[9]

Within these patterns of thought which constitute phenomenological investigations as a paradigm of research in the human sciences (1) **person** and person cannot be rendered identical, and (2) neither **person** nor person can be reduced to the other. Both of these are excluded within the paradigm of phenomenological research. But they are fallacies committed at the very outset of research which proceeds according to the paradigms of research offered generally by conventional statistical approaches, for example which among other things are committed to treating persons as unitized fictions interchangeable with each other to fit the statistical model. And they are unable to investigate **person** at all.

Behavioristic models are tarred with the same brush, since they can be charged with the commission of the same fallacies. Both statistical models and behavioristic models are paradigms of science as I have defined these. Researchers committed to the presuppositions and methods of these models hold them to be patterns of thought which constitute a design or model held to be superior to other designs and models and which 'ought' to be followed in all systematic investigations of determinate subject-matters, or in such investigations of the same subject-matters. If they did not think so, what principal reason(s) would they have for using these models? Habits of research? Their professors and mentors used these? What are the reasons? The best reason would seem to be that researchers in adult education who use these models do so because they consider them to be paradigms of research in the sense in which I have defined the latter.

But **person** and person are not the same subject-matter for systematic investigation. This is a point I have made repeatedly throughout this essay. Persons are constituted of being, action (doing), and speaking-out, and whereas these structures are fundamental expressions of **person**, no paradigm of 'objectivistic' science can investigate these structures as founded in (but not reduced to) feeling, experiencing, and consciousing; and these very structures, however essential to the expression of **person** through persons, are summarily ruled out of court by 'objectivistic' paradigms of rigorous scientific research in adult education.

**Person** is the content of the fullest and richest possible expression of the eductions, the flowings-forth and flowings-through, the actions of feeling, experiencing, and consciousing, of adults. And adults therefore are the adult eductions of **person**. Persons are the subjects, agents, actors, egos, *propria*, which are the vehicles and carriers of **person**. Without the contents, there is nothing for the vehicles and carriers to carry. Persons without **person** might still be carriers, but empty carriers. Persons are said to be 'carriers of value', but values are essentially **person**, and so persons carry **person**, and intersubjectively so, within the coexistence of persons. But as empty carriers, persons, bereft of **person**, would be exactly the fictive abstractions statistically-based and behaviorally-based paradigms of research in adult education necessarily presuppose them to be, empty, bereft of feeling, experiencing, and consciousing. This is a paradigm characteristic of much of the social sciences even today (early 1987), and surely is characteristic of 'role' theory investigation of persons (since it cannot by its paradigmatically-occasioned exclusions investigate **person**). The latter kind of 'objectivistic' paradigm as used in social sciences' investigations of persons cannot possibly investigate **person**, primarily because feeling and experiencing are excluded summarily by the fiat of method, as values are also by these positivistically-based, 'value-free sciences'. Therefore, these approaches to research, these paradigms of research, as they are commonly in vogue in adult education research, cannot possibly reach into essential structures in adult learning and adult education. Not surprisingly many adult educators, and even many researchers, conduct much of their professional work at the level of 'nuts-and-bolts'. And some even count this a virtue in research. In some ways, this kind of research may be termed 'by-the-seat-of-the-pants-research', with far more 'answers' being generated than concrete, deeper, grounding questions being asked. And how does one know what an 'answer' is or how it answers a question without concrete knowledge of that theoretical foundation upon which the question rests?[10]

Conversely, phenomenological investigations, as a new paradigm of research in adult education conceived as a rigorous human science constituted of systematic investigations into the adult eductions of **person**, investigates not only feelings as eductions of **person**, but experiencings and consciousings as well, and they move on toward rich accounts of the expression, behavior, and conduct of persons as the basis of understanding per-

sons. Although they do not focus on adult human behavior as most central, phenomenological investigations
cannot possibly negate or neglect these (as 'objectivistic' paradigms must negate **person**). And whereas
phenomenological investigations may be used in developing measuring scales, instruments, statistical models,
research questions, projects, and programs, and courses
and curricula, and all the rest which may lead to practices, these investigations ground all of these important discoveries and constructions in the firmest possible theoretical foundations, never to be lost or washed
away. Hence, 'nuts-and-bolts' practices and solutions
to practical problems continue to be as important as
they have; indeed, their importance is both more clearly
understood and enhanced, since now they can be fitted
(with appropriate necessary alterations toward the ends
of coherency and consistency) to the firmest foundations
of theory which are the products of careful reflections
within a rigorous human science called adult education.

## B. A New Program of Research: The Theory and Practice of Learning

It is important to distinguish the concepts of
'structure' and 'function'. Structure (from **struere**, to
build) refers to the coexistence in a whole of distinct
parts which have a definite manner of arrangement. The
structure of something is the manner in which it is put
together as constituted, or it is the mutual relation of
the constituent parts or elements of a whole as making
up its character or nature. In biology, for example, a
structure is an organized body or combination of mutually connected and dependent parts or elements.

The 'FEC Structure' is the feeling, experiencing, and
consciousing structure in the sense just defined. Who
am I? I am a person. Whatever else it may mean for
something to be a person, the 'who' which I am, and
which each person is, it is at least to be a coexistence
of a whole of distinct but inseparable activities of
feeling, experiencing, and consciousing, layers of
person which have a definite manner of arrangement which

is constituted as mutually connected and dependent. By 'definite manner of arrangement' I do not claim a 'causal', deterministic, or necessitated manner of arrangement, but still a system which can be investigated phenomenologically.

The 'HRM Structure' is the coexistence in a whole of distinct activities which constitute me as a person insofar as I seek to know anything at all. There is an orderly and definite arrangement of habit(s), relevancy systems, and metaphorization of my relationships with my world. My habituations of my feelings, my experiencings, and my consciousings within the world are the ways through which knowing anything at all is facilitated. What can I know? I can know my habituations and from within these (and must some be changed or eliminated?), the means through which my purposes, goals, and ends are achievable and achieved. These always take place within relevancy systems which are the matrices of all actual and possible knowledge. And new knowledge is first of all expressed and measured out through metaphors or felt meanings within the world. Therefore, the 'HRM Structure' is the coexistence in a whole (I or you as a person) of distinct activities of personal habituations, relevancing of the world, and metaphorizing of newly-felt meanings moving toward the status of knowledge within the world.

The 'EvLV Structure' is the coexistence in a whole of distinct activities which constitute one as a person who knows something about the world and who responds in terms of what one feels, experiences, and consciouses one ought to do in the world. Again there is a definite manner of arrangement, hence a structure, or a coexistence of the 'everydayness' of a person's life, the languages of the relevancy systems in terms of which I live, move and express myself in the world, and the vital quality of my life. Within my 'everydayness', I speak-out and live as I feel, experience, and conscious that I ought to, within situations and their circumstances of greatest relevance to me, always attempting to live as significantly and as vitally as I conceive I ought to.

I have tried to clarify what a structure is and what the **FEC, HRM,** and **EvLV** structures are in persons. These are among the principle essential structures which phenomenological investigations disclose in investigating the subject-matter of adult education.

It is necessary next to clarify what a 'function' is, and what the **FEC, HRM,** and **EvLV** functions are as uncovered through phenomenological investigations of adult eductions of **person** in adult education.

A function (from **fungar,** to perform) refers to the action of performing, of discharging, or to activity in general. A function might be the performance of something, a special kind of activity proper to something, or a special mode of action by which something fulfills its purpose. Hence, just as there is an 'FEC Structure' of person there is also an 'FEC Function', and an 'HRM Structure' and an 'HRM Function', and an 'EvLV Structure' and 'EvLV Function'.

The 'FEC Function' is always at least (1) a structuring of feeling, experiencing, and consciousing (the 'FEC Structure') through which all three of these layers of **person** perform special activities fulfilling appropriate performances together and as a whole. The 'FEC Function' is also (2) the activities of the whole with a special focus on one or more of the distinguishable but inseparable layers of person, as follows: F̲EC, FE̲C, FEC̲, F̲EC̲, F̲E̲C, and FE̲C̲. The bar in each case signifies focus or foci of priority. The 'HRM Function' is always at least (1) a structuring of habit, relevance, and metaphor (the 'HRM Structure') such that all three move through to the constitution of new meanings together and as a whole. But the 'HRM Function' is also (2) the activity of the whole, with a special focus on one or any two of these as follows: H̲RM, HR̲M, HRM̲, H̲R̲M, H̲RM̲, and HR̲M̲.

The 'EvLV Function', too, is always at least (1) a structure of 'everydayness', languages of relevancy, and the vital life (the 'EvLV Structure') through which one resolves new acts and determines a new placement and position within a new situation and its circumstances within the world. The 'EvLV Function' is also (2) the actions of this constituted whole, with a special focus on one action, or any two of the actions, of these clusterings of phenomena, for example, as: E$\underline{v}$LV, Ev$\underline{L}$V, EvL$\underline{V}$, $\underline{Ev}$LV, $\underline{Ev}$L$\underline{V}$, and EvL$\underline{V}$. The bar in each case signifies a focus of priority.

Each **person** presents unique and non-duplicatable **FEC**, **HRM**, and **EvLV** Structures and Functions. This fact is easily ascertainable for oneself by simple phenomenological investigations in both personal and cooperative contexts of investigation. These are of the utmost importance for the human 'scientific' study of persons, whether as individuals or as groups of persons. This fact alone again negates even the possibility of applying to the 'scientific' study of **person** and persons only reductionistic quantitative methodologies and methods which have been used with such stunning success in constructing new knowledge of the physical world. These latter approaches rest, for example, on such presuppositions at bottom as that one atom or wave of energy in principle, and in the accordance with the principle of reduction, is interchangeable, respectively with every other atom or wave of energy. But no two instances of **person** are interchangeable. This is what the **FEC**, **HRM**, and **EvLV** structures of **person** present to us. No two **FEC** structures, for example, are the same. Neither are two **FEC** functions the same.

Each of us always has our own unique **FEC**, **HRM**, and **EvLV** structures and functions by virtue of who we uniquely are, by what we uniquely know, and through our actions which are functions of what and whom we understand we ought to be and to become. These are and express hopes as our **person** as well. Ultimately we must walk the lonesome valleys alone and climb our own peaks to those heights to which our motives carry us.

But adult education is heavily based on the premise that each person can be assisted in significant ways in understanding oneself and one's relationships within the world. This means assistance in understanding such essential structures and functions of **person** as the **FEC**, **HRM**, and **ELV** structures and functions. Through all the years of adult education practices more than ample evidence has been adduced to substantiate the claim that adult education can indeed provide this assistance to persons. Moreover, having identified, described, and analyzed the phenomena constituting what I call the **FEC, HRM,** and **EvLV** structures and functions, it now also becomes possible to show how 'self-help' and 'self-directed' learning can take place, on the one hand, and how adult educators can be of profound assistance to persons, on the other hand.

## C. New Problems for Research in Adult Education

Edmund Husserl claimed that phenomenology could provide the foundation for all sciences. I do not make that claim in this essay. I maintain that in the beginning stages of a research project, and in the later stages which have more to do with interpretations of the results and conclusions of the investigations, reasoning, and experiments, phenomenological investigations (under whatever name) either are actually performed in some degree or would be useful to that research project if they were to be carried out. I suggest also that phenomenological methods would be very useful in many, if not most, research projects in scientific studies (see the discussion in Part I, C). Moreover, phenomenological approaches, in my judgment, are immensely valuable to much contemporary research in adult education, whether one takes it to be a rigorous human science or not. These claims do move in the direction of Husserl's claim, but they do not affirm his absolutistic judgment that phenomenology is the foundation of all science.

In addition to these several claims about the general values of phenomenology as an alternative paradigm and program of research in adult education, I want to show briefly how new kinds of questions and problems for research and practice open up in adult education through the kinds of phenomenological investigations I have tried to provide in this essay. Before offering some examples of these, however, it will be useful to summarize briefly a number of points which have become the ground for these new kinds of questions and problems and the examples to be mentioned.

Throughout the essay I have tried to show how the methods of phenomenological investigations are uniquely appropriate to research in adult education defined as systematic investigations into the determinate subject-matter of the adult eductions of **person** as these are expressed through the feeling, experiencing, and consciousing actions of persons. In support of this position I have laid out carefully focused phenomenological accounts of, and have constructed abbreviating acronyms for, the following clusterings of phenomena: feeling, experiencing, and consciousing (**FEC**); habituatings, relevancies, and metaphors (**HRM**); and 'everydayness', languages of relevancies, and vital life (**EvLV**). I have also presented phenomenological explorations of feeling, habituating, and 'everydayness' (**FHEv**); experiencing, relevancies, and languages of relevancies (**ERL**); and consciousing, metaphor, and vital life (**CMV**).

An especially attentive reader already will have grasped these relationships while moving through the essay. If one has failed to see these thus far, it should be necessary only to glance back through the "Table of Contents" and then to reflect briefly on the location of each **Part** and **chapter** in relation to the others, and on the meanings of the acronyms standing for these special relationships of the various subject-matters presented.

Although no specific chapters have been devoted to them, two additional items remain briefly to be clarified. *First,* it should be noted that 'everydayness' made relevant in some specific episodes and instances evolves as consciousing at work. Consciousing is a person's knowing-with 'objects' which have become relevant, or a focusing on relevant 'objects', within 'everydayness'. This is another way of saying what consciousing really is, and is a point often treated in the essay. For this particular adult eductive relationship of **person**, the clustering of the phenomena of 'everydayness', relevancies, and consciousing, I have constructed the acronym **EvRC**.

Second, feeling which grows in strength and intensity becomes the font of the energizing force in the vital lives of persons. These clusterings of the adult eductions of **person** also have been discussed in various places, and I suggest the acronym **FRV** for them.

All of these points are laid out in the following RESEARCH CONFIGURATIONS I. (1) Concepts encased by the signs '[ ]' refer to the clustered phenomena discussed in detail in the appropriate places in the essay and are easily recognizable. (2) The **arrows,** ⟶, designate the 'Function' of each cluster of phenomena, as **FEC, CMV, ERL, FHEv** Function, and so on, and refer to the flow of the eductions toward what can be identified as greater actualization and realization of the phenomena constituting these adult eductions of **person.** For example, the relationships of the clusterings of the phenomena of **FEC, feeling -----> experiencing -----> consciousing,** mean: feeling flows into experiencing, and both flow into consciousing, under the conditions and in the midst of the circumstances described in detail in the appropriate places in the essay. Feelings, experiencings, and consciousings are related to one another in the same ways, *mutatis mutandis.* These phenomena are all possible 'objects' of phenomenological research, individually and/or in clustered groups.

## RESEARCH CONFIGURATIONS I

The most immediately obvious feature of the whole presentation of RESEARCH CONFIGURATIONS I is that this is the entirety of this essay presented in schematic form: RESEARCH CONFIGURATIONS I is in fact adult education and phenomenological research. We are given new directions in theory, practice, and research.

Another significant feature of this presentation is that it conforms to what I described in various places as **eductive investigation.** Look back at the last paragraph of Chapter 2, for example. There I stated that eductive investigation [as phenomenology] consists in examining relevant ingredients within a person's life, or within persons' (as a group) lives, which are issued forth or educed. Emphasis here would be placed upon the processes of drawing forth, upon the ways of appearing through which parts-of learning, for example, become wholes or wholes-of parts are dissembling into these parts. Elicited meanings and values would be investigated. This kind of reflection would be performed by clarifying all of these ingredients and their processes through the stages, phases and stretches of their development out of conditions and circumstances of their rudimentary, latent, and tacit (or even their merely potential or possible) existence within persons' lives. All of these investigations necessarily would be investigations of the eductions of **person**. These ways of exploring phenomena, and many additional ways, have all been discussed in some detail in the course of the essay.

## RESEARCH CONFIGURATIONS I

### Eductive Phenomenology of Adult Eductions
### of <u>Person</u>

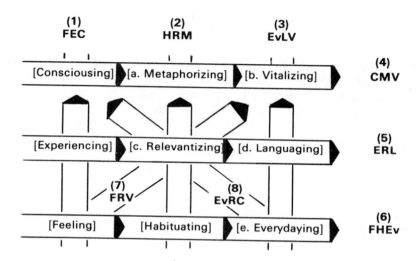

## Notes to RESEARCH CONFIGURATIONS I

a. 'Metaphorizing' compromises the phenomena of the process of disclosing, uncovering, and creating new perspectives of the adult eductions of **person**. A metaphor is first the felt meaning of the originative language of active judgment. See Chapter 8.

b. 'Vitalizing' comprises the phenomena of vigor, energy, life-giving and life-engendering, strength and intensity of the liberative adult eductions of **person** expressed by persons. See Chapter 9.

c. 'Relevantizing' is a more forced construction comprising the processes whereby some phenomena from within the repertory of all phenomena become 'objects' of interest, more apt, fitting, appropriate to some personal action(s), by virtue of some perspective, expressive of the adult eductions of **person**. See Chapters 5 and 6.

d. 'Languaging' comprises the phenomena of linguistic expressions and disciplining constructions through which relevant phenomena comprising the adult eductions of **person** are presented by persons through literal, technical, and metaphorical presentations.

e. 'Everydaying' is perhaps the most forced of these constructions. It is the clustering of phenomena of the 'everydayness' of persons' lives in the midst of which, within the days blurring into the normal routines of each and every day, the adult eductions of **person** take place.

## RESEARCH CONFIGURATIONS II

The research configurations which follow are essentials of **constitutive** investigations as phenomenology. I have discussed these kinds of phenomenological investigations in several places throughout the essay. Look back at the penultimate paragraph of Chapter 2, for example. There I characterized constitutive phenomenology as the examination of relevant ingredients within a person's life through exploring these phenomena 'backwards', or retrospectively, toward the more primal stages, phases, or stretches of these constitutions in relation to the circumstances of these lives in the midst of situations of 'everydayness', for example. How did these phenomena come to be presented in these ways? What have been the conditions for these and for their relationships to come to be what they are? Remember that all questions about the 'existence' or 'non-existence', and 'causal' matters are held in abeyance, or put aside, in these investigations. Constitutive investigation is the personal retrospective investigation of the increasingly more tacit, latent, implicit, and covert stages of these phenomena which constitute, for example, consciousing, experiencing, and feeling as adult eductions of **person**. In what ways did each relevant ingredient come to be what it now is as an adult eduction of **person** through becoming the 'object' of reflection for some person who has become interested in it?

It may be immediately obvious already to some readers that RESEARCH CONFIGURATIONS II also 'catch up' and comprise the entirety of this essay, although the contents of the essay become transposed into a different mode. The cast of the essay has been written in a more obvious **eductive** form through the present participial, gerundial, and adverbial uses of language. But it would not be possible to take those steps if the **constitutive** phenomenological chores had not been cared for along the way as well.

This is one side, or one direction, an example of what I have argued for in several places as *reflexive* experimentation which should be the kind of 'double-pronged' or 'two-directional' experiment used in almost every (I have even said 'every' in places, I suppose) experiment, study, or investigation within research in adult education. The other side, or the other direction, of *reflexive experimentation*, is **eductive** investigation as phenomenology. This side was laid out in RESEARCH CONFIGURATIONS I above.

Even if researchers do not accept the definition of adult education I have argued for, even if they do not wish to employ phenomenological investigations of any kind and in any degree in their research, and insist on using nothing but one or another kind of statistical method or behavioristic method, the questions addressed by this *reflexive experimentation* must also be addressed by them. But how can they do so with their unidimensional and reductionistic methods?

*What are these questions?*

## RESEARCH CONFIGURATIONS II

### Constitutive Phenomenology of Adult Eductions of <u>Person</u>

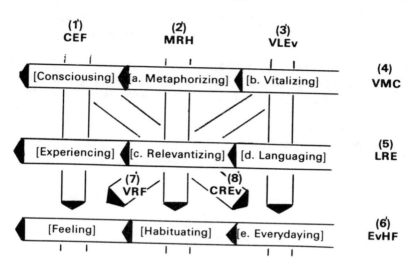

**Notes** to RESEARCH CONFIGURATIONS II

a. 'Metaphorizing' compromises the phenomena of the process of disclosing, uncovering, and creating new perspectives of the adult eductions of **person**. A metaphor is first the felt meaning of the originative language of active judgment. See Chapter 8.

b. 'Vitalizing' comprises the phenomena of vigor, energy, life-giving and life-engendering, strength and intensity of the liberative adult eductions of **person** expressed by persons. See Chapter 9.

c. 'Relevantizing' is a more forced construction comprising the processes whereby some phenomena from within the repertory of all phenomena become 'objects' of interest, more apt, fitting, appropriate to some personal action(s), by virtue of some perspective, expressive of the adult eductions of **person**. See Chapters 5 and 6.

d. 'Languaging' comprises the phenomena of linguistic expressions and disciplining constructions through which relevant phenomena comprising the adult eductions of **person** are presented by persons through literal, technical, and metaphorical presentations.

e. 'Everydaying' is perhaps the most forced of these constructions. It is the clustering of phenomena of the 'everydayness' of persons' lives in the midst of which, within the days blurring into the normal routines of each and every day, the adult eductions of **person** take place.

## CONCLUSION

### The Questions

Indeed, what are the questions addressed by adult educators? Questions involve problems, 'calling into account', challenges, accusations, disputations, doubtings, oppositions, inquiries, examinings, subjects for discussion, difficulties, investigations. . . . The list seems endless, and the number of questions in principle must be endless. All of these actions are what persons do, and questions are nothing at all if not what persons do. That is, persons enact questions as they call any phenomenon into account.

Writing in the 'analytic' tradition in the philosophy of adult education, but strongly supportive of 'liberal'[1] values and goals which ought to be effected through adult learning and education, K. H. Lawson has claimed

> What we call adult education may . . . be much more than initiation into new fields of activity. It is also critical evaluation of those activities and an exploration of new ways of looking at things and a feeling forward to new values. On this view therefore it is not enough to say that when adult educators are encouraging personal development they should offer opportunities for learning within conventional frameworks of skills and knowledge. There is also an expectation that there shall be an ongoing *questioning* of the validity of the conventional and the traditional.

> We do not only teach history and dressmaking, but also *ask* whether what is taught is valid and whether the techniques involved are the most useful. Beyond these *questions* are further *questions* about the worthfulness of what is being learned. This is not a redefinition of adult education, nor of education, but a recognition of what is already implicit in both concepts. To engage in education is to engage in rational intentional activities, and this presupposes that *questions* are asked about the intentions and the activities themselves, and what we mean when we talk of developing as a person includes the development of just these things. A person is someone who can ask *questions* as well as try to answer them.[2] (My emphasis)

What are the questions raised in the context of adult education? Any and all in principle which deal with the adult eductions of **person**. But some questions are more immediately relevant than others. For example, during the first few pages of the essay I called attention to two kinds of questions. *First,* I set out the four prime philosophical questions; **Who am I? What can I know? What ought I to do? What may I hope?** These are important questions in philosophy precisely because they are asked crucially, either tacitly or overtly, by every person, and asking them calls into account eductions of **person**, and therefore necessarily adult eductions of **person**.

*Second,* important questions logically arise with Robie Kidd's claim (quoted in the Preface) that four tasks are needed in adult education today: **conceptualization, persuasion, curriculum, and method.** Consider these once again, and more carefully now in the context of these phenomenological investigations.

1) **Conceptualization** - to take these tattered strands of ideas and make of them a woven garment.

2) **Persuasion** - persuading men and women to give care and attention to what in themselves is most human.

3) **Curriculum** - to develop the content and learning experiences that will enrich and enlarge us to goals for the advancement of the entire human family.

4) **Method** - to choose and organize and refine the means to learning that help men and women to be free. (My emphasis)

This second group of questions therefore includes these: (1) What degree and kind of conceptualization do adult learners and educators require to be successful in what they desire to accomplish? (2) How hard, stubbornly, persistently, and persuasively are we willing to attend to the qualities of what is most 'human' in us all in both individual and global contexts? (3) How do we go about assisting, in both informal and formal contexts, adults in learning experiences which will enrich and enlarge the goals, ends, and purposes of the advancement of the entire human community? (4) And what are the means and methods toward these variegated purposes and goals?

A third grouping of immediately relevant questions can be identified. These are the questions which emerge as serious candidates for specific research projects and which are born logically in the midst of or following other projects, through intuitions, hunches, announced sources of funding (!), and all of the other ways in which a research project **originates** and is formally launched, or **begins.**

I have tried to discuss both the theory and the practice of ways and means of responding to all of these kinds of questions. The ways of phenomenological investigations offer the tools and the discipline necessary to the re-exploration, and the re-investigation of old regions and territories[3] of adults, education, and philosophy. **Feeling,** habits and the will-to-learn, and 'everydayness'; **experiencing**, relevancies, and languages of relevancies; **consciousing**, 'metaphorizing life', and vital life. These all have been discussed and analyzed in great detail both through phenomenological investigations and as exemplars of phenomenological research.

Innumerable possibilities for research projects have been laid out both overtly and heuristically. A large body of notes to the text has been even more explicit in these respects and in citing a rich mass of literature relevant to adult education, a good deal of which (the work of C. S. Peirce, R. G. Collingwood, José Ortega y Gasset, and Alfred Schutz, for example) is probably now unknown (1987) to many students and researchers in adult education.

In addition to these offerings, the essay presents an additional mode of mapping out nodules of new searchings through phenomena which typically have not undergone research in adult education. Important examples are the adult eductions of **person**. These phenomena, newly focused upon, require new search and **re**-search.

So here it is. **Adult education through phenomenological research:** Phenomenological investigations constitute a way through to the theory and practices of adult education conceived as the most rigorous of human sciences. These have as their special subject-matter systematic investigations of the performative enactments of, and the systematic investigation of, the essential structures of the phenomena constituting adult eductions of **person**. These phenomena most specifically are of the deliberate liberative actions of consciousing and responsible persons whereby they become transformed and empowered with vital motives for acting.

The conclusion of a project always forms the originative grounds for new beginnings. . . . And it is this awareness of, and commitment to, the 'infinite tasks' of adult education that I conclude this essay with Spinoza's last words in his *Ethics,* his eloquent witness to the unfinishable, transforming, and empowering work of the mind in all personal quests.

His work attests the clear fact that all consciousing, all concrete reflecting, is indeed performed for

the purpose of personal enactments of one's place in the
world, and that philosophizing therefore may be most
responsibly and successfully performed through the adult
eductions of **person**.

If the way which I have pointed out as leading
to this result seems exceedingly hard, it may
nevertheless be discovered. Needs must it be
hard, since it is so seldom found. How would it
be possible, if salvation were ready to our hand,
and could without great labor be found, that it
should be by almost all men neglected? But all
things excellent are as difficult as they are
rare.[4]

## APPENDIX I

The 'case study' referred to frequently in Parts I, Section B, and II, Section A, was prepared by one of my students at Bowling Green State University to meet an introductory requirement. It is included here with her kind permission.

### *WHO WAS I?*

Claire Smith

Cold,
     Black,
          Nothingness.

Stretches before me,
Below me,
Behind me.

I sit precariously upon
A three pronged stool,
And gaze into--
Cold,
     Black,
          Nothingness.
Gaze, and grope, and strain,
With aching eyes,
Searching for something,
    anything,
Beside myself,
And this stool.

Above me is a glare,
As a sun broken loose from
    its orbit,
And too close to perceive,
Illuminating my solemn
    existence,
My nothingness.

I have memory of what was;
I hope,
But I am alone,
So alone
I am no longer sure that
I am.
I am either alone and dead,
Or else
The world has died.
O God, where are you?

Has the world ceased to be?
No--
I am here, by body, my mind,
This three pronged stool;
These defy an end of existence.

And yet I must be dead,
For I can see nothing beyond
    me but
Endless--
Cold,
      Black,
           Nothingness.

I can remember being alive,
A woman of twenty years,
A student of Bowling Green,
In Springtime.

Yet where am I now?
I am alone, sitting here,
Knowing not where here is,
Knowing only who I am.

Who I am is the same as
Who I was, when I lived;
And yet Who was I?

I was a living human being,
Living my life as a name--Claire Smith.
It could have been X or Y as well as Claire,
For a name is only a designation of a collection of
    somethings
That were uniquely me, and no one else.

I did not live life as Bishop Berkeley would suggest,
"Conscious of what we call ourself, we feel its
    existence,
And are certain of its identity and simplicity."
I did not live life consciously realizing that I was a
Living human being, a collection marked Claire Smith.

* * *

Leaving me in the darkness,
O starry universe, hung in the clear
Bell of my mind, be living in me now!
Dwell in me for a moment here!

How often, in the many minds of men,
Have you been born, only to pass away,
Dying with every mind again!

This is a thought that is too hard for me:
It is a bitter thing to think upon,
That, to myself, all this shall be
As if it had not been, when I am gone.

Existing with a constant purpose in mind,
I lived life blindly, from minute to minute,
And day to day, worrying about petty little problems,
Crying over nothings, escaping into a dream world when
    life
Became too hard to take.

I was Claire Smith, and yet what exactly made me that,
Myself instead of someone else, some other claire
    smith.
I was myself uniquely on the surface.
I am still Claire Smith, myself on the surface.
I still have chewed fingernails, the scars, the
    freckles,
The fillings in my teeth, that mark me myself and
No one else.
I am still Claire Smith as an outer shell.
I can now add nothing to my present self through injury
    or
Artificial aid--no paint or polish will change me
From my present state.

More important I am now what I never was before, a
    determined inner self,
Something I can look at and evaluate exactly because
It will change no more, except in my own re-evaluation.
I have my intelligence gleaned from life.
I know X amount about Y subject and no more.
I will never now add to this knowledge.
I will never know calculus, or zoology, or ancient Greek
    history.
I will have a collection of knowledge which is unique
within itself.

As far as personality is concerned, I am also finite.
My sense of humor, my moods, my abilities (positive or
    negative),
My loves, my hates--all these will remain a part of me.
I will always have my fears, fears of specific things
Which have happened to me or been told to me, in my
    life.
My fears are a part of me, representative of every other
    part of me
In that they are mine.

They are thus because they represent everything in my
    life
Which has been fearful to me.
I am a culmination of all these things.

From the time I was a one-celled being, born to Mr. and
    Mrs. Smith,
My being has been shaped by my experiences.
I was born into a strained marriage,
One threatening to split into divorce.
I was as a ping pong ball on a table called home,
With parents as players, whacking away at me,
Bouncing me back and forth
In a desperate attempt to make a house a home.

Mine was a strange situation, yet one which was similar
To countless others.
I grew up reveling in its uniqueness, certain that I
    alone
Suffered the tortures of Hell in home life.
I was a jealous child, jealous of others around me.
Those with happy homes and loving parents, who did
    things
As a family.
I grew up alone, and certain that the world owed me
    something
For all my trouble.
I blamed my parents for all the sorrow they were causing
    me.

I grew up unaware that these two people, my parents,
were people.
I did not understand, nor did I try to understand, their
plight.
From my beginning came a certain part of my
personality,
An insecurity, a rebellion, which is still a part of
me.

Minute by minute, day by day, I increased in other
ways.
Knowledge added to my self, first informal knowledge and
then
The formal knowledge of school.
I learned to think and reason, to memorize and solve
problems.
Some of the knowledge I gleaned helped me to solve
everyday problems.
Most of the knowledge, however, served as nothing more
than
Mere memorization.
My knowledge involved a number of various areas,
centered around
No particular field or specialty.
I scratched the surface of many areas, yet never went
beyond this surface.

Looking back now I wish that I could have learned more,
much more.
Knowledge opens the door to so many questions.
The questions and the ability to go on questioning
endlessly--
This to some would lack purpose, to me it would have
been happiness.
But I did not continue or use the brain which was mine,
And this, not what I would have liked to have done, is
what
Determines me, as me.

A knowledge of a God was a very important part of my
    life.
As a young child, I accepted the teachings of a grey
    haired
Old lady in Sunday school class as wonderful
    unbelievable stories.
I did not know or understand the word belief, and it
    didn't bother me.
I learned of a God and his son and the wonderful things
    he did.
But mine was a God who brought ponies to little girls,
And so it was him I prayed to at night.
Prayers and hymns were so many words to me.

Not until a day when I realized that I was alive did a
    God mean anything.
When I began to believe that there was truly a God,
I wanted to know about him.
I investigated various religions to find which suited me
    the best.
However, up until the day of my death I did not know
Which religion of all the various ones I investigated
Seemed the best to me.
I had a very definite belief in a God, and yet I could
    not
Especially define him as this or that type of a God.
I did not believe in a kindly old gentleman with white
    hair,
Who caused oceans to roll back and other miracles to
    happen,
Beyond the miracles of everyday life.
He was also a higher being that I could turn to in time
    of trouble
And generally forget to thank except on Christmas and
    Easter.

Where he is now, I do not know.
If there is to be no splendor for eternity,
If this is death and there is no eternity except
What I am seeing now, I shall be sorely disappointed
But will have to accept the situation.
I will not disbelieve in my God, because I do not think
That I ever really did expect white powdery clouds and
   angel's wings.
I will still believe in his existence, yet he has not
   changed me
From my present eternity.

The realization of myself as a human being was one of
   the greatest
Changes in my life.
Until this point I was preoccupied with everyday
   worries,
Or I will assume so, because I can remember nothing of
   any great significance.
I planned half-heartedly for a future,
But never took the time really to live the future.

I was a freshman in college and had been dating a boy
   named X.
X was a wonderful friend, more of a friend than a
   lover.
We laughed and talked and enjoyed spending time
   together.
At the end of the term X and I said goodbye to each
   other.
X was flying home to Alaska and I was driving to
   Philadelphia.
The goodbye was the same as any goodbye with promise of
   tomorrow.
There was nothing terribly unusual about it.
A few days later I received a postcard from him at my
   home.
He had sent the card from Chicago on his way home.
I happened to notice in the paper that day that a plane
   had

Crashed over the coast of Washington, but I thought
    nothing more of it.
The next day I received two letters in the mail,
One from X and one from a sorority sister of mine.
As I read the sorority sister's words of sympathy I
    became a different
Person than I had been before.
She expressed sympathy for me in comforting words and
    told me
The Bowling Green paper had printed a story about X
    being killed
In a plane crash off the coast of Alaska.
The other letter was no longer real, it was written by
    someone
Who no longer existed, and I did.
Existence was a great shock to a dreamer.
The greatest tragedy of the incident was not personal
    loss,
Because I had not known X really that well.
The great realization was in fact that life is not a
Predetermined length to be planned on and expected.
We as human beings have not the right
To expect any such continuance in life from instant to
    instant.
I learned to appreciate each moment for what it was
    worth,
To look beyond the surface situation and try to perceive
    a meaning,
An importance in the incident.

I learned to appreciate exactly what it meant to be
    alive.
I came to the realization through fear,
A blinding fear that I would die. I lived afraid to go
On planes or in dangerous situations.

Before my death I smothered this fear enough to enjoy
  life,
Yet within me it still remained.

As men come and go in a woman's life as in mine,
The women change and mature because of these men.
Because of the type of a person I was, living in
  insecurity
And fear, men were a very important leaning post.
They provided the security I needed to a great extent.

Alone I would probably dream up a pleasant incident if I
Felt fear.
Until the day of my death I was a dreamer,
Remembering the dreams I had invented as a child to
  cover
The unpleasant surroundings I existed in
As a more mature person, I attempted to realize myself
  more
And dream myself less.
I accepted the fact that physically I could be merely 97
  cents
Worth of atoms, plus additional worth of the filling in
  my teeth.
I determined I was going to do something, however, with
  this
Mass of atoms to give it meaning.
A great difference occurred, however, between thinking
  and
Determining I was going to do this, and getting right
  down
To putting words into action.
There were many times that I did live purposefully;
However, there were also many in which I got off the
  track
And ended up merely thinking and dreaming about it.

So life was a constant conflict between reality and non-
    reality,
A conflict between life and death.

And so up until time of my death I existed as a living,
Breathing human being in a society.
Even the society shaped me into what I was.
Had I been exactly the same person up to X number of
    years
In my life and then suddenly lived in a different
    country
Or life situation, all the years beyond X would have
    shaped
Me differently.
I do not even now like to think of myself as a
    prejudiced
Person, and yet I am very prejudiced.
I believe what I have been taught about my country and
    its
Principles to be right.
I believe those opposing it to be wrong.
Upon investigation through knowledge, I can see that
    both
Sides have merit in their existence.
Yet the deep-seated feeling of wrongness is within me.
This is a prejudice as well as any other I have.
Had I existed in another part of the world, I probably
Would have been prejudiced in another direction,
Maybe even against what I believe in now.
This is my own private collection of prejudices, unlike
Any other, because my existence is a synthesis of a
    particular
Collection of happenings unlike any other,
These happenings forming not only my knowledge, my
    prejudices,
My future desires, but also my being.
My friends, my enemies, my nation, my status within my
    society--

All these formed a part of this synthesis.
And thus I was a person: changing, indefinite,
Ever increasing as a be-ing,
Increasing as I lived, every minute of my life,
Until I became what I am now--a self.

If I were to diagram my self as a simple be-ing,
As I am now in my death,
I would be:
SELF = CONCEPTION + EXPERIENCE THROUGH
TIME (AFTER DEATH)
The experience through time is a synthesis of unique
happenings
Which are mine alone and which shape me into me.
Thus man is not only a synthesis, but synthesis of
himself.
I who have never been a self before can now fully
Appreciate my self as something which can be defined,
equated,
And examined.

And here I am, in this selfsame state,
And here I may sit in a timeless forever,
On a three pronged stool,
Surrounded by
Cold,
Black,
Somethingness!

This paper is me; and yet a realization has
occurred within the time of writing and
rewriting it. A realization that I have
changed in my-self while writing it, and hence
it is immediately obsolete. If I were to
rewrite it tomorrow or even a minute from now,
it would be different than it is now, for I
cannot contain myself and describe myself in
definite terms while a living human being.

## APPENDIX II

Course Syllabus

## PHENOMENOLOGY AND ADULT EDUCATION

Evening Seminar, 6:00-8:40 p.m.

## COURSE DESCRIPTION

This course will move through introductory phenomenological accounts of the eductive (and in this special sense, educative) processes of teaching/learning, theory/practice, and research within adult education considered as a rigorous human science. Within the contexts of phenomenology, the human sciences, and adult education, lectures, discussion, and writing will focus on subjects selected from among, but not limited to, the following topics: 'Everydayness' and Adult Learning; Lifeworld/Life Stages; Lifelong Learning; Competency-based Adult Learning; Voluntarism and Learning; Conscientization; Person, Self, and Ego; Willing/Choosing/ Deciding; Obligation; Empowerment; Responsibility.

Other kinds of topics could include: "Qualitative/ Quantitative" Research; Reductive/Eductive Teaching Methods and Research Methods; Adult Education and the Social Sciences; Adult Education and the Humanities; Charles Sanders Peirce, William James, John Dewey, American Pragmatism and late 19th century and early 20th century Phenomenology.

Clearly no single course can cover all of these kinds of topics adequately. Professor Stanage and all seminar participants will jointly select the problems and themes to be investigated as the seminar progresses. Some of these topics will be investigated through projects, papers, and Critical Logbooks. Seminar members with an introductory background in phenomenology and adult education will pursue more advanced projects.

Finally,
1. (1)  All seminar participants will *do* phenomenology.
2. (2)  All participants will be challenged to develop a working knowledge of the theory and the practice of phenomenology.
3. (3)  The potentialities of the methods of phenomenology for professional career, teaching, and research programs will be explored.

## FORMAT

The seminar will feature a number of lectures, much discussion, and a major phenomenological investigation of a theme in adult education or of a phenomenon central to adult eductions of **person**. This investigation will continue throughout the course and will be presented in three stages. A Critical Logbook will be kept throughout the course.

## REQUIRED TEXTBOOKS AND READINGS

Donald Polkinghorne, *Methodology for the Human Sciences*
Sherman Stanage, *Adult Education and Phenomenological Research*
Richard M. Zaner, *The Way of Phenomenology*

### READING ASSIGNMENTS/DISCUSSION TOPICS

Session I — Introductory remarks, discussion of course requirements, textbooks and other readings, explanations covering the major phenomenological investigation(s) of a theme in adult education, the nature and the purpose of the Critical Logbook.
Lecture and general discussion relating to such key notions as: Philosophy, Science (including Physical Science, Social Science, and **Human Science**) Humanities, Education, Phenomenology, and Phenomenology of Adult Education.

Session 2          Donald Polkinghorne, *Methodology for the Human Sciences: Systems of Inquiry*, "Preface," "Introduction," pp. ix-13; "Appendix," pp. 283-289. Sherman Stanage, *Adult Education and Phenomenological Research*, "The Subject-matter of Adult Education: The Phenomenology of Adult Education as Rigorous Human Science." The bulk of *Adult Education and Phenomenology* will be assigned at intervals throughout the course.)

Session 3          Polkinghorne, MHS, Chapter 7, "Human Science Research," pp. 241-281. R. G. Collingwood, *An Essay on Metaphysics*, "Causation," pp. 285-312.
Lecture and general discussion of such key notions as: Cause, Causal, Causality, Causation, Presuppositions, Essence, Existence/Nonexistence, Being, and Consciousness.
Shared observations from the Critical Logbook.

Session 4          Polkinghorne, MHS, Chapter 1, "The Original Debate," pp. 15-57; Collingwood, "Causation," pp. 313-343.
Continuation of lecture and general discussion of key notions involved in the juxtaposition of early positivism and early investigations termed **human sciences**. Brief seminar presentations of the *Workbench Draft I* of the major phenomenological investigation of a theme in adult education or of a phenomenon central to the adult eductions of **person**.
Shared observations from the Critical Logbook.

Session 5    Herbert Spiegelberg, *The Phenomenological Movement*, "The Essentials of the Phenomenological Movement," pp. 653-659.
Polkinghorne, MHS, Chapter 2, "The Received View of Science," pp. 59-91.
Lecture and general discussion concerning phenomenological method(s).
Shared observations from the Critical Logbook.

Session 6    Spiegelberg, PM, "The Essentials of the Phenomenological Movement," pp. 659-676; Polkinghorne, MHS, Chapter 3, "Pragmatic Science," pp. 94-133.
Lecture and general discussion concerning key notions employed within phenomenological method(s), e.g., Method, Reduction, Reductionism, Phenomena, Phenomenological Description, Intuiting, Analyzing, Describing. In addition, the "mind/body problem" and problems relating to the subjectivity/objectivity split will be explored.
Shared observations from the Critical Logbook.

Session 7    Spiegelberg, PM, "The Essentials of the Phenomenological Method," pp. 676-684; Polkinghorne, MHS, Chapter 4, "Systems and Structures," pp. 135-167.
Lecture and general discussion concerning key notions employed within phenomenological method(s), e.g., Essences/General Essences, Apprehending Essential Relationships, Modes of Appearing.
Lecture and general discussion of Stanage, **RESEARCH CONFIGURATIONS I.**
Shared observations from the Critical Logbook.

Session 8    Spiegelberg, PM, "The Essentials of the Phenomenological Method," pp. 684-701; Polkinghorne, MHS, Chapter 5, "Human Action," pp. 169-199.
Lecture and general discussion concerning key notions employed within phenomenological method(s), e.g., the Constitution of Phenomena in Consciousness, Suspending Belief in the Existence of Particular Objects of Consciousness, Epochē, Hermeneutics.
Lecture and general discussion of Stanage, **RESEARCH CONFIGURATIONS II.**
Shared observations from the Critical Logbook.

Session 9    Polkinghorne, MHS, Chapter 6, "Existential-Phenomenological and Hermeneutic Systems," pp. 201-240.
Seminar presentations of the *Workbench Draft II* of the major phenomenological investigation of a theme in adult education or of a phenomenon central to the adult eductions of **person**.
Shared observations from the Critical Logbook.

Session 10   REVIEW: Polkinghorne, MHS, Chapter 7, "Human Science Research," pp. 241-281, "Appendix," pp. 283-289.
Seminar presentations of the *Workbench Draft II* of the major phenomenological investigation of a theme in adult education or of a phenomenon central to the adult eductions of **person**.
Shared observations from the Critical Logbook.

Session 11    Richard M. Zaner, *The Way of Phenomenology,* "Preface," "Prologue," pp. xi-
40.
Lecture and discussion of general phenomenological themes and their possible
applications to the **theory** and **practice**
of adult education and to **research** in
adult education.

Session 12    Zaner, WP, Chapter One, "Ways to Phenomenology," pp. 41-78. Continuation of
lecture and discussion themes as above.
Shared observations from the Critical
Logbook.

Session 13    Zaner, WP, Chapter Two, "The Sense of
Phenomenology," pp. 79-124. Continuation
of lecture and discussion themes as
above.
Shared observations from the Critical
Logbook.

Session 14    Zaner, WP, Chapter Three, "The Theory of
Consciousness," pp. 125-174.
Seminar presentations of the *Final
Draft* of the major phenomenological
investigation of a theme in adult educa-
tion or of a phenomenon central to the
adult eductions of **person**.
Shared observations from the Critical
Logbook.

Session 15    Zaner, WP, Chapter Four, "The Exigency
for Transcendent Philosophy," "Epilogue,"
pp. 175-207.
Seminar presentations of the *Final
Draft* of the major phenomenological
investigation of a theme in adult education or of a phenomenon central to the
adult eductions of **person**.

Shared observations from the Critical Logbook.

Session 16        REVIEW OF THE COURSE: Theory, practice, and research via phenomenological investigations into adult eductions of **person**, and in the light of adult education constituted as a rigorous **human science.**
Final observations from the Critical Logbook.

## APPENDIX III

Doctoral Dissertations in Adult Education
Which Present Phenomenological Investigations

Collins, Michael. *Competency in Adult Education: Applying a Theory of Relevance.* Washington, D.C. Unpublished doctoral dissertation, Northern Illinois University, 1980)

Griffith, Gwyneth Proctor. *Images of Interdependence: Meaning and Judgment in Learning/Teaching.* Unpublished doctoral dissertation, University of Toronto, 1982.

Hardin, Paula. *Generativity in Middle Adulthood.* Unpublished doctoral dissertation, Northern Illinois University, 1985.

Ilsley, Paul. *The Relevance of the Future in Adult Education: A Phenomenological Analysis of Images of the Future.* Unpublished doctoral dissertation, Northern Illinois University, 1982.

Murphy, Steven. *Resistance in the Professions: Adult Education and the New Paradigms of Power.* Unpublished doctoral dissertation, Northern Illinois University, 1986.

Quigley, Benjamin Allan. *The Resisters: Non-Participation in Adult Basic Education.* Unpublished doctoral dissertation, Northern Illinois University, 1986.

Samuels, Sandra Lee. *The Creation of Meaning Through the Structure of Necessary Acts: A Hermeneutic Study of Survival.* Unpublished doctoral dissertation, University of Toronto, 1983.

326 / Appendix III

Sarkisian, Ellen. *Motivation and Personal Meaning of Learning: A Phenomenological Study of the Relationship of Life Events and Life Stages to the Participation of Older Adults in Community College Courses.* Unpublished doctoral dissertation, Boston University, 1982.

Trussler, Terrence Andrew. *The Discovery of Critical Experience in the Social Invention of Everyday Life.* Unpublished doctoral dissertation, University of Toronto, 1982.

# NOTES

## NOTES TO TABLE OF CONTENTS

*Plato, *Letter VII,* in Edith Hamilton and Huntington Cairns, eds., *Plato: Collected Dialogues,* Princeton: Princeton University Press, 1963, translated by L. A. Post, p. 1589.

[1]"Phenomenology is, in the 20th century, mainly the name for a philosophical movement whose primary objective is the direct investigation and description of phenomena as consciously experienced, without theories about their causal explanation and as free as possible from unexamined preconceptions and presuppositions." Herbert Spiegelberg, "Phenomenology," *Encyclopedia Britannica,* Chicago: Encyclopedia Britannica, Inc., 1973. See also note 3 in **Notes to Preface.**

[2]That which is *educed,* from **e,** out + **ducere,** to lead. The emphasis here is deliberately placed upon the processes of drawing forth, bringing out, or eliciting means and values; and the processes of clarifying these through the stages of their development from conditions of latent, rudimentary, or merely potential existence through to their actual and concrete development.

[3]This is my construction and it is crucial to these phenomenological investigations. The term 'consciousing' is constructed from **con,** with, together, and **scire,** to know. Hence, **consciousing** means knowing-together, or knowing in such intimate, and logically primitive, form that all knowing and all cognitive activities of persons are constituted partly through it. My use of 'consciousing' is pointed toward, but not entirely captured, by Henri Bergson's use of 'intuition' as a way of knowing in his *Introduction to Metaphysics,* trans. T. E. Hulme, Indianapolis: The Bobbs-Merrill Company, Inc., 1976, *passim,* but esp. pp. 23-24, 60-62. All structures of knowing and knowledge have consciousing already

present. Consciousness already has consciousing within it. Consciousings are not each a something (**res**), but a flow, a stream of processes (**Erlebnisse**) and activities (**Ich-Akte**), that is, consciousings always with an 'I' - presence. 'To conscious' as an infinitive parallels 'to feel' and 'to experience'. 'Consciousing' is used both as a gerund and as a present participle. As a gerund it is a form of a (my constructed) Latin verb, 'to conscious', capable of being considered as a substantive, but retaining the regimen of the verb 'to conscious'. As a participle it is a derivative of my constructed verb, 'to conscious', which has the function and construction of an adjective (qualifying a noun) while retaining some of those of the verb (e.g., tense, government of an object).

The infinitive form of this neologism is 'I conscious,' and this parallels the infinitive forms 'I feel' and 'I experience'. The model of **person** I intend throughout this essay may be presented as follows:

'I conscious' - - - - - - - - - - Consciousing
'I experience' - - - - - - - - Experiencing
'I feel' - - - - - - - Feeling

## NOTES TO PREFACE

[1]James Robbins Kidd, *Relentless Verity: Education for Being-Becoming-Belonging,* Syracuse: Syracuse University Press, 1973, pp. 23-24.

[2]There are many positions or 'schools' in philosophy which can be (and in some cases have been) developed into theoretical approaches to adult education. Typically these might be characterized as classical realism, materialism, naturalism, idealism, logical positivism, linguistic philosophies of various kinds, analytic philosophy, existentialism, etc. This listing is limited to positions in philosophy in the West. Eastern philosophy provides many more positions and 'schools.'

In each of these it is necessary to begin investigations into subjects with concepts and conceptual tools
which are as clear, sharp, and as clean as possible in
the light of the subject-matter under study. Moreover,
in all of these positions philosophers should do philosophy cooperatively.

According to Edmund Husserl's ideal development of
phenomenology as a rigorous science, each of these
schools of philosophy and the sciences themselves must
be grounded firmly through the results of phenomenological investigations uniquely appropriate to the determinate subject-matter.

This applies also, I believe, to such distinctions
within 'philosophies' of adult education as: 'Liberal',
'Progressive', 'Behaviorist', 'Humanist', 'Analytical',
and 'Radical' philosophies. (See John L. Elias and
Sharan B. Merriam, *Philosophical Foundations of Adult
Education,* Melbourne, FL: Robert E. Krieger Publishing
Co., 1980).

Each approach as disciplined *praxis* and as a
theoretical orientation is practiced and named on the
basis of selectings of phenomena considered most relevant to situationally circumscribed problems adults
encounter. And certain relevancy systems are operative.
Phenomeological investigations, Husserl claimed, may
deal with all phenomena in ways preparatory for all of
the sciences. See Edmund Husserl, *Phenomenology and
the Crisis of Philosophy,* translated by Quentin Lauer,
New York: Harper and Row, 1965, pp. 71-147, esp. 147.

[3]See note 1 to **Notes to Table of Contents**. In addition to Herbert Spiegelberg's definition of 'phenomenology' there, two additional statements may prove
helpful: (1) the first is J. N. Findlay's definition
which first appeared in the *Encyclopedia Britannica* in
1974.

[Phenomenology is] a school of thought that arose at
the turn of the 20th century with the work of Edmund
Husserl. Its primary approach has been to take a fresh
approach to concretely experienced phenomena through the

direct investigation of the data of consciousness--
without theories about their causal explanation and as
free as possible from unexamined presuppositions and to
attempt to describe them as faithfully as possible. By
carefully exploring examples one can thus fathom the
essential structures and relationships of phenomena.

(2) The second is the English translation of Edmund
Husserl's definition of phenomenology in an article
which was not published until 1971 (although it was to
have been included in the *Encyclopedia Britannica* in
1927):

The term 'phenomenology' designates two things: a new
kind of descriptive method which made a breakthrough in
philosophy at the turn of the century, and an a priori
science derived from it; a science which is intended to
supply the basic instrument (**Organon**) for a rigorously
scientific philosophy and, in its consequent application, to make possible a methodical reform of all the
sciences. Together with this philosophical phenomenology, but not yet separated from it, however, there also
came into being a new psychological discipline parallel
to it in method and content: the a priori pure or 'phenomenological' psychology, which raises the reformation-
al claim to being the basic methodological foundation on
which alone a scientifically rigorous empirical psychology can be established. An outline of this psychological phenomenology, standing nearer to our natural
thinking, is well suited to serve as a preliminary step
that will lead up to an understanding of philosophical
phenomenology.

Husserl, "Phenomenology," revised translation by
Richard E. Palmer (as "'Phenomenology'," Edmund
Husserl's Article for the *Encyclopedia Britannica*
[1927]), Peter McCormick and Frederick Elliston, editors, *Husserl: Shorter Works*, Notre Dame, University
of Notre Dame Press, 1981, p. 22. For an account of the
regrettable circumstances surrounding the failure to
include Husserl's own article on phenomenology in the
*Encyclopedia Britannica*, see Herbert Spiegelberg's
excellent philosophical detective work in "On the Mis-
fortunes of Edmund Husserl's *Encyclopedia Britannica*

*Article 'Phenomenology',* in *Husserl: Shorter Works*, pp. 18-20. A major reason for mentioning this point in an essay on adult education and phenomenological research is that the badly translated and chopped version (by C. V. Salmon) of Husserl's original article probably contributed greatly to several decades of gross misperceptions and misunderstandings of phenomenology in the English-speaking world.

[4]A *human science* is an orderly and systematic investigation and description of a person's (and persons') felt experiences of conscioused 'objects' of direct phenomena through the various forms in which a selected and relevant phenomenon may appear or be manifested. A *human science* deals necessarily with both facts and values and does not formally exclude the latter in the midst of its scientific investigations. A *fact* is any phenomenon intersubjectively structured, explored, investigated, and analyzed as an objecting agreement of intersubjectively felt experience. A *value* is any phenomenon intersubjectively structured, explored, investigated, and analyzed as a subjecting agreement of intersubjectively felt experience. See, also, the excellent discussion of what a human science is in Donald Polkinghorne, *Methodology for the Human Sciences: Systems of Inquiry,* Albany: State University of New York Press, 1983, pp. 283-289 ("Appendix: The term 'Human Science'") and *passim.* See also Introduction, Section D.

[5]See Appendix III.

[6]This was Edmund Husserl's early claim concerning the goal of phenomenological investigations. See Edmund Husserl, *Philosophy as Rigorous Science* (published in 1911) in *Phenomenology and the Crisis of Philosophy*, translated by Quentin Lauer, New York: Harper and Row, 1965, pp. 71-147. Phenomenology is intended to be philosophy as a rigorous science in this grounding and foundational sense. As *the necessary basis for all philosophy and for all sciences* phenomenology does not

have to be a final, absolute, complete, or even completeable, basis. I address these issues frequently in a variety of contexts in the book.

7'Everydayness' is the world in which one lives, moves, and has one's being in the midst of routineness, repetitiveness, mundanity and all of the qualities, human actions, events of our daily lives. I discuss this conception of our daily, lived-world in detail in Chapter 3. See the **Glossary of Terms.**

8The lifeworld is simply the world as it is lived through its structures and its structurings by persons through all the years of their lives. The lifeworld is the world of my life, the world of your life, the worlds of the others' lives as these are lived through temporal and spatial structures. That is, I am here and there, and now and then, in life within the world. So are you, and so is every other person in his own life.

9In various places in the book I discuss the issues of competence, performance, and discipline and the ways in which these are brought about and enhanced through work, especially through language forms. See, for example, Part III, Chapters 5 and 6, and *passim.*

10Cf. the very important work of Jack Mezirow in this regard, for example, *Education for Perspective Transformation,* New York: Center for Adult Education, 1978.

11I discuss these matters in detail--and with great emphasis upon the basic essentials and ingredients of what constitutes *research* in the most fundamental sense--very frequently in the book, and especially in Part VI.

12The distinction between **person** and person is absolutely vital to the claims and arguments in this essay. Clarification can only be provided progressively. Provisionally, it can be said here that **person** is the full eduction of what persons are and have in common; it makes possible communication on the basis of intersubjectivity within the coexistence of persons. **Person** is what is drawn forth, pulled out, or what flows forth from persons in their lifeworlds. See Introduction, Section D, especially. See n. 3, **Notes to Table of Contents.**

[13]Bertrand Russell, *The Problems of Philosophy*, Oxford: Oxford University Press, 1912, p. 161.

## NOTES TO INTRODUCTION

[1]José Ortega y Gasset, *Meditations on Quixote*, translated by Evelyn Rugg and Diego Marin, New York: W. W. Norton and Company, Inc., 1961, pp. 59-60. Ortega justly may be considered the most prominent 'adult educator' in Spain in the twentieth century. Candidates for research projects of the greatest urgency and significance abound in his writings.

[2]D. H. Cranage, "The Purpose and Meaning of Adult Education," in *Cambridge Essays in Adult Education*, edited by Reginold St. John Parry, Cambridge: The University Press, 1920, p. 34.

[3]*1919 Report: The Report of the Committee on Adult Education* (Cd. 321.1919).

[4]Alfred Cobham, "A Student Experience," in *Cambridge Essays in Adult Education*, pp. 206 and 215.

[5]George F. Aker, *Education Procedures, Methods and Techniques: A Classified and Annotated Bibliography, 1953-1963* (compiled under the direction of George F. Aker), Syracuse University, 1965, *passim*.

[6]José Ortega y Gasset, *Some Lessons in Metaphysics*, translated by Mildred Adams, New York: W. W. Norton and Company, Inc., 1969, "Lesson 1", pp. 13-27 and *passim*. An 'immediate need' to know comes from one's own **person,**

whereas the 'mediate' need to know is impressed on a person, say a student in a class, by someone else such as the teacher.

[7]René Descartes, *Discourse on Method*, translated from the Latin by Donald A. Cress, Indianapolis: Hackett Publishing Company, 1981, pp. 5-6.

[8]By the accounts we give of things in accordance with our ways of viewing the world. It is difficult to claim with any assurance that there really are 'beginnings' of things in the world apart from the kinds I have indicated. In Spinoza's philosophy, for example, there is only one 'nature', 'substance', 'reality,' 'God' (they are all one), as 'self-caused'.

[9]Cobham, pp. 215-216.

[10]Rene Descartes, *Meditations on First Philosophy*, translated from the Latin by Donald A. Cress, Indianapolis: Hackett Publishing Company, 1979, p. 13.

[11]Robin G. Collingwood, *Speculum Mentis: Or the Map of Knowledge*, Oxford, The Clarendon Press, 1924, p. 16.

[12]Plato, *Republic*, translated by Paul Shorey, in *The Collected Dialogues of Plato*, edited by Edith Hamilton and Huntington Cairns, Princeton: Princeton University Press, 1961, pp. 745-747.

[13]John Dewey, *Logic: The Theory of Inquiry*, New York: Henry Holt and Company, 1938.

[14]Dewey, *op. cit.*, p. 66.

[15]See Chapter 3.

[16]Stanley Sworder, in "What is Adult Education? Nine Working Definitions," *Adult Education*, vol. 5, pp. 131-145, Spring, 1955, p. 135.

[17]Wilbur C. Hallenbeck, in *op. cit.,* p. 132.

[18]UNESCO, *The General Conference Adopts a Recommendation on Adult Education* (Adult Education Information Notes, no. 1), 1977, p. 2. (As quoted in Gordon G. Darkenwald and Sharan B. Merriam, *Adult Education: Foundations of Practice,* New York: Harper and Row, 1982, p. 9.

[19]Darkenwald and Merriam, p. 9.

[20]Jerold W. Apps, *Problems in Continuing Education,* New York: McGraw-Hill Book Company, 1979, p. 68. Apps discusses a number of definitions of adult education which appeared in "What is Adult Education? Nine Working Definitions," *Adult Education,* vol. 5, pp. 131-145, Spring, 1955.

[21]I discuss the topic of relevance and related matters principally in Chapters 5 and 6. Much theoretical research could be done on questions relating to the matters discussed in this paragraph.

[22]John L. Elias and Sharan B. Merriam, *Philosophical Foundations of Adult Education,* Huntington, New York: Robert E. Krieger Publishing Company, 1980.

[23]See n. 2 in **Notes to Preface.**

[24]See R. G. Collingwood, *An Essay on Philosophical Method,* Oxford: The Clarendon Press, 1933, pp. 1-91.

[25]In the latter pages of Chapter 9 and in the Conclusion I reformulate this definition as follows: Adult education is the performative enactment of, and systematic investigation of, the essential structures of the phenomena constituting *adult eductions* of **person,** specifically of the deliberate liberative actions of consciousing and responsible persons whereby they are transformed and empowered with vital motives for acting. Before this restated definition of the subject-matter of

adult education can be presented with sufficient confi-
dence that it will withstand criticism, presuppositions,
claims, and arguments foundational to it must be fleshed
out in orderly fashion in the intervening chapters.

26In *An Essay on Metaphysics*, Oxford: The Clarendon
Press, 1940. This volume is a rich mine for adult
educators interested in theory and philosophy of adult
education. See Sherman M. Stanage, "Collingwood's
Phenomenology of Education: **Person** and the Self-Recogni-
tion of the Mind," in Michael Krausz, editor, *Critical
Essays on the Philosophy of R. G. Collingwood*, Oxford:
The Clarendon Press, 1972, pp. 268-295.

27Collingwood, pp. 285-287. Readers especially
interested in Collingwood as adult educator will find
Chapters XXIX - XXXII (pp. 285-327) particularly reward-
ing. See also his *The New Leviathan*, Oxford: The
Clarendon Press, 1947, throughout, but especially Part
III, "Civilization", pp. 280-341. Again, adult educators will find this work of Collingwood's of the greatest value to their reflections and research. Indeed,
Collingwood's entire writings constitute a coherent and
consistent position of great significance to philosophical reflections on adult education practices and research.

28See the distinction between 'generic concepts' and
'class concepts' above, and n. 24.

29See Preface, n. 4.


**NOTES TO PART I**

1See **Table of Contents**, n. 1, and **Notes to Preface**,
n. 3.

2Alexander Pfänder, "Introduction to **Logic**," in
*Phenomenology of Willing and Motivation*, translated by

Herbert Spiegelberg, Evanston: Northwestern University, 1967, pp. 66-67.

[3]See **Table of Contents**, n. 3.

[4]See Introduction, Section C. for the discussions of Plato and Dewey and the ways in which thinking is con-sciousing's turning around and reconsidering the ob-ject(s) which it has grasped. A person comes to know some things, and in 'turning around' (reflecting, re-flexing), knows that (s)he knows them, and comes to know them better . . . and better in these ways. See also the discussion of 'learning-to-learn' in Part I, Section A.

[5]An 'object' of thought or of consciousing is not simply a material object. It is anything attended-to, grasped, and held, however fleetingly, by a person's in-terest and thought. Every instance of thinking is necessarily a thinking-of *something*, whether this something is a desk, mountain, hope, plan, a moment of anger, or an episode of surprise.

[6]Pfänder, p. 66.

[7]Pfänder, p. 66.

[8]Edmund Husserl, *Cartesian Meditations,* translated by Dorion Cairns, The Hague: Martinus Nijhoff, pp. 1-2.

[9]'I' and 'my consciousness' are the same thing at the level of **person** termed 'consciousing'. See **Table of Contents**, n. 3. Chapter 7 deals with this concept in detail.

[10]See **Table of Contents**, n. 2. I discuss the crucial notion of 'adult education' at length in Part III, and *passim.*

[11]J. L. Austin, *Philosophical Papers,* Oxford: The Clarendon Press, 1961, p. 130. Also quoted in Herbert Spiegelberg, "'Linguistic Phenomenology': John L. Austin

and Alexander Pfänder," *Memorias del XIII Congreso Internacianal de Filosofia,* Vol. IX, Mexico, D.F., Universidad Nicional Autonomia de Mexico, 1964, p. 511.

12Spiegelberg, p. 511.

13Spiegelberg, p. 510.

14Georges Gusdorf, *Speaking,* Evanston: Northwestern University Press, 1965, p. 4.

15Gusdorf, p. 119.

16Maurice Merleau-Ponty, *Phenomenology of Perceptions,* London: Routledge and Kegan Paul, 1962, p. 193.

17Robin G. Collingwood, *The Principles of Art,* Oxford: The Clarendon Press, 1938, p. 248.

18Collingwood, 317.

19**Person**-speaking is the direct eduction of **person**, the drawing forth, bringing out, of feelings, experiencings, and consciousings and the continuing process of clarifying these through to their actual and concrete development. See **Notes to Table of Contents,** n. 2.

20See Appendix I, Claire Smith, "Who Was I?," and Part II, Section A.

21See the discussion of distinctions between *possessing* the power which knowledge is and *having* this power in hand in Part IV, Section B.

22This is José Ortega y Gasset's view of the function of any *concept.*

23For the interested reader, these are examples of what Edmund Husserl termed the 'noematic object' and the 'noetic object', respectively. See n. 27 below, and p. 721 of the work noted.

[24]Cf. R. G. Collingwood, *An Essay on Philosophical Method,* Oxford: The Clarendon Press, 1933, p. 3.

[25]All of this is laid out with great clarity in Collingwood, *An Essay on Metaphysics,* Oxford: The Clarendon Press, 1948, Chapter IV, "On Presupposing," pp. 21-33.

[26]See n. 23 above.

[27]I call attention here to his classic presentation of "The Essentials of the Phenomenological Method," in his definitive history, *The Phenomenological Movement: A Historical Introduction,* Second Edition, 1965, pp. 653-701. His statement of these 'essentials of the method' has been as absolutely indispensable to my work in phenomenology as I know others in adult education who are interested in phenomenological research will surely find them.

[28]Norwood Hanson, *Patterns of Discovery,* Cambridge: Cambridge University Press, 1958. See Part VI, n. 7, for citations of literature of the 'new philosophy of science', in which this notion is especially important.

[29]A devastating critique of this set of presuppositions which carry on a long-standing version of 'cartesian' philosophy is offered in R. G. Collingwood, *An Essay on Philosophical Method,* Oxford: The Clarendon Press, 1933. See Chapters I-III and especially pp. 1-91.

[30]See Introduction, Section D., for a discussion of 'cause', 'causality', and 'causation', especially as these conceptions are used in any human science, and thereby in adult education as a human science.

[31]See Introduction, late in Section D., for a discussion of these motives. These are very fundamental notions in Alfred Schutz's phenomenology, and also of the most critical importance to practices and theories in adult education. Cf., for example, Alfred Schutz, *The Phenomenology of the Social World,* translated by George Walsh and Frederick Lehnert, Evanston, IL: Northwestern University Press, 1967, especially pp. 86-96, but *passim* in almost all of his writings.

[32]'This may involve two things: the attempt either (1) 'to leave off certain components [of the "essentials" or "essence" of some 'object'] completely or (2) to replace them by others.' See Spiegelberg, *The Phenomenological Movement,* p. 680f., and n. 27 above.

[33]In *Some Lessons in Metaphysics,* p. 15.

## NOTES TO PART II

[1]Martin Buber, *I and Thou,* translated by Walter Kaufmann, New York: Charles Scribner's Sons, 1970, lines from pp. 111-115. Buber provides much content for what I intend by **person,** as what flows from the intersubjectivity of persons coexisting in their lifeworlds.

[2]R. G. Collingwood, *The Principles of Art,* Oxford: The Clarendon Press, 1938, pp. 248-249. Collingwood emphasizes *persona,* speaker. **Person**-speaking is a mode of the eduction of **person** in my account.

[3]See Richard M. Zaner, *The Way of Phenomenology,* Indianapolis: The Bobbs-Merrill Company, Inc., 1970, pp. 122, 180-187, and *passim.* In many places and in many ways throughout this essay I have been guided by Richard

Zaner's brilliantly original phenomenological investigations.

[4]See Søren Kierkegaard, *Fear and Trembling* and *The Sickness Unto Death,* Princeton, NJ: Princeton University Press, 1944, 1954, pp. 146-147.

[5]But Edmund Husserl did so fully in a famous set of investigations. See his *The Phenomenology of Internal Time-Consciousness,* Bloomington, IN: Indiana University Press, 1964.

[6]Spiegelberg, *The Phenomenological Movement,* p. 688.

[7]See the definitions of 'phenomenology' in notes 1 and 3 in the **Notes to Table of Contents** and **Notes to Preface,** respectively.

[8]This would have to be the case if theoretical approaches to adult education allegedly built on those philosophies are consistent with these philosophies. Behavioristic psychology of the older variety is most closely based on logical positivism.

[9]See Part III, Introduction, for a listing of many other expressions of **person,** and regions and sectors of persons' lives in their coexistence within their 'everydayness', which cannot be genuinely researched by use of those other methods.

[10]I deal with this question in detail primarily in Part VI, but also in very many other places in the form of recommendations for specific research projects.

[11]Jerold W. Apps, *Problems in Continuing Education,* New York: McGraw-Hill Book Company, 1979.

12Throughout the volume.

13I discuss a number of these relevancy systems at work in Chapter 5 and Chapter 6 primarily, but also *passim.*

14Cf. the 'New Philosophy of Science' as cited in Part VI, and some of its important literature in **Notes to Part VI**, ns. 6 and 7.

15John Dewey, *Logic: The Theory of Inquiry,* pp. 66-67.

16The etymologies of 'concrete' and 'theory' are probably surprising to most readers, and surely instructive to the focus on problems in adult education. 'Concrete' derives from the Latin **conscrescere**, to grow together, and 'theory' derives from the Greek, θεωρία, a looking at, viewing, contemplation, speculation, or sometimes a sight or spectacle.

### NOTES TO PART III

1Ortega y Gasset, pp. 41-42.

2See n. 6 below. I use this qualified notion of a 'critical' synthesis', whereas I have been tempted to use the metaphor 'critical mass' of adult eductions of **person** as constituting an 'adult'. There are problems with that metaphor, but I still like it.

3For example, Erik H. Erikson, *Childhood and Society,* 2nd ed., New York: Norton, 1963, Chapter 7; Abraham Maslow, *Toward a Psychology of Being,* Princeton, NJ: Van Nostrand, 1968; George Vaillant, *Adaptation to Life,* Boston: Little, Brown and Company, 1977; and *Identity and the Life-Cycle: A Reissue,* New York: Norton, 1980, pp. 51-107; Daniel J. Levinson, et al.,

*The Seasons of a Man's Life,* New York: Knopf, 1978; Lawrence Kohlberg, *The Philosophy of Moral Development,* San Francisco: Harper and Row, 1981; Carol Gilligan, *In a Different Voice: Psychological Theory and Women's Development,* Cambridge: Harvard University Press, 1982. A brief but very helpful bibliography of works on adult development is provided in Sharan B. Merriam, ed., *Themes of Adulthood Through Literature,* pp. 417-418.

[4]Sharan B. Merriam, ed., *Themes of Adulthood Through Literature,* pp. 417-418.

[5]See these listings in the bibliography.

[6]I am tempted to invoke either one, or both, of two metaphors here and say that an 'adult' is a 'critical mass' of certain kinds of eductions of **person**, or a 'LASER-like' cluster of activities among kinds of eductions of **person**. As metaphors these familiar conceptions in physics of certain relationships of activities in nature would be carried over into other felt relevancy systems (see Chapters 5 and 6), viz., those indigenous to adult education. Very briefly,

> The *critical size* [or *critical mass]* of a system containing fissile (and fissionable) material is defined as the size for which the number of neutrons produced in the fission process just balances those lost by leakage and by capture. The critical size is not a constant, but depends on the isotopic composition of the uranium, the proportion of moderator, the shape and arrangement of the materials, and the presence of various substances causing parasitic capture of neutrons. If a system is smaller than the critical size, i.e., `subcritical,* neutrons are lost at a greater rate than they are replenished by fission, and so a self-sustaining, chain reaction will be impossible. It is essential, therefore, that the size of the uranium-moderator

> lattice should be equal to or larger than the critical value, i.e., *supercritical,* if the fission chain is to be maintained.

(Samuel Glasstone, *Sourcebook on Atomic Energy,* 3rd ed., Princeton: D. Van Nostrand Company, 1950, 1958, 1967, p. 518 [14.45].)

The value of the use of this possible metaphor would rest on the phrase 'critical size' as permissibly usable in two distinguishable but inseparable ways. It would refer: (1) to certain distinguishable eductions of **person** as having sufficient strength and force to qualify as *adult* eductions of person, and (2) to a sufficiently large and rich cluster of these distinct and unique *adult* eductions of person to qualify as being of sufficient 'critical size' as to qualify some person as an 'adult'.

The other possible metaphor might relate to the laser. A laser (or an *optical* maser) may be described in the following way:

> In 1960 a new word, LASER, an acronym standing for *light* amplification by stimulated emission of radiation, was added to the popular and scientific vocabulary of the world. Light amplification is *what* a laser does, and stimulated emission of radiation is *how* it accomplishes this feat.

(William V. Smith and Peter P. Sorokin, *The Laser,* New York: McGraw-Hill Book Company, 1966, p. 1.)

Perhaps this possible metaphor becomes too playful a use, but I confess that I am still intrigued by the metaphor of an adult being a 'LASER-like' cluster of activities among kinds of eductions of **person**. Consider the following compilings:

| LASER | - | 'ADULT' |
|---|---|---|
| Light | - | Person |
| Amplification | - | Strength and force of expression |
| Stimulated | - | Charged with feeling |
| Emissions | - | Personal actions |
| Radiation | - | Expressing degrees and kinds of eductions in the world. |

The 'laser' metaphor of 'adult' gives us the following construction: An 'adult' is **person** whose strength and force of expression is charged with feeling as a persons' personal actions expressing degrees and kinds of eductions in the world. And this is very close indeed to what I have been trying to say an 'adult' is.

Although my colleague, physicist Richard S. Preston, has helped me with my sources here, and has helped me to understand what lasers (or optical masers) and 'critical size' (or 'critical mass') are, he cannot be saddled with my interpretations and metaphorizings. In fact, he remains skeptical, and he may be right. But since I understand a metaphor to be an originative language of active judgment, the two metaphors above constitute (at least for me!) originative languages of active judgment. So . . . are they useful to anyone else?

## NOTES TO CHAPTER 1

[1] I discuss relevance and relevancy systems in Chapters 5 and 6.

[2] In one sense the distinction between feeling and *a* feeling is obvious. One might say that feeling is the genus and *a* feeling is a species; or that feeling is a class of all particular feelings. But as I use these terms 'feeling' is more like the generic essence of 'feeling' as a generic concept, and feelings are its variable attributes. See Collingwood, *An Essay on Philosophical Method*, Chapter III.

But more to the point here, feeling is an eduction of
**person**, and feelings are expressions of persons. Feeling is made concrete, and instantiated, in the feelings
of persons.

3R. G. Collingwood, *The New Leviathan,* Oxford: The
Clarendon Press, 1942, pp. 21-22.

4 *Op. cit.,* p. 18.

5William P. Alston, "Emotion and Feeling," in *The
Encyclopedia of Philosophy,* Vols. 1-8, edited by Paul
Edwards, New York: Macmillan and Company and The Free
Press, 1967, Vols. 1 and 2, pp. 479-486.

6José Ortega y Gasset, *Obras Completas,* Tomos I-XI,
Madrid: Revista de Occidente, 1966-1973, VII, p. 124.
Cf. George Herbert Mead, *The Philosophy of the Act,*
Chicago: The University of Chicago Press, 1938, 1972,
pp. 174-204, for a discussion of this same idea. Mead's
writings deserve a very careful re-examination by researchers in adult education.

7Ortega y Gasset, p. 124.

8Ortega y Gasset, p. 124 (my translation).

9Ortega y Gasset, *Some Lessons in Metaphysics,*
translated by Mildred Adams, New York: W. W. Norton and
Company, 1969, p. 36, but see pp. 28-45.

10Collingwood, *An Essay on Metaphysics,* p. 109.

11 *Op. cit.,* p. 10.

[12] *Ibid.*

## NOTES TO CHAPTER 2

[1]Both Ortega and Schutz refer often to all of these matters, and to *usages* (in Ortega's case, especially).

[2]This is a term which frequently occurs in Schutz's writings, especially in reference to 'multiple realities' and to the everyday world of work. It is defined in the text.

[3]I am indebted to my colleague, James Hudson, for this term. How many generations into the 'future' constitute the context for even our most serious plannings? And in adult education contexts?

[4]Charles Sanders Peirce, *Collected Papers*, Volumes I-VI, edited by Charles Hartshorne and Paul Weiss, Cambridge, MA: The Belknap Press of Harvard University Press, 1960, Volumes I-VIII. Both William James and John Dewey credit Peirce with having developed the principal modern foundations of 'pragmatism', the only major philosophical position which has been developed in the United States. His writings, and especially so as they have been rediscovered by phenomenologists (along with the rediscoveries of those of James and Dewey in phenomenological contexts) are of critical importance to phenomenological research in adult education. See, for example, the section entitled "Phenomenology", in Book III of Vol. I, pp. 141-308.

[5]Peirce, *Collected Papers*, Vol. I, pp. 312-313.

[6]I make extensive use of these writings in Chapters 2 and 7, especially, and what I have presented in Chapter 1 also is closely related to Peirce's views on feeling.

[7]Peirce, *Collected Papers,* Vol. I, pp. 206-207.

[8]See William James, *The Principles of Psychology,* I, II; New York: Henry Holt Co., 1890, Vol. II, p. 534.

[9]This is my neologism. When added to the verb, the "-ive" suffix always creates a word on Latin analogies intending "having a tendency to," or "having the nature, character or quality" of that verb. Words so constructed sometimes may be used as nouns.

[10]Carefully designed research programs should investigate the specific emergence of the will-to-learn in given persons' willingness to learn in carefully circumscribed projects within their lived worlds. What I do in this chapter, and in the essay generally, is philosophical exploration basic to such research programs.

[11]Alfred Schutz, *Collected Papers,* I, ed. Maurice Natanson, The Hague: Martinus Nijhoff, 1962. Alexander Pfänder, *Phenomenology of Willing and Motivation,* ed., Herbert Spiegelberg, Evanston, Northwestern University Press, 1967. See also Nicholai Hartmann, *Ethics,* Vols. I, II, and III, trans. Stanton Coit, New York: The Macmillan Company, 1932. See also Alfred Schutz, *Reflections on the Problem of Relevance,* ed. Richard M. Zaner, New Haven: Yale University Press, 1970. See also William James, *The Will to Believe,* Cambridge, MA: Harvard University Press, 1979.

[12]James, *The Principles of Psychology,* Vol. II, p. 559.

[13] *Ibid.,* pp. 568-569.

[14]Schutz, *Collected Papers,* I., pp. 68-69.

[15]Pfänder, *Phenomenology of Willing and Motivation,* p. 7.

[16]I owe the use of this construction to Richard M. Zaner. See Chapter 8, "'Metaphorizing' Life", also.

[17]Hartmann, Vol. II, p. 357.

[18]Schutz, *Reflections on the Problems of Relevance*, pp. 55-56.

[19]The most significant feature of persons as the subject-matter of adult education, of the adult eductions of **person**, specifically is speaking, or **person**-talk, as I developed this conception in part I, Section B. If the adult eductions of **person**, as persons' presentations and expressions through speaking are not allowable in all investigations involving persons, then the 'scientific' methods and models disallowing these are not sufficiently rigorous to stand the test of the phenomena which constitute the most relevant features of this subject-matter.

[20]In one sense this is the whole thrust of this essay on meaning, specifically of gaining meaning through careful phenomenological investigations of the adult eductions of **person**. See Chapter 8, "'Metaphorizing' Life", also.

## NOTES TO CHAPTER 3

[1]Ortega y Gasset, *Obras Completas*, III, "El tema de nuestro tiempo" ["The Theme of Our Time"], pp. 143-203. Translated as *The Modern Theme* by James Cleugh, New York: Harper and Row, 1961. See pp. 11-18. 'The generation is a dynamic compromise between mass and individual, and is the most important conception in history. It is, so to speak, the pivot responsible for the increments of historical evolution.' This conception of 'generation' has much to offer by way of serious research projects in adult education.

[2]Schutz, *Collected Papers*, I, pp. 222-223.

[3]Pages 208-209.

## NOTES TO PART IV

[1]R. G. Collingwood, *Speculum Mentis*, Oxford: The Clarendon Press, 1924, 1946, pp. 316-317.

[2]The reader by now is familiar with the construction of 'consciousing' as the intimacy of 'knowing-with' anything. I now use this construction adverbially, since I know my own intention intimately and immediately.

[3]P. 316.

[4]Collingwood, *Speculum Mentis*, p. 15.

[5]See the fine work of Jack Mezirow, for example, "A Critical Theory of Adult Learning and Education," in Sharan B. Merriam, editor, *Selected Writings on Philosophy and Adult Education*, Malabar, FL: Robert E. Krieger Publishing Company, 1984, pp. 123-139. Mezirow defines (p. 124) 'perspective transformation' as the emancipatory process of becoming critically aware of how and why the structure of psycho-cultural assumptions has come to constrain the way we see ourselves and our relationships, reconstituting this structure to permit a more inclusive and discriminating integration of experience and acting on these new understandings. It is the learning process by which adults come to recognize their culturally induced dependency roles and relationships and the reasons for them and take action to overcome them. See my Chapters 8 and 9 also.

[6]I discuss these matters in Chapters 5 and 6.

[7]These metaphors are borrowed from José Ortega y Gasset.

⁸'Looping' is computer language, although Douglas R. Hofstadter, in that magnificent book, *Gödel, Escher, Bach: An External Golden Braid*, New York: Vintage Books, 1979, 1980, has extended its intension as a characterization of features of works of art and music. See p. 149, for example: '[A *bounded loop:*] . . . perform some series of related steps over and over, and abort the process when specific conditions are met. Now sometimes, the maximum number of steps in a loop will be known in advance; other times, you just begin, and wait until it is aborted.' A *free loop* is 'dangerous' since it goes on forever . . .

⁹Jerold Apps, *Problems in Continuing Education*, New York: McGraw-Hill Book Company, 1979, p. 64.

¹⁰Paulo Freire, *Pedagogy of the Oppressed*, New York: The Seabury Press, 1968, Chapter 2, especially.

¹¹In the Introduction, Section C.

¹²Plato, *Theaetetus*, 197A-199C, tr. Francis M. Conford, *Plato's Theory of Knowledge*, Indianapolis: Bobbs-Merrill Company, 1957, pp. 131-135. In the text I have substituted and italicized as follows: 'empowering' for 'knowing'; 'power' for 'knowledge'; 'empowers' for 'knows'; 'empower' for 'know'; and 'empowered' for 'knew'.

¹³Cf. Ludwig Wittgenstein's notion of a person as a 'form of life'. See Dallas M. High, *Language, Persons, and Belief*, New York: Oxford University Press, 1967, pp. 102-103: "For Wittgenstein, language is intimately bound to the concept 'man' or 'person'. This is in part, at least, what Wittgenstein means by the notion 'form of life'. The phrase 'form of life' functions as a logically primitive concept. To speak or to do things with words other than what we do (past, present, and future) is logically not imaginable. There is no situation logically more primitive. The point is reached and the 'spade is turned'; 'Then I am inclined to say: "This is simply what I do."' The 'human condition' is not a

barrier to language and knowledge; rather, it is the
**conditio sine qua non** for all modalities of meaning and
comprehension, and, therefore, the condition of language
and knowledge. . . .

The inclination to divide off certain kinds of activities as constituting a 'form of life' is what is to be
avoided. Deduction and induction, too, are involved in
what is meant by 'form of life.' I purposely use the
blessedly vague word 'involved' since the point I wish
to underscore is not to say that logic or rationality is
a 'form of life' (though the practice of rationality
might be) or simply that persons and their actions are
logic or rational; rather it is to say that what counts
as logical and rational (e.g., deduction and induction)
is dependent upon the human 'form of life' and what is
done by persons. Concerning the related concept, 'justification', Wittgenstein puts it this way: 'What
people accept as a justification--is shown by how they
think and live.'". . . .

[14]I owe this insight to Edmund Husserl, and through
him to Descartes. Cf. the former's *Cartesian Meditations,* tr. Dorion Cairns, The Hague: Martinus Nijhoff,
1960, p. 2: 'If someone were to object that, on the
contrary, science, philosophy, takes its rise in the
cooperative labor of the scientific community of philosophers and, at each level, acquires its perfection only
therein, Descartes' answer might well be: I, the solitary individual philosophizer, owe much to others; but
what they accept as true, what they offer me as allegedly established by their insight, is for me at first only
something they claim. If I am to accept it, I might
justify it by a perfect insight on my own part. Therein
consists my autonomy--mine and that of every genuine
scientist.'

[15]This matter was discussed in the Introduction,
Section A., and Part I., Section A.

[16]By precisely the kinds of phenomenological investigations I am presenting and proposing in this essay.

[17]Edward Cell, *Learning to Learn from Experience.* Albany, NY: State University of New York Press, 1984, p. 18.

[18]Robert M. Smith, *Learning How to Learn.* Chicago, IL: Follett Publishing Company, 1982, p. 28.

## NOTES TO CHAPTER 4

[1]Herbert Spiegelberg, "Toward a Phenomenology of Experience," *American Philosophical Quarterly,* Vol. I, Number 4, October, 1964, pp. 325-332.

[2]If the 'mind/body problem' is really a problem in the special sense that the 'mind' and the 'body' are mutually exclusive of one another, how can it be 'solved'? If really mutually exclusive, then how can they *not* be really mutually exclusive?! But if there are 'solutions' to it, this must mean that either 'mind' and 'body' are not mutually exclusive, or one or the other is 'reduced' to the other, or that there is some third notion which facilitates their relationship.

[3]The 'mind', or perhaps (and better) 'person'. 'Effortive' ways are ways which express power, strength, energy, and intensity, or have these qualities, or have the tendency to express these. And these really are persons' expressions of eductions of **person**. See **Notes to Chapter** 2, n. 9.

[4]An excellent discussion of perceptions and conceptions (especially for students and researchers interested in phenomenological research in adult education) is contained in William James, *Some Problems of Philosophy: A Beginning of an Introduction to Philosophy,* New York: Longman's, Green, and Co., 1911, pp. 47-112.

[5]Spiegelberg, p. 327.

[6]Spiegelberg, p. 328.

[7]See Chapters 5 and 6, especially the discussions of J. L. Austin on 'action'.

[8]See the excellent discussion of 'relevance' (especially the views of Alfred Schutz) as applied to crucial problems in adult education in Michael Collins, *Competency in Adult Education: Applying a Theory of Relevance,* unpublished doctoral dissertation, Northern Illinois University, 1980.

## NOTES TO CHAPTER 5

[1]From the Latin **per**, through, and **specere**, to look. 'Perspective' is one of the most important concepts in Ortega's phenomenological philosophy. His philosophy, in fact, has often been referred to as 'perspectivism.' Thus, Ortega's usage involves a wider connotation than I intend here, but it would be valuable to study fully the relationships between Ortega's notion of perspectivism and a phenomenology of relevance.

'Through' is a *preposition, adverb,* and *adjective.* As a *preposition,* it is used to suggest something going into one side, end, or point, and out the other, or to present during the period of, as in the sense of 'from the first through the last.' As an *adverb,* it presents continuity from one end, side, surface, etc., to or beyond another, or from beginning to the end: 'He is wet through and through', or 'He pulled through.' As an *adjective* it bespeaks going from beginning to the end without stops, or with very few stops, as in the phrases, 'a through train,' or a 'through road.' I intend all of these senses when speaking of any action which is *through.*

I shall be concerned here only with the phenomena of *human action* and *acts,* and not with kinds of activities other than those which have been found to constitute activities of persons. Many of these other kinds of activities deserve thorough phenomenological investigation on other occasions: the 'activities' of animals generally (and of plants, perhaps), of the smallest through the largest spatial-temporal bodies such as particles, planets or stars, and of such 'happenings' or 'events' as earthquakes, floods, tornadoes, and the like.

[2]The emphasis in this latter case is on the present plans which persons may have for future actions.

[3]The actions of persons are shaped by interests and goals, such that various forms of the relevancy matrix of personal action are operative within the circumstances of specific situations.

[4]'Here' and 'there', 'now' and 'then', are what Husserl termed 'idealities' of repetitions of persons' actions.

[5]See Alfred Schutz and Thomas Luckmann, *Structures of the Lifeworld,* translated by Richard M. Zaner and Tristam Englehardt, Jr., Evanston, IL: Northwestern University Press, 1974, p. 178.

[6]José Ortega y Gasset, *Obras Completas,* IV, p. 428. (My translation.)

[7]J. L. Austin, *Philosophical Papers,* Oxford: Oxford University Press, 1961, pp. 129-130; see also 126, 127, and 133.

[8] *Op. cit.,* pp. 129-130. See also pp. 126, 127, and 133. (My emphasis.)

[9]The full and rich meaning of language beyond mere speaking through the use of words is of course all we have as tools, ultimately, for calling attention to, and gaining some 'power' within the natural world. Metaphorically, of course, there is also what could be called the technical languages of 'the languages of

nature', or physics, chemistry, biology, for example. See Chapters 6 and 8 also.

[10]Paulo Freire, *Pedagogy of the Oppressed*, translated by Myra Bergman Ramos, New York: The Seabury Press, 1973, pp. 85-86: 'The language of the educator or the politician (and it seems more and more clear that the latter must also become an educator, in the broadest sense of the word), like the language of the people, cannot exist without thought; and neither language nor thought can exist without a structure to which they refer. In order to communicate effectively, educator and politician must understand the structural conditions in . . . the thought and language of the people.'

[11]Edmund Husserl, *Logical Investigations*, Volumes I and II, translated by J. N. Findlay, London: Routledge and Kegan Paul, 1970, in a total of six investigations, following his classic refutation of 'psychologism' in logic. There are ample grounds and evidence for arguing that this two-volume work is the most impressive single work among the writings so far constituting 'the phenomenological movement'. It was Husserl's greatest and most important work, and contains the foundational concepts of most of his later phenomenology.

[12]Spiegelberg, *The Phenomenological Movement*, II, p. 673.

[13]These 'idealities', repeated and repeatable actions are articulated also through habituations within 'everydayness'.

[14]R. G. Collingwood, *The Idea of History*, Oxford: Oxford University Press, 1946, Galaxy Book, 1956, pp. 282, 297, and see pp. 282-302.

[15]Michael Collins, "Phenomenological Perspectives: Some Implications for Adult Education," in Sharan B. Merriam, *Selected Writings on Philosophy and Adult Education*, Malabar, FL: Robert E. Krieger Publishing Company, 1984, p. 185, and: 'The systematic design of

learning projects arising from typified ingredients which point the way, via purposive planning, to appropriate resources requires effort and is sometimes different. But it is the *best* we can do.'

[16]J. L. Austin, *Philosophical Papers,* pp. 127-128. (My emphasis.)

[17]See Part VI, Section C., and **"Research Configurations II,"** especially.

[18]But perspectivally, from different points of view, and differing kinds of ordering systems, with none of them necessarily being 'causal' reductionisms and orderings. Or at least 'causal' questions, according to phenomenology, are held in abeyance.

[19]See Part VI, Section C., and **Research Configurations I**, especially.

## NOTES TO CHAPTER 6

[1]Adult eductions of **person** are expressed by persons who have larger stocks of feelings, experiences, and consciousings (thoughts) generally. The 'objects' of their conscious lives are all shaped in degree and kind by these larger stocks.

[2]Innumerable research questions and projects have been suggested throughout the essay, with each chapter containing many possibilities. I address questions about research programs and alternative possibilities provided through phenomenological investigations most directly in Part VI, **New Beginnings: Phenomenology as a New Paradigm and Program of Research in Adult Education.**

[3]Ludwig Wittgenstein, *Philosophical Investigations,* 2nd edition, translated by G. E. M. Anscombe, New York: the Macmillan Company, 1953, 1958 (Basil Blackwell and Mott, Ltd.), pp. 11e-12e, 20e, 31e-32e.

[4]Paulo Freire, *Pedagogy of the Oppressed*, p. 75.

## NOTES TO PART V

[1]Benedict de Spinoza, *The Improvement of the Understanding*, translated from the Latin by R. H. M. Elwes, New York: Dover Publications, 1951, pp. 3-5.

[2](1) 'Knowledge is identified with perception.' (2) 'Knowledge is true judgment.' (3) 'Knowledge is true belief accompanied by an account or explanation.' See Plato, *Theaetetus*, translated by F. M. Cornford, Indianapolis, IN: The Bobbs-Merrill Company, 1957, pp. 29, 109, and 142. Socrates of course criticizes all three of these definitions in great detail.

[3]Plato, *Theaetetus*, translated by Benjamin Jowett, Indianapolis, IN: Bobbs-Merrill Educational Publishing, 1949, p. 17 (Steph. 155).

[4]Robert Graves, *The Greek Myths*, New York: George Braziller, Inc., 1959, Vol. I, p. 58.

[5] *Ibid.*

[6]Plato, *Symposium*, translated by Benjamin Jowett, *The Dialogues of Plato*, New York: Random House, Vol. I, p. 335 (Steph. 211-212).

## NOTES TO CHAPTER 7

[1]Cf. Michael Polanyi, *Personal Knowledge: Towards a Post-Critical Philosophy*, New York: Harper and Row, 1958, 1962. See, for example, p. x: '. . . tacit knowledge is more fundamental than explicit knowing: we can know more than we can tell and we can tell nothing without relying on our awareness of things we may not be able to tell.' And p. xi: 'The power of science to grow by the originality of individual thought is . . .

established within a cosmic perspective of steadily emergent meaning. Science, conceived as understanding nature, seamlessly joins with the humanities, bent on the understanding of man and human greatness. Man's ideals, unfolding in action, come into view. . . .

Indwelling is being-in-the-world. Every act of tacit knowing shifts our existence, re-directing, contracting our participation in the world. Existentialism and phenomenology have studied such processes under other names. We must re-interpret such observations now in terms of the more concrete structure of "tacit knowing."'

[2]Thinking always refers to an 'object', to something which is thought. Husserl also distinguished the act which intends (intentional act) and the object intended (intentional object). The former is *noetic intentionality,* and the latter, *noematic intentionality.* See Spiegelberg, *The Phenomenological Movement,* p. 719. See also William James, *The Principles of Psychology,* I, Chapter IX, "The Stream of Thought," pp. 224-290.

[3]José Ortega y Gasset, *The Idea of Principle in Leibniz and the Evolution of Deductive Theory,* translated by Mildred Adams, New York: W. W. Norton, 1971, pp. 280-81.

[4]Charles Sanders Peirce, *Collected Papers,* Volumes I-VIII, Cambridge, MA: The Belknap Press of Harvard University Press, 1960, Vol. I, p. 326. Hereafter, all references in this chapter to Peirce's writings will refer in the text to Vol. I and paragraph number, for example here as 1.591.

[5]My neologism. The reader by now is familiar with my use of 'consciousing'. 'Consciousing' means an intimate 'knowing-with', and 'consciousive' refers to a use of the word 'conscious' on a Latin analogy, with the sense of 'having a tendency to', 'having the nature', 'character', or 'quality of' 'knowing-with'.

[6]She has given herself over to the power or effort to change, the power of resolving to change. The proprietorship of her **person** is moving into the threshold of determining a change, but the movement is not quite yet the action of 'deciding'.

## NOTES TO CHAPTER 8

[1]The particular eductions, and the number, of these constituting this 'critical synthesis' will surely vary from one person to another.

[2]See **Research Configurations I and II** in Part VI, Section C. (1) The **FEC Structure** is: **feeling, experiencing, and consciousing**. These constitute the **person** of each and every person. See, for example, n. 3 in **Notes to Table of Contents**. (2) The **HRM Structure** is this: Habits are the foundations of most of my actions as a person, but within relevancy systems, I create Metaphors (as originative language of active judgment) and these express new perspectives, and hence this is what I can know. (3) The **ELV Structure** is this: Within my 'everydayness' as a person the languages of relevancy systems express the constitutive ends and goals which I ought to seek in my lifeworld.

[3]By 'model' of **person** (and not of a person) I mean descriptions of the most relevant phenomena which can be the ground for a framework and structure of rigorous phenomenological investigations of what persons are and do.

[4]Talcott Parsons and Edward A. Shils, "Values, Motives, and Systems of Actions" in *Toward a General Theory of Action*, edited by Parsons and Shils, Cambridge, MA: Harvard University Press, 1951, pp. 190, 191, and 194.

[5]And no doubt, even if they remember that 'role' is a metaphor, the 'role' theorists may forget that it is a

metaphor *of* a metaphor (person, from **persona**, or mask).

[6]And it turns out to be another instance in which a major theory in the 'social sciences' is based on a reductionism characteristic of logical positivism.

[7]'Facts' and 'values' clearly may be *distinguished*, but is it possible to *separate* them entirely? See n. 4 in **Notes to Preface.**

[8]Which is related to those other dichotomies or mutual exclusions: objective/subjective, objectivity/subjectivity, extension/thought, and of course body/mind.

[9]Here and elsewhere 'conscious' and its various forms ('consciousing', 'consciousingly', 'consciousive') are used as forms of an intentional 'knowing-with'. In any '-ing' forms the focus is upon the present, dynamic, and processional intentionality of the meaning and the use of these words as forms of 'knowing-with'.

[10]See, for example, Sherman M. Stanage, "Order, Violatives, and Metaphors of Violence," *Thought: A Review of Culture and Idea,* Vol. LVI, No. 220, March, 1981. Power, force, and strength are metaphors of violence whenever used in relation to discussions of violence, as in the expressions, 'violence is power,' 'violence is force,' or 'violence is strength.'

[11]In Terence Hawkes, *Metaphor,* London: Methuen and Company, 1972.

[12]José Ortega y Gasset, *Obras Completas,* VI, p. 261, n., my translation.

[13]In, for example, her edited volume, *Themes of Adulthood Through Literature,* New York: Teachers College Press, 1983.

[14]Monroe Berger, *Real and Imagined Worlds*, Cambridge, MA: Harvard University Press, 1977, p. 159.

[15]Merriam, *op. cit.*, p. 7.

[16]Pearl Gasarch and Ralph Gasarch, *Fiction: The Universal Elements*, New York: Van Nostrand Reinhold, 1972, xiii.

[17]Martin Buber, *I and Thou*, translated by Walter Kaufmann, New York: Charles Scribner's Sons, 1970, p. 62.

[18]Something which has been further created from one or more 'intentional objects'.

[19]R. G. Collingwood, *The Principles of Art*, Oxford: The Clarendon Press, 1938, p. 336.

## NOTES TO CHAPTER 9

[1]James Robbins Kidd, *Relentless Verity: Education for Being-Becoming-Belonging*, p. 23.

[2]Jonathan Edwards, *Freedom of the Will*, edited by Paul Ramsey, New Haven: Yale University Press, 1957, pp. 163-164.

[3]Nicolai Hartmann, *Ethics*, Volumes I-III, translated by Stanton Coit, London: George Allen and Unwin, Ltd., 1932, *passim*, especially Volume II.

[4]In his *Nicomachean Ethics*, in, for example, *The Basic Works of Aristotle*, translated by Richard McKeon, New York: Random House, 1941, pp. 925-1112.

[5]Alasdair MacIntyre, *After Virtue: A Study of Moral Theory*, Second Edition, South Bend, IN: Notre Dame University Press, 1984, especially chapters 14 and 15, pp. 181-225. See Robin G. Collingwood, *Speculum*

*Mentis, or the Map of Knowledge,* Oxford: The Clarendon Press, 1924, especially the "Prologue," pp. 15-38.

[6]Collingwood, pp. 15-38; MacIntyre, *passim,* especially pp. 256-278.

[7]Hartmann, p. 144.

[8]Albert Camus, *The Rebel,* New York: Vintage Books, 1959, p. 13.

[9]Camus, p. 14.

[10]John Rawls, *A Theory of Justice,* Cambridge, MA: Harvard University Press, 1971, *passim,* but see p. 244, for example: 'the precedence of liberty means that liberty can be restricted only for the sake of liberty itself. There are two sorts of cases. The basic liberties may either be less extensive, the representative citizen must find this a gain for his freedom on balance; and if liberty is unequal, the freedom of those with the lesser liberty must be better secured. In both instances the justification proceeds by reference to the whole system of the equal liberties.'

[11]Hallenbeck, Wilbur, "What is Adult Education?" *Adult Education,* v. 3, Spring, 1955, pp. 132-133.

[12]Sworder, Stanley, "What is Adult Education?" *Adult Education,* v. 3, Spring, 1955, pp. 135-136.

[13]Perhaps all of the theoretical approaches and practices ought to do this, but sadly not all do so. For example, if persons are treated mainly as 'objects' in training sessions and projects, empowerment and transformation of these persons (as 'objects') do not really take place.

[14]Elias, John, and Sharan B. Merriam, *Philosophical Foundations of Adult Education,* Huntington, New York: Robert E. Krieger Publishing Company, 1980.

15Robin G. Collingwood, *An Essay on Philosophical Method* , Oxford: The Clarendon Press, 1933, pp. 1-53.

16See Introduction, Section D, particularly the discussion of Collingwood's account of the three senses of 'cause'. 'Sense I. Here that which is "caused" is the free and deliberate act of a conscious and responsible agent, and "causing" him to do it means affording him a motive for doing it.'

17Alfred Schutz, *The Phenomenology of the Social World*, translated by George Walsh and Frederick Lehnert (Evanston: Northwestern University Press, 1967), pp. 86-97. In the former case, 'reasons-why' as motives refer to the past and may be called 'causes'. In the latter case, 'reasons-for' as motives refer to the future and are the object or purpose for the realization of which the action itself is a means.

18See Edmund Husserl, *Cartesian Meditations*, translated by Dorion Cairns (The Hague: Martinus Nijhoff, 1960), p. 2.

19In the Introduction, Section D. Phenomenologists have long argued that there are kinds of studies which can be called **human sciences**. A phenomenological investigation is always a case of human science. Moreover, a central claim of this paper is that adult education is potentially the paradigm of rigorous human science. A human science is an orderly and systematic description and investigation of a person's, and persons', felt experience of direct phenomena through the various forms in which relevant phenomena may appear or be manifested. Realizing, evidencing, and certifying are three of the many possible ways in which we speak of our valuational feeling, felt values, and our constructions of facts within our lifeworlds. Within our adult lifeworlds we learn most fundamentally and lastingly through the assurances of our values through commitments and in terms of the facts situated within a unity of values. These value commitments and consequent constructed and situated facts flow through indeterminately long streams of personal lives.

## NOTES TO PART VI

[1]Edmund Husserl, *Die Krisis der europaischen Wissenschaften und die transzendentale Phanomenologie*, Bd. 1, *Gesammelte Werke*, auf Grund des Nachlasses veroffentlicht vom Husserl-Archiv (Louvain) unter Leitung von H. L. van Breda, Haag: Martinus Nijhoff, 1950-62.

[2]Maurice Natanson, *Edmund Husserl: Philosopher of Infinite Tasks*, Evanston, IL: Northwestern University Press, 1973, p. 207. This is an excellent study of Husserl's phenomenology by one of the 'phenomenological movement's' finest philosophers. It won the 1974 National Book award for Philosophy and Religion.

[3]Suppose that research no longer is viewed in the special terms of or on the foundation of a natural and straightforward view of the world as their research models it. In other words, put *habits* of research aside for the time being. Cf. Natanson, *op. cit.*, pp. 58-59.

[4]Richard M. Zaner, *The Way of Phenomenology: Criticism as a Philosophical Discipline*, Indianapolis, IN: The Bobbs-Merrill Company, 1970.

[5]See Edmund Husserl, *Phenomenology as Rigorous Science*, in *Phenomenology and the Crisis of Philosophy*, translated by Quentin Lauer, New York: Harper and Row, 1965, pp. 71-146.

[6]Published in 1962 by the University of Chicago Press. But see Thomas S. Kuhn, *The Structure of Scientific Revolutions*, Second Edition, Enlarged *(International Encyclopedia of Unified Science*, Vols. I and II, *Foundations of the Unity of Science*, Volume II, No. 2), Chicago: The University of Chicago Press, 1970. See the "postscript," especially pp. 174-210.

[7]Imre Lakatos and Alan Musgrave, editors, *Criticism and the Growth of Knowledge*, Cambridge: The Cambridge University Press, 1970. In this volume, Margaret Masterman, in "The Nature of a Paradigm," claims that Kuhn uses "'paradigm' in not less than twenty-one different senses in his *The Structure of Scientific Revolutions*, 1962, first edition, possibly more, not less', and then lays out these diverse uses in detail; Harold I. Brown, *Perception Theory and Commitment*, Chicago: Precedent Publishers, 1977; see also John Ziman, *Reliable Knowledge: An Exploration of the Grounds for Belief in Science*, Cambridge: Cambridge University Press, 1978.

[8]I refer here to Herbert Spiegelberg's "The Essentials of the Phenomenological Method," and to my discussions in Parts I and II.

[9]Refer to the several definitions of 'phenomenology' in n. 1 in **Notes to Table of Contents** and n. 3 in **Notes to Preface**.

[10]Cf. R. G. Collingwood, *An Essay on Metaphysics*, Oxford: The Clarendon Press, 1948, Chapter IV, "On Presupposing," pp. 21-33.

## NOTES TO CONCLUSION

[1]This means that the 'analytic' and 'liberal' approaches to philosophy of adult education (identified by Elias and Merriam in *Philosophical Approaches to Adult Education)* overlap, as do the so-called 'progressive', 'humanistic', 'behavioristic', and 'radical' approaches. 'Adult education' as a concept must be a generic concept constituted of overlapping concepts rather than a class concept bringing together a variety of mutually exclusive classes or sub-classes. Both the generic essence and the variable attribute of 'adult education' as a generic concept are the adult eductions of **person**.

[2]K. H. Lawson, *Philosophical Concepts and Values in Adult Education,* Revised Edition, 1979, pp. 100-101. Lawson's last sentence raises a claim which I discussed in detail in Part I, Section B. It is also vital to the foundation of any account of 'learning to learn.'

[3]And *territorialities* of habituated research paradigms and programs as well. Alternative and competitive approaches to adult education do not necessarily militate against ultimately cooperative research and practices dedicated to the most worthful projections of, and enactment of, persons' vital living within the 'everydayness' of their lifeworlds.

[4]Benedict de Spinoza, *Ethics,* translated by R. H. M. Elwes, New York: Dover Publications, Inc., pp. 270-271.

# BIBLIOGRAPHY

References are grouped into three broad classifications: **I. Adult Education, II. Phenomenology and Phenomenological Research, and III. Philosophy and "New Philosophy of Science".**

## I.

## Adult Education

Adams, Frank. "Highlander Folk School: Getting Information, Going Back and Teaching It." *Harvard Educational Review,* 1972, *2,* 497-520.

Adams, F. *Unearthing Seeds of Fire.* Winston-Salem: John F. Blair, 1975.

Adult Performance Level Staff. *Adult Functional Competency: A Summary.* Austin, Texas: University of Texas, March 1975.

Aker, George F. *Adult Education Procedures, Methods and Techniques: A Classified and Annotated Bibliography, 1953-1963* (compiled under the direction of George F. Aker). Syracuse: Syracuse University, 1965.

Apps, J. W. *Problems in Continuing Education.* New York: McGraw-Hill, 1979.

Archambault, R. D. (ed.). *Philosophical Analysis and Education.* London: Routledge and Kegan Paul, 1965.

Beck, George A. "Aims in Education: Neo-Thomism." In T. Hollins (ed.), *Aims in Education: The Philosophic Approach.* Manchester: Manchester University Press, 1964.

Belth, M. (ed.). *Education as a Discipline.* Boston: Allyn and Bacon, 1965.

Benne, Kenneth. "Some Philosophical Issues in Adult Education." *Adult Education,* 1956, *7,* 67-82.

Bergevin, Paul. *A Philosophy for Adult Education.* New York: Seabury, 1967.

Bergevin, Paul and John McKinley. *Design for Adult Education in the Church: The Indiana Plan.* New York: Seabury, 1958.

Bergevin, Paul, Dwight Morris, and Robert Smith. *Adult Education Procedures: A Handbook of Tested Patterns for Effective Participation.* New York: Seabury, 1963.

Bergevin, Paul and John McKinley. *Participation Training for Adult Education.* New York: Seabury, 1965.

Blakely, Robert J. *Adult Education in a Free Society.* Toronto: Guardian Bird Publications, 1958.

Blakely, R. J. "Adult Education Needs a Philosophy and a Goal." *Adult Education* 3 (Fall 1952): 2-10.

Blakely, Robert J. *Toward a Homeodynamic Society.* Boston: Center for the Study of Liberal Education for Adults, 1965.

Boone, Edward J. and others. *Programming in the Cooperative Extension Service: A Conceptual Scheme.* Raleigh: The North Carolina Agricultural Extension Service. Misc. Extension Publication 73, 1971.

Boshier, R. *Towards a Learning Society.* Vancouver: Learning Press, Ltd., 1980.

Bowers, C. A. *The Progressive Educator and the Depression: The Radical Years.* New York: Random House, 1969.

Bowles, Samuel and Herbert Gintis. *Schooling in a Capitalist Society.* New York: Basic Books, 1975.

Boyle, Patrick and Irwin Johns. "Program Development and Evaluation." In Robert M. Smith, George F. Aker, and J. R. Kidd (eds.), *Handbook of Adult Education.* New York: MacMillan Co., 1970.

Bridenbaugh, C. and J. Bridenbaugh. *Rebels and Gentlemen* (2nd ed.). New York: Oxford University Press, 1962.

Broudy, Harry. *Aims in Adult Education: A Realist's View.* New York: Seabury, 1967.

Broudy, Harry and John Palmer. *Exemplars of Teaching Method.* Chicago: Rand McNally, 1965.

Bugental, James F. T. *Challenges of Humanistic Psychology.* New York: McGraw-Hill, 1967.

Carlson, Robert A. *The Quest for Conformity: American-ization Through Education.* New York: John Wiley Sons, 1975.

Cell, Edward. *Learning to Learn from Experience.* Albany, New York: State University of New York Press, 1984.

Champion, A. "The Concept of 'Liberal'". *Adult Education, 41* (3), 1968.

Champion, A. "Towards an Ontology of Adult Education." *Studies in Adult Education, 7* (1), 1975.

City University of New York. *Report on Task Force on Adult and Continuing Education.* New York: City University of New York, 1980.

Cobham, Alfred. "A Student Experience." In Reginold St. John Parry (ed.), *Cambridge Essays in Adult Education.* Cambridge: The University Press, 206-223.

Collins, Michael. *Competency in Adult Education: Applying a Theory of Relevance.* Unpublished doctoral dissertation, Northern Illinois University, 1980.

Combs, Arthur W., Donald L. Avila, and William W. Purkey. *Helping Relationships: Basic Concepts for the Helping Professions.* Boston: Allyn and Bacon, 1971.

*Commission on Nontraditional Study. Diversity by Design.* San Francisco: Jossey-Bass, 1973.

Competency-Based Vocational Education: Participants Guide for Inservice Teaching. Richmond, VA: Division of Vocational Education, VA State Department of Education, 1977.

Coombs, P. *New Paths to Learning.* New York: International Council for Educational Development, 1973.

Cranage, D. H. "The Purpose and Meaning of Adult Education." In Reginold St. John Parry (ed.), *Cambridge Essays in Adult Education.* Cambridge: The University Press, 1920, 16-34.

Cremin, Lawrence. *American Education: The Colonial Experience, 1607-1783.* New York: Harper and Row, 1970.

Cremin, Lawrence A. *The Transformation of the School: Progressivism in American Education, 1876-1957.* New York: Random House, 1961.

Davidson, Thomas. "Education for All: Problem for the 20th Century." In C. Hartley Gratton (ed.), *American Ideas about Adult Education, 1710-1951.* New York: Teachers College Press, 1959.

Davis, James. *Great Books and Small Groups.* New York: Free Press, 1961.

Dearden, R. F., P. H. Hirst, and R. S. Peters. *Education and the Development of Reason.* Routledge and Kegan Paul, 1972.

De Lima, Agnes. "Education for What?" *The New Republic,* 71 (August 3, 1932).

Downie, R. S., E. M. Loudfoot, and E. Telfer. *Education and Personal Relationships.* Methuen, 1974.

Doyle, J. F. (ed.). *Educational Judgements.* London: Routledge and Kegan Paul, 1975.

Elias, John L. "Neither Andragogy nor Pedagogy, but Education." *Adult Education,* 1979, *29,* 525-526.

Elias, John L. and Sharan B. Merriam. *Philosophical Foundations of Adult Education.* Huntington, New York: Robert E. Krieger Publishing Company, 1980.

Erickson, Erik H. *Childhood and Society,* 2nd ed. New York: Norton, 1963.

Fischer, Joan K. "A Review of Competency-Based Adult Education," *Report of the USOE Invitational Workshop in Adult Competency Education.* Washington, D.C.: U.S. Government Printing Office, 1978.

Fowler, James W. *Becoming Adult, Becoming Christian.* San Francisco: Harper and Row, 1984.

Franklin, Benjamin, *The Autobiography of.* In Leonard Laboree (ed.), *The Writings of Benjamin Franklin.* New Haven: Yale, 1964.

Freire, Paulo. *Conscientization and Liberation.* Geneva: Institute of Cultural Action, 1972.

Freire, Paulo. *Education for Critical Consciousness.* New York: Seabury, 1973.

Freire, Paulo. *Pedagogy of the Oppressed.* New York: Herder and Herder, 1970.

Friedenberg, Edgar. "Liberal Education and the Fear of Failure." *Leader Digest,* Vol. 3, Washington: Adult Education Association, 1956, 51-54.

Friedenberg, Edgar. "The Purpose of Liberal Study versus the Purpose of Adult Students." *Adult Leadership*, May 1958.

Gilligan, Carol. *In a Different Voice: Psychological Theory and Women's Development.* Cambridge: Harvard University Press, 1982.

Grabowski, S. M. (ed.). *Paulo Freire: A Revolutionary Dilemma for the Adult Educator.* Syracuse, N.Y.: Syracuse University Publications in Continuing Education, 1972.

Grattan, C. Hartley. *In Quest of Knowledge: An Historical Perspective on Adult Education.* New York: Association Press, 1955.

Grattan, C. Hartley. *American Ideas about Adult Education, 1710-1951.* New York: Columbia University Press, 1962.

Graves, Robert. *The Greek Myths,* Vol. I. New York: George Braziller, Inc., 1959.

Greene, Maxine. *Teacher as Stranger: Educational Philosophy for the Modern Age.* Belmont, CA: Wadsworth, 1973.

Griffith, William S. and Ronald M. Cervero. "The Adult Performance Level Program: A Serious and Deliberate Examination," *Adult Education,* 1977, *27,* 209-224.

Gross, R. and Dimenderg, E. *Meeting the Needs of Independent Scholars.* New York: College Board, 1980.

Guttierrez, Gustavo. "A Latin American Perception of a Theology of Liberation." In Louis Colonnese (ed.), *Conscientization for Liberation.* Washington, D.C.: United States Catholic Conference, 1971.

Hallenbeck, Wilbur. "What is Adult Education?" *Adult Education, 3,* Spring 1955, 132-133.

Hansen, Kenneth. *The Educational Philosophy of the Great Books Program.* Unpublished doctoral dissertation, University of Missouri, 1949. A lengthy abstract appears in L. Little (ed.), *Toward Understanding Adults and Adult Education,* Department of Religious Education, University of Pittsburgh, 1963.

Heaney, T. "Adult Learning and Empowerment: Toward a Theory of Liberatory Education." Unpublished doctoral dissertation, Union Graduate School, 1980.

Heilbroner, Robert. *Between Capitalism and Socialism.* New York: Random House, 1972.

Henle, Robert. "A Roman Catholic View of Education." In Philip Phenix (ed.), *Philosophies of Education.* New York: Wiley, 1965.

Herndon, James. *How to Survive in Your Native Land.* New York: Simon and Schuster, 1971.

Hirschberg, Cornelius. *The Priceless Gift.* New York: Simon and Schuster, 1960.

Highet, Gilbert. *The Art of Teaching.* New York: Knopf, 1950.

Homme, L. W. and A. P. Csanyi. *Contingency Contracting: A System for Motivation Management in Education.* Albuquerque, N.M.: Southwestern Cooperating Training Laboratories, 1968.

Horowitz, Louis. *Three Worlds of Development.* New York: Oxford University Press, 1966.

Houghton, V. and K. Richardson (eds.). *Recurrent Education.* Ward Lock Educational, 1974.

Houle, C. O. "Deep Traditions of Experiential Learning." In M. T. Keeton (ed.), *Experiential Learning.* San Francisco: Jossey-Bass, 1977.

Houle, Cyril. *The Design of Education.* San Francisco: Jossey-Bass, Inc., 1972.

Houle, Cyril O. *The Inquiring Mind: A Study of the Adult Who Continues to Learn.* Madison, Wisconsin: University of Wisconsin Press, 1963.

Hutchins, Robert. *The Higher Learning in America.* New Haven: Yale University Press, 1936.

Hutchins, Robert. *The Conflict in Education in a Democratic Society.* New York: Harper and Row, 1953.

Hutchins, Robert. *The Learning Society.* New York: Britannica Books, 1968.

Illich, Ivan. *Deschooling Society.* New York: Harper and Row, 1970.

Illich, Ivan. *Tools for Conviviality.* New York: Harper and Row, 1973.

Ilsley, Paul J. *The Relevance of the Future in Adult Education: A Phenomenological Analysis of Images of the Future.* Unpublished doctoral dissertation, Northern Illinois University, 1982.

Institute for Cultural Action. *Liberation of Woman: To Change the World and Re-Invent Life.* Geneva: Institute for Cultural Action, 1974.

Institute for Cultural Action. *Toward a Woman's World.* Geneva: Institute for Cultural Action, 1975.

James, B. J. "Can 'Needs' Define Educational Goals?" *Adult Education* (USA), 7 (1), 1956.

Jarvis, Peter. *Adult and Continuing Education: Theory and Practice.* London: Croom Helm, 1983.

Jensen, Gale, A. A. Liveright, and Wilbur Hallenbeck (eds.). *Adult Education: Outlines of an Emerging Field of University Study.* Chicago: Adult Education Association of the U.S.A., 1964.

Jones, H. A. "A Rationale for Adult Education." In M. D. Stephens and G. W. Roderick (eds.), *Teaching Techniques in Adult Education,* David and Charles, 1971.

Kallen, Horace. *Philosophical Issues in Adult Education.* Springfield, IL: Charles C. Thomas, 1962.

Karen, Robert L. *An Introduction to Behavior Theory and its Application.* New York: Harper and Row, 1974.

Karrier, Clarence, Paul Violas, and Joel Spring. *Roots of Crisis: American Education in the Twentieth Century.* Chicago: Rand McNally, 1973.

Katz, Michael. *The Irony of Early School Reform.* Boston: Beacon, 1968.

Keller, Fred. "Behaviorism." *Collier's Encyclopedia* (Vol. 4). New York: MacMillan Educational Corporation, Inc., 1977.

Kidd, J. R. *How Adults Learn* (Rev. ed.). New York: Association Press, 1973.

Kidd, James Robbins. *Relentless Verity: Education for Being-Becoming-Belonging.* Syracuse: Syracuse University Press, 1973.

Kinkade, Kathleen. *A Walden Two Experiment: The First Five Years of Twin Oaks Community.* New York: William Morrow, 1972.

Kirk, Russell. "A Conservative View of Education." In P. Phenix (ed.), *Philosophies of Eduction.* New York: Wiley, 1965.

Kneller, George. *Existentialism and Education.* New York: Wiley, 1958.

Knowles, M. S. *The Adult Learner: A Neglected Species.* Houston: Gulf Publishing, 1973.

Knowles, Malcolm. *The History of the Adult Education Movement in the United States* (Rev. ed.). New York: Krieger, 1977.

Knowles, Malcolm S. *The Modern Practice of Adult Education: Andragogy Versus Pedagogy.* New York: Association Press, 1970, 1977.

Knowles, M. S. "Philosophical Issues that Confront Adult Educators." *Adult Education* (USA), Vol. VII.

Knowles, Malcolm. *Self-Directed Learning.* Chicago: Association Press/Follett, 1975.

Knox, Alan B. *Adult Development and Learning.* San Francisco: Jossey-Bass, 1977.

Kohlberg, Lawrence. *The Philosophy of Moral Development.* San Francisco: Harper and Row, 1981.

Kolesnik, Walter B. *Humanism and/or Behaviorism in Education.* Boston: Allyn and Bacon, Inc., 1975.

Lawson, K. H. "The Concept of Purpose." *Adult Education, 43* (3), 1970.

Lawson, K. H. "The Justification of Objectives in Adult Education." *Studies in Adult Education, 5* (1), 1973.

Lawson, K. H. *Philosophical Concepts and Values in Adult Education.* Nottingham, England: Barnes and Humby, Ltd., 1975.

LeClerq, Jacques. *The Love of God and the Love of Learning.* New York: Fordham University Press, 1961.

Lenz, Elinor. "Values in Transition." *The Forum for Continuing Education,* 1979, *2,* 8-11.

Levinson, Daniel J., et al. *The Seasons of a Man's Life.* New York: Knopf, 1978.

Lindeman, Eduard C. *The Meaning of Adult Education.* Montreal: Harvest House, 1961. (Originally published 1926.)

Lindeman, Eduard C. *The Democratic Man: Selected Writings of Eduard Lindeman.* Edited by Robert Glessner. Boston: Beacon, 1956.

Londoner, Carroll A. "The Systems Approach as an Administrative and Program Planning Tool for Continuing Education," *Educational Technology,* August 1972, 24-30.

Lusterman, Seymour. "Education in Industry." *Lifelong Learning: The Adult Years,* 1978, *1,* 8-9, 38-39.

McGuchen, William. "The Philosophy of Catholic Education." In *Philosophies of Education,* National Society for the Study of Education, Forty-First Yearbook, Part I. Chicago: University of Chicago Press, 1942.

McKenzie, L. *Adult Education and the Burden of the Future.* Washington, D.C.: University Press of America, 1978.

McLeish, J. "The Philosophical Basis of Adult Education, Part I and II." *Researches and Studies,* No. 11 and No. 12, 1955, University of Leeds.

Malcolm X. *The Autobiography of Malcolm X.* New York: Grove Press, 1964.

Maritain, Jacques. *Education at the Crossroads.* New Haven: Yale University Press, 1943.

Marrou, H. I. *A History of Education in Antiquity.* New York: Sneed and Ward, 1956.

Martin, Everett Dean. *The Meaning of a Liberal Education.* New York: Norton, 1926.

Marx, Karl. *Economic and Philosophic Manuscripts.* In Erich Fromm's *Marx's Concept of a Man.* New York: Frederick Ungar, 1961.

Maslow, Abraham. "Education and Peak Experience." In Courtney D. Schlosser (ed.), *The Person in Education: A Humanistic Approach.* New York: Macmillan, 1976.

Maslow, Abraham. *Toward a Psychology of Being.* Princeton, N.J.: Van Nostrand, 1968.

Mattran, K. J. "Mandatory Education Increases Professional Competence." In B. W. Kreitlow and Associates, *Examining Controversies in Adult Education.* San Francisco: Jossey-Bass, 1981.

Merriam, Sharan B. "Ben Franklin's Junto Revisited." *Lifelong Learning: The Adult Years,* 1979, *2,* 18-19.

Merriam, Sharan B. "Philosophical Perspectives on Adult Education: A Critical Review of the Literature." *Adult Education,* 1977, *27,* 195-208.

Merriam, Sharan B. (ed.). *Selected Writings on Philosophy and Adult Education.* Malabar, FL: Robert E. Krieger Publishing Company, 1984.

Merriam, Sharan B. (ed.). *Themes of Adulthood Through Literature.* New York: Teachers College Press, 1983.

Mezirow, Jack. *Education for Perspective Transformation: Women's Re-entry Programs in Community Colleges.* New York: Center for Adult Education, Teachers College, Columbia University, 1975, 1978.

Mezirow, Jack. *Evaluating Statewide Programs of Adult Basic Education: A Design with Instrumentation.* New York: Center for Adult Education, Teachers College, Columbia University, 1975.

Mezirow, Jack. "Program Analysis and Evaluation: An Alternative Approach." *Literacy Discussion* 5, Fall 1974.

Mezirow, Jack and Amy Rose. *An Evaluation Guide for College Women's Re-entry Programs.* New York: Center for Adult Education, Teachers College, Columbia University, 1978.

Mezirow, Jack, Gordon Darkenwald, and Alan Knox. *Last Gamble on Education; Dynamics of Adult Basic Education.* Washington, D.C.: Adult Education Association of the U.S.A., 1973.

Miller, H. and G. McGuire. *Liberal Education: An Evaluative Study.* Chicago: Center for the Study of Liberal Education of Adults, 1961.

Minzey, Jack. "Community Education--Another Perception." *Community Education Journal,* 1977, *4,* 3, 58-61.

Misiak, Henryk and Virginia Standt Sexton. *Phenomenological, Existential, and Humanistic Psychologies: A Historical Survey.* New York: Grune and Stratton, 1973.

Monette, Maurice L. "The Concept of Need: An Analysis of Selected Literature," *Adult Education,* 1977, *27,* 116-127.

Monette, Maurice L. "Need Assessment: A Critique of Philosophical Assumptions." *Adult Education,* 1979, *29,* 83-95.
Moody, H. R. "Philosophical Presuppositions of Education for Old Age." *Educational Gerontology,* 1976, *1,* 1-16.
Morris, Van Cleve. *Existentialism in Education.* New York: Harper and Row, 1966.
Murchland, Bernard. "Reviving the Connected View; Reforming the Liberal Arts," 1979, *106.*
Nash, P. *Authority and Freedom in Education.* New York: Wiley, 1966.
Nash, P. *Models of Man.* New York: Wiley, 1968.
*1919 Report: The Report of the Committee on Adult Education* (Cd. 321.1919).
Nye, Robert D. *Three Views of Man.* Monterey, CA: Brooks/Cole Publishing Company, 1975.
Oakeshott, M. "Education: The Engagement and Its Frustration." In R. F. Dearden, P. H. Hirst, and R. S. Peters (eds.), *Education and the Development of Reason.* London: Routledge and Kegan Paul, 1972.
Ohliger, J. "Dialogue on Mandatory Continuing Education." *Lifelong Learning: The Adult Years,* 1981, 4(10), 5-7.
Ohliger, John. "Is Lifelong Adult Education a Guarantee of Permanent Inadequacy:" Public lecture at Saskatoon, Saskatchewan, March 1974. Available from John Ohliger, University of Wisconsin.
Parson, Steve. "Cooperative Extension Guide to Community Education Development." In *Yearbook of Adult and Continuing Education, 1978-1979.* Chicago: Marquis Academic Media, 1978.
Paterson, R. W. K. "The Concept of Discussion." *Studies in Adult Education,* 1970, *2* (1).
Paterson, R. W. K. "Philosophical Aspects of Adult Education." *Studies in Adult Education,* 1971, *3* (2).
Paterson, R. W. K. "Social Change as an Educational Aim." *Adult Education,* 1973, *45* (6).
Paterson, R. W. K. "Values in Adult Education." *Rewley House Papers,* 1964-65, *4* (3).

Paterson, R. W. K. *Values, Education, and the Adult.* London: Routledge and Kegan Paul, 1979.

Patterson, C. H. *Humanistic Education.* Englewood Cliffs, N.J.: Prentice-Hall, 1973.

Perkinson, Henry. *The Imperfect Panacea: American Faith in Education, 1865-1976* (2nd ed.). New York: Random House, 1977.

Peters, R. S. *Authority, Responsibility and Education.* London: Allen and Unwin, 1959.

Peters, R. S. (ed.). *The Concept of Education.* London: Routledge and Kegan Paul, 1967.

Peters, R. S. *Ethics and Education.* London: Allen and Unwin, 1966.

Popham, W. James. "Probing the Validity of Arguments Against Behavioral Goals." In Miriam B. Kapter (ed.), *Behavioral Objectives in Curriculum Development.* Englewood Cliffs, N.J.: Educational Technology Publications, 1971.

Popham, W. James. "The New World of Accountability: In the Classroom." In Julia DeCarlo and Constant Mason (eds.), *Innovations in Education for the Seventies: Selected Readings.* New York: Behavioral Publications, 1973.

Robinson, James. *The Humanizing of Knowledge.* New York: George H. Doran, 1924.

Rockhill, K. "Professional Education Should Not Be Mandatory." In B. W. Kreitlow and Associates, *Examining Controversies in Adult Education.* San Francisco: Jossey-Bass, 1981.

Rogers, Carl R. "The Place of the Person in the New World of the Behavioral Sciences." In Frank T. Severin (ed.), *Humanistic Viewpoints in Psychology.* New York: McGraw-Hill, 1965.

Rogers, Carl R. "The Process of the Basic Encounter Group." In James F. T. Bugental (ed.), *Challenges of Humanistic Psychology.* New York: McGraw-Hill, 1967.

Rush, Benjamin. "Thoughts Upon the Mode of Education Proper in a Republic" (1786). In S. Alexander Rippa (ed.), *Educational Ideas in America: A Documentary History.* New York: McKay, 1969.

Scheffler, Israel. *The Language of Education*. Boston: Allyn and Bacon, 1960.

Schroeder, W. L. "Adult Education Defined and Described." In R. M. Smith, G. F. Aker, and W. Hallenbeck (eds.), *Handbook of Adult Education*. Adult Education Association of the USA, 1970.

Schroeder, W. L. "Adult Education Defined and Described." In R. M. Smith, G. F. Aker, and J. R. Kidd (eds.), *Handbook of Adult Education*. Adult Education Association of the USA, 1970, 33-34.

Seller, Maxine S. "Success and Failure in Adult Education: The Immigrant Experience, 1914-1924." *Adult Education*, 1978, *28*, 83-99.

Sheats, Paul. *Education and the Quest for a Middle Way*. New York: Macmillan, 1938.

Simpson, E. L. "Some Dimensions of Nontraditional." *Thresholds in Education*, 1977, *3* (3), 2-3.

Simpson, Elizabeth Leonie and Mary Ann Gray. *Humanistic Education: An Interpretation*. Cambridge, MA: Ballinger, 1976.

Simpson, J. A. *Today and Tomorrow in European Adult Education*, 1972.

Skinner, B. F. *About Behaviorism*. New York: Alfred A. Knopf, 1974.

Skinner, B. F. *Beyond Freedom and Dignity*. New York: Alfred A. Knopf, 1971.

Skinner, B. F. *Walden Two*. New York: Macmillan, 1948.

Smith, B. O. and Ennis, R. H. (eds.). *Language and Concepts in Education*. Chicago: Rand McNally, 1961.

Smith, Robert M. *Learning How to Learn: Applied Theory for Adults*. Chicago: Follett Publishing Company, 1982.

Snook, I. A. (ed.). *Concepts of Indoctrination*. London: Routledge and Kegan Paul, 1972.

Spikes, Frank. "A Multidimensional Program Planning Model for Continuing Nursing Education." *Lifelong Learning: The Adult Years*, 1978, *1*, 4-8.

Spring, Joel. "Anarchism and Education: A Dissenting Tradition." In *Roots of Crisis: American Education in the Twentieth Century*, Clarence Karier, Paul Violas, Joel Spring. Chicago: Rand McNally, 1973.

Spring, Joel. *A Primer of Libertarian Education.* New York: Free Life Editions, Inc., 1975.

Stirner, Max. *The False Principle of Education.* Translated by Robert Beebe. Colorado Springs: Ralph Myles, 1967.

Stubblefield, Harold. *The Aims of the American Education Movement in the Nineteen Twenties: A Historical Analysis.* Paper presented at the Adult Education Research Conference, Ann Arbor, Michigan, April 1979.

Sworder, Stanley. "What is Adult Education? Nine Working Definitions." In *Adult Education,* Spring 1955, 5, 131-145.

## II.

### Phenomenology and Phenomenological Research

Appel, Karl-Otto. *Towards a Transformation of Philosophy.* Translated by Glyn Adey and David Frisby. London: Routledge and Kegan Paul, 1980.

Berger, Peter L. and Thomas Luckmann. *The Social Construction of Reality: A Treatise in the Sociology of Knowledge.* Garden City, N.Y.: Doubleday, 1966.

Brentano, Franz. *Psychology From an Empirical Standpoint.* 1874. Edited by Linda L. McAlister and translated by Antos C. Rancurello, D. B. Terrell, and Linda L. McAlister. New York: Humanities Press, 1973.

Bruzina, Ronald. *Logos and Eidos: The Concept in Phenomenology.* The Hague: Mouton, 1970.

Buber, Martin. *I and Thou.* Translated by Walter Kaufmann. New York: Charles Scribner's Sons, 1970.

Buchler, Justus. *Charles Peirce's Empiricism.* New York: Barnes and Noble, 1938.

Casey, Edward. *Imagining: A Phenomenological Study.* Bloomington: Indiana University Press, 1976.

Chapman, Harmon M. *Sensations and Phenomenology.* Bloomington: Indiana University Press, 1966.

Collingwood, Robin G. *An Essay on Metaphysics*. Oxford: The Clarendon Press, 1948.

Collingwood, Robin G. *An Essay on Philosophical Method*. Oxford: The Clarendon Press, 1933.

Collingwood, Robin G. *The Idea of History*. Oxford: Oxford University Press, 1946. Galaxy Book, 1956.

Collingwood, Robin G. *The New Leviathan*. Oxford: The Clarendon Press, 1942.

Collingwood, Robin G. *The Principles of Art*. Oxford: The Clarendon Press, 1938.

Collingwood, Robin G. *Speculum Mentis: Or the Map of Knowledge*. Oxford: The Clarendon Press, 1924.

Derrida, Jacques. *Speech and Phenomena: And Other Essays on Husserl's Theory of Signs*. Translated by David B. Allison. Evanston, IL: Northwestern University Press, 1973.

Dewey, John. *Art as Experience*. G. P. Putnam's Sons, 1934, 1958.

Dewey, John. *Democracy and Education*. New York: Macmillan, 1916, 1964.

Dewey, John. *Experience and Education*. New York: Macmillan, 1938, 1963.

Dewey, John. *How We Think*. Chicago: University of Chicago, 1910, 1933.

Dewey, John. *Human Nature and Conduct*. New York: Henry Holt andCompany, 1922.

Dewey, John. *Logic: The Theory of Inquiry*. New York: Henry Holt and Co., 1938.

Dewey, John. *The Quest for Certainty: A Study of the Relation of Knowledge and Action*. New York: G. P. Putnam's Sons, 1929, 1960.

Ellison, F. A. and P. McCormick (eds.). *Husserl: Expositions and Appraisals*. Notre Dame, Indiana: University of Notre Dame Press, 1977.

Embree, Lester E. (ed.). *Life-world and Consciousness: Essays for Aron Gurwitsch*. Evanston, IL: Northwestern University Press, 1972.

Farber, Marvin. *The Foundation of Phenomenology: Edmund Husserl and the Quest for a Rigorous Science of Philosophy*. 3d ed. Albany, N.Y.: State University of New York Press, 1967.

Farber, Marvin (ed.). *Philosophical Essays in Memory of Edmund Husserl.* Cambridge, MA: Harvard University Press, 1940; reprinted, New York: Greenwood Press, 1968.

Gadamer, Hans-Georg. *Wahrheit und Methode.* Tubingen: J. C. B. Mohr, 1960. *Truth and Method,* translated by Garren Burden and John Cumming. New York: Seabury Press, 1975.

Gadamer, Hans-Georg. *Philosophy Hermeneutics.* Edited and translated by David E. Linge. Berkeley: University of California Press, 1976.

Gadamer, Hans-Georg. *Reason in the Age of Science.* Translated by Frederick G. Lawrence. Cambridge, MA: MIT Press, 1981.

Garfinkel, Harold. *Studies in Ethnomethodology.* Englewood Cliffs, N.J.: Prentice-Hall, 1967.

Gendlin, Eugene T. *Experiencing and the Creation of Meaning: A Philosophical and Psychological Approach to the Subjective.* New York: Free Press, 1962.

Giorgi, Amedeo. *Psychology as a Human Science.* New York: Harper and Row, 1970.

Gurwitsch, Aron. *The Field of Consciousness.* Pittsburgh, PA: Duquesne University Press, 1964.

Gurwitsch, Aron. *Studies in Phenomenology and Psychology.* Evanston, IL: Northwestern University Press, 1966.

Habermas, Jürgen. *Knowledge and Human Interests.* Translated by Jeremy J. Shapiro. Boston: Beacon Press, 1971.

Habermas, Jürgen. "Postscript to *Knowledge and Human Interests.*" *Philosophy of Social Sciences,* 1973, *3,* 157-189.

Habermas, Jürgen. *Theory and Practice.* 1971. Translated by John Viertel. Boston: Beacon Press, 1973.

Hartman, Nicholai. *Ethics.* Vols. I, II, and III. Translated by Stanton Coit. New York: The Macmillan Company, 1932.

Heidegger, Martin. *Being and Time.* 1927. Translated by John Macquarrie and Edward Robinson. New York: Harper and Row, 1962.

Husserl, Edmund. *Cartesian Meditations: An Introduction to Phenomenology*. Translated by Dorion Cairns. The Hague: Nijhoff, 1960.

Husserl, Edmund. *The Crisis of European Sciences and Transcendental Phenomenology: An Introduction to Phenomenological Philosophy*. Translated with an Introduction by David Carr. Evanston, IL: Northwestern University Press, 1970.

Husserl, Edmund. *Experience and Judgment*. Translated by James Spencer Churchill and Karl Ameriks, with a Foreword by Ludwig Landgrebe and an Afterword by Lothar Eley. Evanston, IL: Northwestern University Press, 1973.

Husserl, Edmund. *Formal and Transcendental Logic*. Translated by Dorion Cairns. The Hague: Nijhoff, 1969.

Husserl, Edmund. *The Idea of Phenomenology*. Translated by William P. Alston and George Nakhnikian with an Introduction by George Nakhnikian. The Hague: Nijhoff, 1964.

Husserl, Edmund. *Ideas: General Introduction to Pure Phenomenology*. ("Ideas I.") Translated by W. R. Boyce Gibson. New York: Macmillan, 1931; reprint, New York: Colliers, 1962.

Husserl, Edmund. *Logical Investigations*. Translated with an Introduction by J. N. Findlay. 2 vols. New York: Humanities Press, 1970.

Husserl, Edmund. *The Paris Lectures*. Translated with an Introduction by Peter Koestenbaum. The Hague: Nijhoff, 1964.

Husserl, Edmund. "Phenomenology." Revised translation by Richard E. Palmer (as "'Phenomenology', Edmund Husserl's Article for the *Encyclopedia Britannica*, 1926"). Peter McCormick and Frederick Elliston (eds.). *Husserl: Shorter Works*. Notre Dame: University of Notre Dame Press, 1981.

Husserl, Edmund. *The Phenomenology of Internal Time-Consciousness*. Translated by James S. Churchill and edited by Martin Heidegger with an Introduction by Calvin O. Schrag. Bloomington, IN: Indiana University Press, 1964.

Ihde, Don. *Experimental Phenomenology: An Introduction.* New York: Putnam's, 1977.

James, William. *Essays in Radical Empiricism.* New York: Longmans, Green, and Co., 1912.

James, William. *Some Problems of Philosophy: A Beginning of an Introduction to Philosophy.* New York: Longmans, Green, and Co., 1911.

James, William. *A Pluralistic Universe.* New York: Longmans, Green, and Co., 1909.

James, William. *Pragmatism: A New Name for Some Old Ways of Thinking.* Longmans, Green, and Co., 1907.

James, William. *The Varieties of Religious Experience.* New York: Longmans, Green, and Co., 1902.

James, William. *Talks to Teachers on Psychology: and to Students on Some of Life's Ideals.* Henry Holt and Co., 1899.

James, William. *The Will to Believe.* New York: Longmans, Green, and Co., 1897.

James, William. *The Principles of Psychology,* vols. I and II. New York: Henry Holt and Co., 1890.

Jonas, Hans. *The Phenomenology of Life: Toward a Philosophical Biology.* Westport, Conn.: Greenwood Press, 1966.

Kersten, Frederick I. and Richard M. Zaner (eds.). *Phenomenology: Continuation and Criticism: Essays in Memory of Dorion Cairns.* The Hague: Nijhoff, 1973.

Kierkegaard, Søren. *Fear and Trembling* and *The Sickness Unto Death.* Princeton, N.J.: Princeton University Press, 1944, 1954.

Kockelmans, Joseph J. *Edmund Husserl's Phenomenological Psychology: A Historico-Critical Study.* Translated by Berndt Jager and revised by the author. Pittsburgh, PA: Duquesne University Press, 1967.

Kohak, Erazim V. *Idea and Experience: Edmund Husserl's Project of Phenomenology in "Ideas I".* Chicago: University of Chicago Press, 1978.

Landgrebe, Ludwig. *The Phenomenology of Edmund Husserl.* Ithaca and London: Cornell University Press, 1981.

Luckmann, Thomas (ed.). *Phenomenology and Sociology: Selected Readings.* New York: Penguin Books, 1978.

McCormick, P. and F. Elliston (eds.). 1981. *Husserl. Shorter Works.* South Bend, IN: University of Notre Dame Press.

Marcel, Gabriel. *Being and Having.* 1935. Translated by K. Farrer. London: Collins, 1965.

Mead, George Herbert. *Mind, Self, and Society.* Chicago: University of Chicago Press, 1934.

Mead, George Herbert. *The Philosophy of the Act.* Chicago: University of Chicago Press, 1938, 1972.

Merleau-Ponty, Maurice. *The Structure of Behavior.* 1942. Translated by Alden L. Fisher. Boston: Beacon Press, 1967.

Merleau-Ponty, Maurice. *Phenomenology of Perception.* Translated by Colin Smith. New York: Humanities Press, 1962.

Merleau-Ponty, Maurice. *The Primacy of Perception: And Other Essays on Phenomenological Psychology, the Philosophy of Art, History and Politics.* Edited with an Introduction by James M. Edie and translated by William Cobb et al. Evanston, IL: Northwestern University Press, 1964.

Merleau-Ponty, Maurice. *Sense and Non-Sense.* Translated with an Introduction by Hubert L. Dreyfus and Patricia Allen Dreyfus. Evanston, IL: Northwestern Illinois Press, 1964.

Merleau-Ponty, Maurice. *Signs.* Translated with an Introduction by Richard C. McCleary. Evanston, IL: Northwestern University Press, 1964.

Minkowski, Eugene. *Lived Time: Phenomenological and Psychopathological Studies.* 1933. Translated by Nancy Metzel. Evanston, IL: Northwestern University Press, 1970.

Mohanty, J. N. *Edmund Husserl's Theory of Meaning.* The Hague: Nijhoff, 1964.

Natanson, Maurice. *Edmund Husserl: Philosopher of Infinite Tasks.* Evanston, IL: Northwestern University Press, 1973.

Natanson, Maurice. *The Journeying Self: A Study in Philosophy and Social Role*. Reading, MA: Addison-Wesley, 1970.

Natanson, Maurice (ed.). *Phenomenology and Social Reality: Essays in Memory of Alfred Schutz*. The Hague: Nijhoff, 1970.

O'Neill, John. *Perception, Expression, and History: The Social Phenomenology of Maurice Merleau-Ponty*. Evanston, IL: Northwestern University Press, 1970.

O'Neill, John. *Sociology as a Skin Trade: Essays Towards a Reflexive Sociology*. London: Heinemann, 1972.

Ortega y Gasset, José. *The Idea of Principle in Leibniz and the Evolution of Deductive Theory*. Translated by Mildred Adams. New York: W. W. Norton, 1971.

Ortega y Gasset, José. *Obras Completas,* Tomos I-XI. Madrid: Revista de Occidente, 1966-1973.

Ortega y Gasset, José. *Obras Completas,* III, "El tema de nuestro tiempo" ["The Theme of Our Time"]. Translated as *The Modern Theme* by James Cleugh. New York: Harper and Row, 1961.

Ortega y Gasset, José. *Man and People*. Translated by Willard R. Trask. New York: Norton, 1957.

Ortega y Gasset, José. *Some Lessons in Metaphysics*. Translated by Mildred Adams. New York: W. W. Norton and Company, 1969.

Ortega y Gasset, José. *What is Philosophy?* Translated by Mildred Adams. New York, N.Y.: Norton and Co., 1964, 216.

Palmer, Richard E. *Hermeneutics: Interpretation Theory in Schleiermacher, Dilthey, Heidegger, and Gadamer*. Evanston, IL: Northwestern University Press, 1969.

Peirce, Charles Sanders. *Collected Papers,* Volumes I-VIII. Volumes I-VI edited by Charles Hartshorne and Paul Weiss, and Volumes VII and VIII edited by Arthur W. Burks. Cambridge, MA: The Belknap Press of Harvard University Press, 1958.

Pfänder, Alexander. "Introduction to **Logic**." In Herbert Spiegelberg (ed and trans.), *Phenomenology of Willing and Motivation*. Evanston, IL: Northwestern University, 1967.

Richardson, W. J. *Heidegger: Through Phenomenology to Thought.* The Hague: Martinus Nijhoff, 1967.

Rickman, H. P. *Understanding and the Human Sciences.* London: Heinemann, 1967.

Rickman, H. P. *Wilhelm Dilthey: Pioneer of the Human Sciences.* Berkeley: University of California Press, 1979.

Ricoeur, P. *Husserl. An Analysis of His Phenomenology.* Trans. E. G. Ballard and L. E. Embree. Evanston, IL: Northwestern University Press.

Ricoeur, P. *Freedom and Nature: The Voluntary and the Involuntary.* 1950. Translated by Erazim V. Kohak. Evanston, IL: Northwestern University Press, 1966.

Ricoeur, P. *History and Truth.* Translated with an Introduction by Charles A. Kelbley. Evanston, IL: Northwestern University Prses, 1965.

Ricoeur, P. "What Is a Text? Explanation and Understanding." 1970. Reprinted in *Hermeneutics and the Human Sciences.* Edited and translated by John B. Thompson. Cambridge: Cambridge University Press, 1981.

Ricoeur, P. *Freud and Philosophy: An Essay on Interpretation.* Translated by Denis Savage. New Haven, CN: Yale University Press, 1970.

Ricoeur, P. "The Model of the Text: Meaningful Action Considered as a Text." 1971. Reprinted in *Hermeneutics and the Human Sciences.* Edited and translated by John B. Thompson. Cambridge: Cambridge University Press, 1981.

Ricoeur, P. *The Rule of Metaphor: Multi-Disciplinary Studies of the Creation of Meaning in Language.* 1975. Translated by Robert M. Czerny. Toronto: University of Toronto Press, 1977.

Ricoeur, P. *Interpretation Theory: Discourse and the Surplus of Meaning.* Fort Worth: Texas Christian University Press, 1976.

Sartre, Jean-Paul. *Being and Nothingness: An Essay on Phenomenological Ontology.* Translated with an Introduction by Hazel E. Barnes. New York: Philosophical Library, 1956.

Sartre, Jean-Paul. *Imagination: A Psychological Critique.* Translated with an Introduction by Forrest Williams. Ann Arbor, MI: University of Michigan Press, 1962.

Sartre, Jean-Paul. *The Psychology of Imagination.* Translated by Bernard Frechtman. London: Rider, 1949.

Sartre, Jean-Paul. *The Transcendence of the Ego: An Existentialist Theory of Consciousness.* Translated and annotated with an Introduction by Forrest Williams and Robert Kirkpatrick. New York: Farrar, Straus, Noonday Press, 1957.

Scheler, Max. *Man's Place in Nature.* Translated with an Introduction by Hans Meyerhoff. Boston: Beacon, 1961; New York: Farrar, Straus, Noonday Press, 1963.

Scheler, Max. *The Nature of Sympathy.* Translated by Peter Heath with an Introduction by W. Stark. New Haven, CN: Yale University Press, 1954.

Scheler, Max. *Ressentiment.* Edited with an Introduction by Lewis A. Coser and translated by William W. Holdheim. New York: Free Press, 1961.

Schrag, Calvin. *Experience and Being: Prolegomena to a Future Ontology.* Evanston, IL: Northwestern University Press, 1969.

Schrag, Calvin. *Radical Reflection and the Origin of the Human Sciences.* West Lafayette, IN: Purdue University Press, 1980.

Schutz, Alfred. *Collected Papers, Vol. I: The Problem of Social Reality.* Edited with an Introduction by Maurice Natanson and a Preface by H. L. Van Breda. The Hague: Nijhoff, 1962. Vol. II: *Studies in Social Theory.* Edited with an Introduction by Arvid Brodersen. The Hague: Nijhoff, 1964. Vol. III: *Studies in Phenomenological Philosophy.* Edited by Ilse Schutz with an Introduction by Aron Gurwitsch. The Hague: Nijhoff, 1966.

Schutz, Alfred. *The Phenomenology of the Social World.* Translated by George Walsh and Frederick Lehnert with an Introduction by George Walsh. Evanston, IL: Northwestern University Press, 1967.

Schutz, Alfred. *Reflections on the Problem of Relevance.* Edited and annotated with an Introduction by Richard M. Zaner. New Haven, CN: Yale University Press, 1970.

Schutz, Alfred and Thomas Luckmann. *The Structures of the Life-World.* Translated by Richard M. Zaner and H. Tristram Engelhardt, Jr. Evanston, IL: Northwestern University Press, 1973.

Spiegelberg, Herbert. "'Linguistic Phenomenology': John L. Austin and Alexander Pfänder." *Memorias del XIII Congreso Internacianal de Filosofia.* Vol. IX. Mexico, D.F.: Universidad Nicional Autonomia de Mexico, 1964, 511.

Spiegelberg, Herbert. "Phenomenology." *Encyclopedia Britannica.* Chicago: Encyclopedia Britannica, Inc., 1965.

Spiegelberg, Herbert. *The Phenomenological Movement: A Historical Introduction.* 3rd edition revised and enlarged. The Hague: Martinus Nijhoff, 1982.

Spiegelberg, Herbert. *Phenomenology in Psychology and Psychiatry: A Historical Introduction.* Evanston, IL: Northwestern University Press, 1972.

Spiegelberg, Herbert. "Toward a Phenomenology of Experience." *American Philosophical Quarterly,* October 1964, *1* (4).

Stanage, Sherman M. "Collingwood's Phenomenology of Education: **Person** and the Self-Recognition of the Mind." In Michael Krausz (ed.), *Critical Essays on the Philosophy of R. G. Collingwood.* Oxford: The Clarendon Press, 1972, 268-295.

Stein, Edith. *On the Problem of Empathy.* Translated by Waltraut Stein with a Foreword by Erwin W. Straus. The Hague: Nijhoff, 1964.

Strasser, Stephan. *Phenomenology and the Human Sciences.* Pittsburgh: Duquesne University Press, 1963.

Strasser, Stephan. *Phenomenology of Feeling: An Essay on the Phenomena of Heart.* Translated by Robert E. Wood. Pittsbugh: Duquesne University Press, 1977.

Straus, Erwin W. *Phenomenological Psychology: Selected Papers.* Translated, in part, by Erling Eng. New York: Basic Books, 1966.

Straus, Erwin W. "Psychiatry and Philosophy." Translated by Erling Eng. In *Psychiatry and Philosophy,* edited by Maurice Natanson, 1-83. New York: Springer, 1969.

Straus, Erwin W. (ed.). *Phenomenology, Pure and Applied: The First Lexington Conference.* Pittsburgh, PA: Duquesne University Press, 1964.

Taylor, Charles. *The Explanation of Behavior.* London: Routledge and Kegan Paul, 1964.

Taylor, Charles. *Philosophy and the Human Sciences.* Cambridge: Cambridge University Press, 1985.

Tiryakian, Edward A. *Sociologism and Existentialism: Two Perspectives on the Individual and Society.* Englewood Cliffs, N.J.: Prentice-Hall, 1962.

Tymieniecka, A. T. *Phenomenology and Science in Contemporary European Thought.* New York: The Noonday Press, 1962.

Wagner, Helmut R. (ed.). *Alfred Schutz on Phenomenology and Social Relations: Selected Writings.* Chicago: University of Chicago Press, 1970.

Wild, John. *Existence and the World of Freedom.* Englewood Cliffs, N.J.: Prentice-Hall, 1963.

Zaner, Richard M. *The Context of Self: A Phenomenological Inquiry Using Medicine as a Clue.* Athens: Ohio University Press, 1981.

Zaner, Richard M. *The Problem of Embodiment: Some Contributions to a Phenomenology of the Body.* The Hague: Martinus Nijhoff, 1964.

Zaner, Richard M. *The Way of Phenomenology: Criticism as a Philosophical Discipline.* New York: Western Publishing, Pegasus, 1970.

## III.

## Philosophy and 'New Philosophy of Science'

Alston, William P. "Emotion and Feeling." In Paul Edwards (ed.), *The Encyclopedia of Philosophy,*

Vols. 1-8. New York: Macmillan and Company and The Free Press, 1967, Vols. 1-2, 469-486.

Arendt, Hannah. *The Human Condition*. Chicago: University of Chicago Press, 1958.

Austin, J. L. *Philosophical Papers*. Oxford: The Clarendon Press, 1961.

Aristotle. *Nichomachean Ethics*. In Richard McKeon (trans.), *The Basic Works of Aristotle*. New York: Random House, 1941.

Brown, Harold I. *Perception, Theory and Commitment: The New Philosophy of Science*. Chicago: University of Chicago Press, 1977.

Camus, Albert. *The Rebel*. New York: Vintage Books, 1959.

Descartes, René. *Discourse on Method*. Translated from the Latin by Donald A. Cress. Indianapolis: Hackett Publishing Company, 1981.

Descartes, René. *Meditations on First Philosophy*. Translated from the Latin by Donald A. Cress. Indianapolis: Hackett Publishing Company, 1979.

Edwards, Jonathan. *Freedom of the Will*. Edited by Paul Ramsey. New Haven: Yale University Press, 1957.

Feyerabend, Paul. *Against Method: Outline of an Anarchistic Theory of Knowledge*. London: Redwood Barn, 1975; Verso Edition, 1978.

Gray, J. Glenn. *The Promise of Wisdom: A Philosophical Theory of Education*. New York: Harper and Row, 1968.

Hanson, Norwood R. *Patterns of Discovery: An Inquiry into the Conceptual Foundations of Science*. Cambridge: Cambridge University Press, 1958. Reprint, 1969.

High, Dallas M. *Language, Persons, and Belief*. New York: Oxford University Press, 1967.

Kuhn, Thomas S. *The Structure of Scientific Revolutions*, 2nd ed. Chicago: University of Chicago Press, 1970.

Lakatos, Imre. "Falsification and the Methodology of Scientific Research Programmes." In Imre Lakatos and Alam Musgrave (eds.), *Criticism and the Growth of*

*Knowledge: Proceedings of the International Colloquium in the Philosophy of Science.* London, 1965, vol. 4. Cambridge: Cambridge University Press, 1970.

Laudan, Larry. *Progress and Its Problems: Toward a Theory of Scientific Growth.* Berkeley: University of California Press, 1977.

MacIntyre, Alasdair. *After Virtue: A Study of Moral Theory,* 2nd edition. Notre Dame: Notre Dame University Press, 1984.

Perry, Ralph Barton. *The Humanity of Man.* New York: George Braziller, 1956.

Plato. *Symposium.* In Benjamin Jowett (trans.), *The Dialogues of Plato.* New York: Random House, Vol. 1.

Plato. *Theaetetus.* Translated by F. M. Cornford. Indianapolis, IN: The Bobbs-Merrill Co., 1957, 29.

Polanyi, Michael. *Personal Knowledge: Towards a Post-Critical Philosophy.* New York: Harper and Row, 1958, 1962.

Polkinghorne, Donald. *Methodology for the Human Sciences: Systems of Inquiry.* Albany: State University of New York Press, 1983.

Rawls, John. *A Theory of Justice.* Cambridge, MA: Harvard University Press, 1971.

Russell, Bertrand. *The Problems of Philosophy.* Oxford: Oxford University Press, 1912.

Spinoza, Benedict de. *Ethics.* Translated by R. H. M. Elwes. New York: Dover Publications, Inc., 1951.

Spinoza, Benedict de. *The Improvement of the Understanding.* Translated from the Latin by R. H. M. Elwes. New York: Dover Publications, 1951.

Wittgenstein, Ludwig. *Philosophical Investigations,* 2nd edition. Translated by G. E. M. Anscombe. New York: The Macmillan Co., 1953, 1958.

Ziman, John. *An Introduction to Science Studies.* Cambridge: Cambridge University Press, 1984.

Ziman, John. *Reliable Knowledge: An Exploration of the Grounds for Belief in Science.* Cambridge: Cambridge University Press, 1978.

## GLOSSARY OF TERMS

**Adult education** - Adult education is the performative enactments of, and systematic investigation of, the essential structures of the phenomena constituting adult eductions of **person**, specifically of the deliberate liberative actions of consciousing and responsible persons whereby they become transformed and empowered with vital motives for acting. The research program I propose throughout this essay includes the presupposition that the adult eductions of **person** constitute the fundamental subject-matter of adult education.

**Adult eductions of person** - Eductions of **person** include (but are not exhausted by) activities, actions and acts of agents and agencies of the following kinds: self-conscious being and activities; feeling, experiencing, and consciousing; reasoning; willing; perceiving; discussing; knowing that one knows; producing, selecting, using, and rejecting concepts, systems, theories, laws; communicating and interpersonal communicating; deliberately habituating oneself with one's circumstances, situations, and environments, and then deliberately altering these habits; purposing, planning, judging, evaluating; describing, analyzing, and defining; planning a system of actions; organizing a system of beliefs; desiring; approving; learning to learn; formulating and appraising kinds and degrees of liberation and ways of being free; transformation; empowerment . . .

These constitute but a mere beginning of a rehearsal of the degrees and kinds of eductions of **person**. **Person** is this kind of being and doing. These are among the sorts of things persons do.

Adult eductions of **person** are at least eductions of **person** like those just presented. All adult educ-

tions of **person** are the expressions and direct presentations of persons who in the context of such
eductions of **person** as the above perceive themselves
to be and/or are perceived by other persons to have
or to be: *more* responsible for their choices,
decision making and actions; *more* accepting of
personal responsibilities in general; *more* self-
supporting; *more* independent of earlier peer-pressures; *more* versed in practical wisdom and prudence
in the 'everyday' world; *more* self-knowledge;
*more* remembrances of a longer chronological aging
coupled with increasing ability to leave them behind. . . . The surveying goes on, and it is a
function of adult education research, in accordance
with the overall research program being presented in
this essay, to continue surveying the blurred boundaries marking adulthood and charting the general
contours of valleys, plains, and peaks of the adult
eductions of **person**. What one is working with all
the while as the fusion of the reality of person and
the concept of **person** are adult eductions actualized
and realized executively in the lifeworlds of
persons.

The concept of **person** and the dynamic realities of
living and breathing persons are fused in the adult
case by the actualizing and realizing executively
within the world of what I call adult eductions of
**person**. Being an 'adult', doing 'adult' things, and
speaking as an 'adult' constitute more a state of
mind. These constitute a state of mind in which a
sufficiently rich and varied cluster of adult eductions of **person** like those in both presentations
above have become instantiated concretely in a given
person whose actions in the 'everydayness' of daily
life manifest these as an identifiable **critical
synthesis** of 'adulthood'. An 'adult' therefore is
what a certain degree and kind of **critical synthesis**
of eductions of **person** called adult eductions of
**person** are and do.

**Consciousing** - The term 'consciousing' is constructed from **con**, with, together, and **scire**, to know. Hence, consciousing means knowing-together, or knowing in such intimate, and logically primitive, form that all knowing and all cognitive activities of persons are constituted partly through it. All structures of knowing and knowledge have consciousing already present. Conscious**ness** already has consciousing within it. Consciousings are not each a something (**res**), but a flow, a stream of processes (**Erlebnisse**) and activities (**Ich-Akte**), that is, consciousings always with an 'I' - presence. 'To conscious,' as an infinitive, transcends 'to feel' and 'to experience.' Consciousing is used both as a gerund and as a present participle. As a gerund it is a form of a (my constructed) Latin verb, 'to conscious', capable of being considered as a substantive, but retaining the regimen of the verb 'to conscious'. As a participle it is a derivative of my constructed verb, 'to conscious', which has the function and construction of an adjective (qualifying a noun) while retaining some of those of the verb (e.g., tense, government of an object).

**Constitutive investigation** - Constitutive investigation consists in examining relevant ingredients within a person's life by exploring these ingredients 'backward' toward the more primal stages, phases, or stretches of its constitution among circumstances within situations. How did each one of these come to be what it is (although not in 'causal' terms)? Constitutive investigation is the investigation of the increasingly more tacit and implicit stages of these ingredients which may be feelings, experiences, or consciousings of **person**. In what ways did each relevant ingredient come to be what it is now as it becomes the 'object' of reflection in a given person's life? Constitutive phenomenology must be distinguished from eductive phenomenology.

**Eductions of person** (See **person** below.) - Eductions of **person** include (but are not exhausted by) activities, actions and acts of agents and agencies of the following kinds: self-conscious being and activities; feeling, experiencing, and consciousing; reasoning; willing; perceiving; discussing; knowing that one knows; producing, selecting, using and rejecting concepts, systems, theories, laws; communicating and interpersonal communicating; deliberately habituating oneself within one's circumstances, situations, and environments, and then deliberately altering these habits; purposing, planning, judging, evaluating; describing, analyzing, and defining; planning a system of actions; organizing a system of beliefs; desiring; approving; learning to learn; formulating and appraising kinds and degrees of liberation and ways of being free; transformation; empowerment. These constitute but a mere beginning of a rehearsal of the degrees and kinds of eductions of **person**. **Person** is this kind of being and doing. These are among the sorts of things persons do.

**Eductive phenomenology** - The term 'eduction' means that which is educed, from **e**, out + **ducere**, to lead. The emphasis here is deliberately placed upon the processes of drawing forth, bringing out, or eliciting meanings and values and the processes of clarifying these through the stages of their development from conditions of latent, rudimentary, or merely potential existence through to their actual and concrete development.

Eductive investigation (as phenomenology) consists in examining relevant ingredients within a person's life which are issued forth or educed or which become, or have become more explicit. Emphasis here is placed upon the process of drawing forth, upon the ways of appearing through which parts-of learning become wholes, or wholes-of parts are dissembling into these parts. Elicited meanings and values are investigated. This kind of reflection is performed by clarifying all of these ingredients and their processes through the stages, phases and stretches of their development out of conditions of their rudimentary, latent, and tacit (or even their merely potential or possible) existence within persons' lives. Eductive phenomenology must be distinguished from constitutive phenomenology.

**'Everydaying'** - 'Everydaying' is the active clustering of phenomena of the 'everydayness' of persons' lives in the midst of which, within the days blurring into the normal routines of each and every day, the eductions of **person** take place.

**Human science** (as contrasted with physical science and social science) - Phenomenologists have long argued that there are kinds of studies which can be called 'human sciences'. A phenomenological investigation is always a case of human science. A human science is an orderly and systematic description and investigation of a person's, and persons', felt experience of direct phenomena through the various forms in which relevant phenomena may appear or be manifested. A human science deals necessarily with both facts and values and does not formally exclude the latter in the midst of its scientific investigations. A **fact** is any phenomenon intersubjectively structured, explored, investigated, and analyzed as an **objecting** agreement of intersubjectively felt experience. A **value** is any phenomenon intersubjectively structured, explored, investigated, and analyzed as a **subjecting** agreement of intersubjectively felt experience. Realizing, evidencing, and certifying are three of the many possible ways in which we speak of our valuational feeling, felt values, and our constructions of facts within our lifeworlds. Within our adult lifeworlds we learn most fundamentally and lastingly through the assurances of our values through commitments and in terms of the facts situated within a unity of values. These value commitments and consequent constructed and situated facts flow through indeterminately long streams of personal lives.

'Languaging' - 'Languaging' comprises the phenomena of linguistic expressions and disciplining constructions through which relevant phenomena comprising the eductions of **person** are presented by persons through literal, technical, and metaphorical presentations.

Linguistic phenomenology - This is a way of articulating as precisely as possible the distinctions within what adults say in direct investigation and description of phenomena which we feel, experience, and conscious (know-with). In this context, a phenomenon is (literally) any showing-of-itself-in-itself, or anything taken as an instance-of-itself, to be focused upon. Linguistic phenomenology is a way as free as possible from unexamined preconceptions and presuppositions. Thus, it is 'presuppositionless' in Husserl's special sense: its presuppositions are under constant re-examination.

There is one complex cluster of phenomena in particular to which the investigations of linguistic phenomenology uniquely apply within the theory and practice of adult education. These are the phenomena which we may refer as the adult eductions of **person**. A **person** is a special kind of phenomenon, a special showing-of-itself-in-itself, a special instance-of-itself, to be focused upon. When we investigate this phenomenon we necessarily do so initially as linguistic phenomenologists, I believe. In the *strong sense*, linguistic phenomenology, properly so-called, focuses upon **person**, a special showing-of-itself-in-itself, a special instance-of-itself. Linguistic phenomenology first attempts to articulate as precisely as possible the distinctions (among inseparables) within **person**-talk. Linguistic phenomenology then will gather the clusterings of all instances of **person**-talk for orderly and systematic description and investigation. It will focus upon key examples of uses of these either as instances-of a structure,

or as a structure-of instances. It will position
these structures at levels of feelings, experiencings, and consciousings of person-talk.

**Metaphor** - Metaphors are new perspectives which are
ubiquitously bursts, jolts, suddennesses of feelings
and consciousings of **person** within persons. Metaphors constitute the language of seminal movement for
the adult learner, a veritable rite of passage into
further, much richer and deeper, reaches of learning
through restructuring, reordering, refashioning the
everyday world through the sudden rise of new perspectives. These make possible the transformations
and new empowerments of life effected via the surrender of one's **person** to the catchings of metaphor
first stages as 'figural' and 'configural' language.
A metaphor is originative language of active judgment. In fleshing out this main thesis I argue that
the word 'metaphor' (from the Greek, **meta**, change of
place, order, condition, or nature, and **pherein**, to
bear, carry), transference and transposition, ind-
icates etymologically the position of one thing in
the place of another. But the transference is always
mutual and reciprocal, and this suggests that the
place where each of the conscioused 'objects' party
to the metaphor is placed is not that of one or the
other parts of the metaphor, but a **felt place** which
is the same for both parts of the metaphor. Metaphor, therefore, consists in the transposition of a
conscioused 'object' from its real placement to a **new
felt place**. It seems to me that this recognition
must be accepted by any successful theory of
metaphor.

**'Metaphorizing'** - 'Metaphorizing' compromises the phenomena of the process of disclosing, uncovering, and
creating new perspectives of the eductions of **person**.
A metaphor is first the felt meaning of the originative language of active judgment.

**Paradigm** - (1) A paradigm is a pattern and patterning of the thoughts and thinking of persons. I prefer to say that a paradigm is a pattern and the patterning process of the conscioused 'objects' and consciousing 'objects' of persons. This meaning derives from the Middle English and late French, **patron** (which continues to mean both 'patron' and 'pattern' in French), and still conveys some vestiges of 'patron' as protector, defender, father, or as one who stands to others as their lord, defender, master, or protector. In other words, the term 'paradigm' still connotes a pattern of transcendence, superiority, and protection which is overriding in its relevance and significance. These connotations already bring us rather close to the meaning(s) the concept has in the discussions in the literature of the 'new science' and the 'new philosophy of science'. A paradigm is a pattern. A pattern is to its copies as the original and 'superior' form and design are to these copies. A paradigm is a model of particular excellence, a superior model from which anything is made, or a plan, design, or outline of supreme importance. To pattern something is to make something in conformance with a model or design, or to work out or construct something according to a model.

(2) A paradigm is a principal example among a number of examples, or what is known as an exemplar (from Latin, **exemplaris**, and Old French, **exemplaire**), or a perfect specimen of some quality, pattern, or model to be imitated or followed, or in accordance with which certain actions in designing something should be taken.

(3) A paradigm is also an action, the action of exhibiting something beside something else, or side by side with something, such that descriptions of both, and comparisons, become unavoidable. It is the action of holding out, or of submitting to view, something of importance and significance, such as the delineation or an embodiment of an idea in words in

such a manner that something is given existence or indicated as existing. When the unavoidable descriptions and comparisons are necessarily offered following the action of exhibiting something side by side with something else, they may take the form of comparisons in virtue of 'better' or 'worse', 'more than' or 'less than', 'of greater importance' or 'of lesser importance', and so on.

We can see clearly that the essential structure of a paradigm is a pattern of thoughts which constitute a design or model held to be superior, as an exemplar, to other designs or models and which 'ought' to be followed in systematic investigations of a determinate subject-matter, when compared with those other models, designs, and patterns of thought which could be followed in investigations into the same determinate subject-matter.

**Person** (contrasted with person) - The distinction between **person** and person is absolutely vital to the claims and arguments in this essay. Clarification can only be provided progressively. Provisionally, it can be said here that **person** is the full eduction of what persons are, have in common, and makes possible communication on the basis of intersubjectivity within the coexistence of persons. **Person** is what is drawn forth, pulled out, or what flows forth from persons in their lifeworlds, or what intimately flows from persons through their feeling, their experiencing, and their consciousing, from within the intersubjectivity of persons coexisting in their lifeworlds.

**Phenomenology** - Phenomenology is, in the 20th century, mainly the name for a philosophical movement whose primary objective is the direct investigation and description of phenomena as consciously experienced, without theories about their causal explanation and as free as possible from unexamined preconceptions and presuppositions. (Herbert Spiegelberg, "Phenomenology," in the *Encyclopedia Britannica*, 1965.)

**Reflexive experimentation** - In a number of places in this essay I suggest that research in adult education should require the use of at least two models (one constitutive and one eductive) in every experiment involving persons. This suggestion if taken seriously by a sufficient number of researchers among adult educators, could have profound influence on all investigations involving **person** in adult education. This two-fold way (or double-pronged research) might lead, with the development of the necessary empirical methods, to what I call reflexive experimentation in both 'qualitatively' and 'quantitatively' based research in adult education. *This would mean that every experiment involving persons' ideas and actions would have to state two forms of any given hypothesis, and test out hypotheses in a double sense, in both a constitutive and an eductive form.* These may be investigated through the constitutive function of phenomenology and the eductive function of phenomenology, respectively. The constitutive form is a model of experiment founded upon the **because motives** of persons, whereas the eductive form is a model of experiment based upon the **in-order-to-motives** of persons. Some of this experimentation could be done as public praxis, but much more remains to be the experience of a thought experiment, or a variant of Husserl's method of 'free imaginative variation.' And, of course, these are all actions, and under appropriate matrices of relevance, acts as well. *The question is how an adult comes to see that it may be possible to find a dramatically different place in the lived world through learning. In investigating the ways in which it may be possible for them to do so, every one of our research projects in adult education should be reflexive. The study should move along in two directions at the same time. If a research project must employ statistical or behavioral methods, then it should pursue two distinct kinds of investigation as equally central at the same time.*

*We may call these constitutive investigation and eductive investigation.*

**Relevance** - Relevance is perspective in, of, and through the world. It is literally a looking-through the world, a process taking place in time and constituted in terms of the relative priority and ordering importance of the ingredients of the world. A **system of relevance** is a way through which are presented the relative priority and ordering importance of the ingredients of the world from a fashioning and structuring point of view. This way is through the medium of a matrix of relatings manifesting themselves in degrees and kinds of phenomena in their presentation and expression from the most tacit through the most explicit constitutions. I call this matrix the **relevancy matrix** of personal action.

**'Relevantizing'** - 'Relevantizing' comprises the processes whereby some phenomena from within the repertory of all phenomena become 'objects' of interest, more apt, fitting, appropriate to some person action(s), by virtue of some perspective, expressive of the eductions of **person**.

**'Vitalizing'** - 'Vitalizing' comprises the phenomena of vigor, energy, life-giving and life-engendering, strength and intensity of the liberative, transforming, and empowering eductions of **person** expressed by persons.

# INDEX

1995